Management for Professionals

More information about this series at http://www.springer.com/series/10101

Arun Kohli

Effective Coaching, and the Fallacy of Sustainable Change

Springer

Arun Kohli
London, United Kingdom

ISSN 2192-8096 ISSN 2192-810X (electronic)
Management for Professionals
ISBN 978-3-319-39734-4 ISBN 978-3-319-39735-1 (eBook)
DOI 10.1007/978-3-319-39735-1

Library of Congress Control Number: 2016942572

Printed on acid-free paper

This Springer imprint is published by Springer Nature
The registered company is Springer International Publishing AG Switzerland

I write this book with a deep sense of gratitude and dedication to the people who have been the strongest inspirations and support for me

Gabriele B. Kohli †
13.04.1965–15.01.1994
My first Coach and beloved wife

Anke Kohli
My beloved wife and the sunny side of life

Mrs Mohini Kohli
My mother and the iron pillar of my life

Neeru and Ritu Kohli
Two strong women and most wonderful sisters without whom I would not have mastered many challenges in India

&

David Ben Adam and Anna Mohini Kohli
My wife's and my reincarnations with a superior operating system

Foreword by Stefan Rau

Coaching and Leadership

Stefan Rau

You are not born a leader. Your rise on the career path is often very fast. The problems of leading teams or individuals are often ignored or underestimated, and potential or rising new leaders are often not sufficiently prepared for their new roles—to both the new leader's and the corporation's disadvantage.

The requirements and demands of employees are very different and more involved today than they once were. The consequences can be seen in the culture of your company which reflects your style of leadership! Employee satisfaction is significantly influenced by your communication through your leadership style and also your personal behaviour. To lead and inspire employees in a manner that they follow you is a key to your success within the company—this is true for all management levels.

With personal coaching you are supported in personal development through self-reflection; you learn about the differences between your self-image and your public image: what you think of yourself and what others do. With coaching it is easier to interpret and to relate to employee reactions to certain management challenges and consequently, where necessary, bring about changed behaviours and increased or better performance.

For me the professional, critical, and honest feedback on my behaviour was the key benefit and opportunity I gained from personal coaching.

It was also important for me to understand the clear difference between managing and leading—for me, personally, it assisted in considering how to lead my reports and reflecting about how to motivate employees. I found that knowing more than their names . . . admitting mistakes does not weaken me but strengthens their respect for me as their leader. Employees value an authentic leader who does not simply copy an off-the-shelf idealistic management style. Coaching has given me the opportunity to discover my own leadership style, on my own terms. I found it was extremely productive to get insight about my self-hood and on the effect I have on others through an honest and unbiased self-reflection, conducted with my coach. The outcome was that it led to an improvement in my leadership style, which affected those around me in a positive way.

Stefan Rau, coaching client. Managing Director/Geschaeftsfuehrer: Global Process Plants Director, TI Automotive (Heidelberg) GmbH. Heidelberg, Germany March 2013

Foreword by Juliana Roth

The Best Coaches for Successful Intercultural Venues

Juliana Roth

Intercultural coaching is a new subject in the world of international business. Theoreticians may still attribute little importance to it; others may even consider it to be only a new buzzword in international business. There is some research on it, but it is based less on original theories than on findings adopted from other bodies of knowledge, such as system theory or intercultural training or competence. As a result, we still lack valid definitions, methodological guidelines, and accepted work formats for intercultural coaching venues.

But in spite of this academic neglect, intercultural coaching has firmly established itself as a tool in personnel development and is regarded as a much needed service for managers in positions of leadership. In today's globalised business, leaders are urged to develop their personality and identity to adapt to quickly varying international contexts. They also have to enhance their personal skills, to include self-reflection, cultural self-awareness, perspective change, and empathy. In my view, the most effective way to gain these competences is in individualised intercultural coaching venues.

Intercultural coaching gained popularity thanks to the efforts of the many practising coaches who quickly grasped the importance of the new educational format and began to enclose in their portfolios intercultural issues such as cultural difference, solution-seeking, or conflict resolution for intercultural situations. Due to the lack of a uniting theory and job profile, the services which intercultural coaches provide can vary a lot. Some rely mainly on the cultural dimension and conduct their venues as simplified mini intercultural training, while others emphasise a systemic approach and tend to minimise the importance of cultural differences. Between these two extremes, there is a variety of formats which coaches use—depending on their affinity to certain topics or on their biographical experience.

Intercultural coaching can also vary, depending on who the coachees are. They can be individual executives, expatriate couples, small groups, or multicultural teams. This text refers to the most frequently applied format of individual coaching for business executives.

With regard to content, intercultural training and intercultural coaching have a lot in common, but they are not identical. There are certain strategic differences that make these two settings distinct from each other. The differences derive primarily from the specificity of the communicative situation in a coaching session where coach and coachee work intensively one-to-one and face-to-face.

In intercultural coaching:

- Coachees receive individual customised support.
- The privacy of the client is guaranteed.
- Coach and coachee are in a closer relationship.
- Coaches can be flexible with their time management and be more responsive to the worries of their clients.
- Coaches can intervene more directly and achieve higher effectiveness of their work.
- Coaching sessions allow for a dynamic reaction to changes in the personal and work environments of the client.
- Problematic issues can be brought in and discussed spontaneously.
- Coach and coachee can develop strategies and solutions for troublesome issues.

All the above points are derived from the personal experience of practitioners. I am sure that there are many more practical insights into the essence of intercultural executive coaching and especially into the criteria for successful coaches. The absence of general academic criteria renders great relevance to the insights of experienced coaches. For the corporations that include intercultural coaching as a tool for the personal development of their business leaders, this means that they have to invest more scrutiny when deciding about coaches and coaching strategies.

Juliana Roth, Professor of Intercultural Communication, Ludwig Maximilians University of Munich, Germany April 2016

Foreword by Dirk Brinkmann

Coaching for Leadership

Dirk Brinkmann

Colleagues become reports, bosses become colleagues, and decisions need to be taken and responded to faster than ever before: Welcome to modern leadership!

Seminars and toolkits alone cannot be the right response for a smooth transition of a young manager from middle to upper management. Coaching that is close to real-life practice—better still, 'shadowing' in the current job—is becoming more and more an elementary necessity and an appropriate support for young managers in transition.

Dirk Brinkmann, coaching client, Director, Arvato Bertelsmann SE Munich, Germany April 2012

Acknowledgments

I would like to express my sincere gratitude to many people who carry large responsibilities and are extremely busy and who helped in providing valuable data for my book by dedicating their precious time for interviews and informal discussions. I have taken care to name only those people who gave me their express consent:

- Andrew Lin, Managing Director Fronter International Co. Ltd., Taipei, Taiwan
- Dirk Brinkmann, Director Arvato Systems, The Bertelsmann SE Group, Germany
- Dr. Dirk Vossmann, Porsche AG, Wiesloch, Germany
- Dr. Wolfgang Heizmann, CIO Tognum, Friedrichshafen, Germany
- Jorg Limberg, Vice President/ General Manager HP Germany
- Helmut Fabry, CEO of Hexal AG, Holzkirchen, Germany
- Holger Fuhrmann, Director Order Processes, Merck AG, Darmstadt, Germany
- Jochen Seitz, Manager at Arval - BNP Paribas Group
- Christian Kuwer, IT Process Manager, Drexelmaier, Germany
- Chris Gueglhoer, Managing Director, GM GmbH, Germany
- Andy Johnston, Senior Director, Open Text, Germany
- Bernd Kueper, Vice President-Head of Sales, MTU Friedrichshafen, Germany
- Sebastian Meier, TI Automotive, Germany

The titles and positions held by the interviewees were valid at the time of the interview, when the draft title of the book was *Do I Need a Coach?* I would also like to thank those people who have chosen to remain anonymous.

I am grateful to those people and institutions who enable access to education, including the online educators providing courses free of charge—www.coursera.org, www.edX.org, www.khanacademy.org, lagunita.stanford.edu, and www.udacity.com—it is a blessing.

A dear friend who I have known for as long as I can remember advised me to move to Cuba, drink good wines, and smoke cigars to get inspiration for my book. According to him that is the only way to write a book. Even though I disagree with his views, I would like to express my sincere gratitude to my friend, Dipam Patel, in London, without whose support this book would never have taken off the ground.

Contents

Introduction 1

This book is about coaching, and about the fallacy that unconditional, sustainable change is possible through coaching. You could ask why there is a need for a book on these two subjects. Of the many claims and books on coaching I have consulted, I think it is important to discuss the ambiguities and distortions in order to remove misconceptions about what a coach does and what coaching is. For example, Astrid Schreyoegg, in her book, *Coaching, eine Einfuehrung fuer Praxis und Ausbildung* (2012, p. 27) (*Coaching, an Introduction for Practice and Education*), talks about coaching as a form of professional management consultancy (Coaching als professionelles Managementberatung), and claims that coaching offers therapy for professional ailments, 'Coaching als Therapie gegen berufliches Leid' (p. 84). The confusion around coaching is prolific. Schreyoegg's publishers claim the book is 'Das Standardwerk ist der fundierteste Leitfaden für Coaching profis und interessierte' (The standard work, the most profound guide for coaching professionals and those interested in it). If there is anything further away from coaching, then it is that coaching is a therapy or professional management consultancy. Another claim is that coaching comes from psychoanalysis; this was broadcast in a TV channel[1] in Germany. Besides my own disagreement and opinion that such claims are detrimental to coaches and clients alike, I am particularly pleased that Manfred F. R. Kets de Vries, a professor at INSEAD, in France, a graduate business school for leadership development and organisational change, writes, in 'Coaching's "good hour": creating tipping points' (in *Coaching: An International Journal of Theory, Research and Practice* (2013) 'outdated perceptions of coaching (confusing the coaching process with more traditional forms of psychoanalysis and psychotherapy) continue, making for the often great hesitancy about asking for help from someone in a helping profession' (p. 153). Other claims around coaching include that coaching comes from business psychology or human resources—see

[1] A German TV channel called 3Sat broadcast the programme on the 6 October 2015 at 20:15 pm. It was called *Der Coaching–Wahn* (*The Coaching–Madness*).

A. Kohli, *Effective Coaching, and the Fallacy of Sustainable Change*, Management for Professionals, DOI 10.1007/978-3-319-39735-1_1

Die Professionalisierung von Coaching—Ein Lesebuch für den Coach (2015, p. 105) (*The Professionalisation of Coaching—A Reader for the Coach*). In addition to the examples cited above, a simple search on the Internet will show the confusion is widespread and coaching is often linked with some other discipline such as psychological coaching. Coaching is a psychological process and it is a standalone service and does not need additives; it is also not an advisory service: *Coaching Theorie—Eine Einfuehrung* (2015, p. 20) (*Coaching Theory—an Introduction*). Even though coaching is not any of these things, people practising different professions can easily learn and implement coaching methods to enhance their competency. That does not give them the right to change the concept of coaching and attempt to refashion it into something other than what it was conceived by the founding fathers.

Of the many books I have read on coaching, let me cite a few: *So Coache Ich* (2012) (*Coaching My Way*); *Coaching—Erfrischend Einfach* (2008) (*Coaching—Plain Simple*); *Führen, Fördern, Coachen: So entwickeln Sie die Potenziale Ihrer Mitarbeiter* (2007) (*Lead, Encourage, Coach: This is how you develop the potential of your employees*); *Coaching Jenseits von Tools und Techniken* (2015) (*Coaching Beyond Tools and Techniques*); *Die Professionalisierung von Coaching—Ein Lesebuch für den Coach* (2015) (*The Professionalisation of Coaching—A Reader for the Coach*); *Emotionen im Coaching, Kommunikative Muster der Beratungsinteraktion* (2015) (*Emotions in Coaching, Communicative Pattern of the Advisory Interaction*); and *Coaching Theorie—Eine Einfuehrung* (2015) (*Coaching Theory—an Introduction*)—with few exceptions, hardly any of them mention where coaching originated.

Why is that necessary? Understanding the origins of coaching will clarify that the new forms of coaching are idiosyncratic, and help both the coaches and clients approach coaching with a sense of clarity and certainty. Yes, they all agree that coaching originated in the USA, but few books about coaching mention that it took its present form due to the contribution of certain people who were responsible for inventing the methodology that underpins modern coaching. A natural consequence of this oversight is confusion.

To validate this point, I asked Sabine Asgodom why she had chosen to call her book (mentioned above) *So Coach Ich* (*Coaching My Way*). To me the title of the book seemed as if she was saying, I coach like this, whatever the others may be saying about it or perhaps, whatever it may be. In an email from her office dated 3rd December 2015 I received the following answer: 'Um Ihre Frage zu beantworten, Frau Asgodom hat das Buch so genannt, weil sie darin die von ihr entwickelte Coaching-Methode vorgestellt hat.' ('To answer your question, Mrs. Asgodom has given her book this title because she presents the coaching method developed by her in it'). There is nothing wrong with developing a style that is personal. I think most coaches do it during their career. Imagine a potential client who is looking for a coach and comes across a title that says, this is how I developed it. What would he think? I think the first thought would be, perhaps there are other ways of coaching too. If that is so, he needs to identify which one is the appropriate one for him. This contributes to his insecurity and causes hesitancy in seeking help through any coach.

The reasons cited above make it difficult to demarcate between what coaching is and is not, and between who is and is not a coach. In the last 10 years, in particular, some of the existing professions have adopted the term 'coach'. A person who once offered his services to tweak your curriculum vitae to increase the likelihood of you getting a new job now calls himself a 'future coach'. The mystical shaman who drummed to communicate with the other side now calls himself a 'shaman coach'. Many management consultants now sell their services as 'business coaches'. Can the 'future' or a 'business' or even 'spirits' on the other side be coached?

The word 'coach', which is now added to many professional titles, is completely whimsical and so are many meanings that are being attributed to it. How can I say that with confidence? Besides learning coaching—personal coaching, as it was introduced for the first time around 1992 in the USA—from an institution that was founded by the person who is recognised as being 'the founder of coaching' in *The Coach U Personal and Corporate Coach Training Handbook* (2005), as a professional coach by conscious and diligent effort and not by accident, I have years of experience in coaching, and the word 'coach' does not signify anything other than the profession I pursue and as it is defined by the people who created coaching for us. I have implemented coaching methodically and observed my clients reap its benefits. The ambiguity that surrounds coaching as a new profession is not solely caused by the idiosyncratic interpretations of people who wilfully add the word 'coach' to their old professions. Coaches and clients alike grapple with the ambiguities of the term 'coaching'. I find some of the claims for coaching extremely problematic.

There is also a common belief with personnel managers that human resources managers are also by default good coaches, as if to imply that, since they have always dealt with human resources, they are best placed to provide coaching. Is that true? Does human resource management training provide the relevant prerequisites of a coach? To substantiate this claim, you will later on encounter Matt (See Sect. 9.5); it is a case study of a person who was coached by a human resources manager engaged by a multibillion-euro company whose decision makers based their selection criteria on this misconception. In addition to the case study of Matt, during my interaction with my clients, I regularly meet with senior personnel managers. It is not uncommon that many discuss their future plans with me. I have recorded 17 statements of HR managers who claimed that after retiring they could become a coach. What is wrong with that? Nothing, but it becomes problematic when they claim that they had been working with personnel and that the natural consequence of their professional experience is to move into coaching. When I wanted to know whether they would learn coaching after retiring, I received different answers but the gist of all of them was, they did not need to. One such statement from an HR manager of a worldwide well-known pharmaceutics company, who was also on the board of directors, was 'I have done it all my life; I know what coaching is'. Exploring these and many other questions about the nature of coaching occupied my research; they inform the basis for this book.

What about the sustainable change from coaching promised by practically every second brochure or website? A change, yes; I agree that coaching can trigger a change, but I disagree with those who claim that coaching provides unconditional, sustainable change.

My conclusion is that the coaching profession does not deserve either the prevailing ambiguity or the confusion surrounding it; neither should it be hijacked by anyone looking for a cosmetic facelift for their profession or job title. The distortion of the definition of coaching from its origins has led to its mutation into something that has nothing to do with coaching, except the use or perhaps abuse of the expression. In my opinion, the problems emerged because the people who created coaching and also the original methodology of coaching are overlooked. Due to the lack of a common understanding of the definition of the words 'coaching' and 'coach', potential clients, as well as coaches, suffer from an inferior quality of service from self-styled coaches, which is handed out to experienced professionals, even those within very large corporations. These practices are not short of shameful. Besides the hesitancy of potential clients to ask for help (as mentioned by Kets de Vries above), coaches face enormous resistance when they offer their services to potential clients. During my research I discovered, due to these difficulties, more than 85 % of new coaches pursue the profession only part-time, because they are unable to sell their services: 'it just does not provide enough revenue to sustain oneself; I have to take up a job where I can earn money regularly', said one coach who I interviewed. Some begin to offer coaching classes to find new ways to use their coaching skills, while others return to their old profession. In all about 8–10 % of the coaches I interviewed pursued coaching as their core profession.

When a coach approaches a client, the client is extremely insecure, if not suspicious, because he is unclear about the efficacy and outcome of coaching. The origins of coaching have been pushed into oblivion and unfortunately a client does not have a benchmark to see what coaching really can do for a person or a company. During my interviews, some clients said that the existing ambiguity became worse when coaches offered fanciful versions of coaching, for example, family constellations or metaphysical solutions for management issues—this adds to the existing difficulties of choosing a coach. One measure of what this confusion has caused in the general public is my personal example: whenever I introduce myself to someone new, I am asked what I do for a living. The moment I say I am a coach, the invariable question that follows in most cases, I would speculate 97 % of the time, is 'what coaching do you do?'

Coaching is not about 'what' it is about 'who'.

These and other reasons make it imperative to begin a new discussion on coaching. Through practical examples and case studies, I will demonstrate the shoddy treatment some professionals in world class corporations have undergone under the name of coaching, paid for by their employers. I will also offer a contrast, showing when and why coaching works; what changes it can bring about, and why it is a fallacy to promise sustainable change.

Research included field research—mainly qualitative—and interviews with many CEOs, entrepreneurs, senior managers, potential clients, and coaches. As a 'participant observer'[2] I enrolled in various courses in order to research the different training methods employed by institutions who offer coaching classes and certificates. The wide-ranging research meant I was able to differentiate between what is and is not coaching. One final and highly significant factor that goes a long way to substantiate my claims is my extensive coaching experience.

Since opening my coaching practice in 2010, my focus and quest, alongside offering a first-class coaching service to my clients, has been to find evidence of the visible and effective results of my coaching methodology. While my clients reported experiencing a positive difference from coaching, particularly the kind of difference they had desired in various areas at the outset of their coaching sessions—such as leadership, personal relationships, and sometimes, extremely challenging situations in many areas of their lives—I wanted to discover why they felt coaching had worked for them.

As I developed my coaching practice, I realised that formal knowledge would enable me to more effectively implement coaching methods in order to bring concrete benefits to my clients, while, at the same time, enhancing my skills. There was also the question of how to determine the difference between a coach and a psychoanalyst, a management consultant, a hypnotherapist coach, an NLP trainer coach, a Systemic coach, an adviser, or a human resources manager. For these reasons, in 2013, I enrolled in a distance-learning psychology degree at a German University. My intentions were very clear: I did not want to study psychology to practice as a psychologist; I enrolled in the course to study psychology to explore one aspect: I knew that in coaching I would primarily face questions about human personality, how human behaviour, emotions and perceptions are influenced by their environments and genetic inheritance. With all the scientific studies and its long history, there is no better discipline than psychology to give in-depth knowledge in this area. In addition, I also undertook around 20 online study courses, offered by institutions, such as, Stanford.[3] The online courses were a blessing because they were instrumental in helping me to understand which subjects to study in detail. I was able to gauge whether I needed more knowledge in methodical and critical thinking, Gamification, irrationality, discipline of logic, research methods, studies in leadership and emotional intelligence, psychology, or philosophy.

The book is ordered according to the different relevant questions arising from the research:

- What is coaching?

[2]The expression has its origins in anthropology. It was coined by Bronislaw Malinowski. I interpret the phrase to mean being part of those who I am with but not being one of them.

[3]The courses were offered from the following institutions: www.coursera.org, www.khanacademy.org, lagunita.stanford.edu, www.udacity.com and www.edX.org

- Can a coach claim to bring about a sustainable change for his clients?
- Do clients want to change through coaching?
- Who needs coaching?
- Does coaching work?
- Why does coaching work?

The reference point of this book is the German coaching and business community and society in general, although my professional activity extends beyond Germany. The decision to focus on the German business community is because the ambiguity around coaching is more prevalent in Germany. That is also the reason why I focused most of my research, interviews, schooling, further studies, and observations there. The German TV programme mentioned earlier, broadcast on 6 October 2015, claimed that there were 16,000 coaches in the US and they were mostly personal coaches or life coaches. In Germany, it was reported in the same broadcast, there are about 8000 coaches. I have no possibility to verify these figures and have quoted them on their face value.

For the sake of inclusiveness, I use gender interchangeably throughout the book. This I have done for convenience of reading and without any intention to disregard gender: reference to one gender should be understood as to the gender of your own preference.

References

Asgodom, S. (2012). *So coache ich*. Munich: Koesel Verlag. English Edition: Asgodom, S. (2014). *Coaching my way* (M. Seisenberger, Trans.). Hamburg: Kreutzfeld Digital.

Böening, U. (2015). *Coaching Jenseits von Tools und Techniken*. Heidelberg: Springer.

Der Coaching–Wahn. (*The Coaching–Madness*), broadcast on SWR, 6 October 2015 at 20:15 pm. http://www.3sat.de/page/?source=/wissenschaftsdoku/sendungen/183147/index.html&cx=12. Accessed 6 Oct 2015.

Haberleitner, E., Deistler, E., & Ungvari, R. (2007). *Führen, fördern, coachen: So entwickeln sie die potenziale ihrer mitarbeiter* [Lead, encourage, coach: *This is how you develop the potential of your employees*]. Heidelberg: Redline GmbH.

Kets de Vries, M. F. R. (2013). Coaching's 'good hour': Creating tipping points. *Coaching: An International Journal of Theory, Research and Practice*, *6*(2), 152–175.

Leonard, T. J. (2005). *The Coach U personal and corporate coach training handbook*. Hoboken, NJ: Wiley.

Loebbert, M. (2015). *Coaching Theorie—Eine Einfuehrung* [*Coaching theory—An introduction*]. Wiesbaden: Springer.

Meier, D., & Szabo, P. (2008). *Coaching—Erfrischend einfach*. Luzern: Solutionsurfers GmbH. English Edition: Meier, D., & Szabo, P. (2009). *Coaching—Plain Simple* (K. Dierolf, Trans.). New York: Norton.

Schreyoegg, B. (2015). *Emotionen im Coaching, Kommunikative Muster der Beratungsinteraktion* [*Emotions in coaching, communicative pattern of the advisory interaction*]. Wiesbaden: Springer.

Schreyoegg, A., & Schmidt-Lellek, C. (2012). *Coaching, eine Einfuehrung fuer Praxis und Ausbildung* [*Coaching, an introduction for practice and education*]. Frankfurt: Campus Verlag. http://deposit.d-nb.de/cgi-bin/dokserv?id=4043001&prov=M&dok_var=1&dok_ext=htm. Accessed 15 Jul 2015.

Schreyoegg, A., & Schmidt-Lellek, C. (Hrsg.). (2015). *Die Professionalisierung von Coaching—Ein Lesebuch für den Coach* [*The professionalisation of coaching—A reader for the coach*]. Wiesbaden: Springer.

2 Leadership and Coaching

The oldest memory that I have about an inspirational leader and of someone thinking of developing new leaders is that of Akio Morita. He also left behind a lasting impression on me through his writing. Morita, along with Masaru Ibuka, were the founders of the electronics giant Sony Corporation in 1946. For me, Morita's foresight left behind a concept of development for future managers that I could not compare to any other. I found it fascinating that a person could select someone who would almost four decades later become the CEO of Sony. At the time when I read *Made in Japan* (1986), I did not have a concrete concept of leadership. After reading it, somehow, I was certain that a business person—a manager—should prepare future managers. I also thought of it as a way to secure the future of your company; make it a sustainable business model. In *Made in Japan* (1986), Morita talks about his young staffers and associates and mentions Norio Ohga in 1950. He says, 'I had had my eyes on him for all those years because of his bold criticism of our first machine. He was a great champion of the tape recorder, but he was severe with us because he didn't think our early machine was good enough' (p. 122). In 1989, 39 years later, Ohga became the CEO of this international giant and is credited for giving us the compact disc (CD).

From Morita, I learnt that executives need to look for people who will criticise their ideas or products and their way of working. It is not just about accepting criticism but also using it as an opportunity to see reason—to notice what others notice. Only then, I thought, will there be greatness in any product, idea, or company or even in human interaction.

In reality, in our daily practice, what is it that we do? We regard those who criticise us as irritating, as a nuisance, as someone who does not understand what our company or what we are about: we shortlist them as a candidate to be fired. On the other hand, what do we do as individuals, as employees? We indulge in the institutional imperative: we agree to what the boss says unconditionally. He must be right, he is the boss. What do we do for the development of future leaders? Nothing; we have no time. Take a look at the comments of a successful young business

A. Kohli, *Effective Coaching, and the Fallacy of Sustainable Change*, Management for Professionals, DOI 10.1007/978-3-319-39735-1_2

leader, Mr. Stefan Rau, in the Foreword, and in particular, what he says about not having time or focus on developing new leaders or managers.

Leadership and coaching have something in common: both are person-centred. Leadership creates a fertile environment for growth; coaching creates awareness and perceptions for growth. Most companies, when they look for a top person, focus on the fact of whether he comes from the same trade. For example, in the companies in which I have gained business experience, we would look for a textiles expert to join us for the top job. In short, we were looking for someone to manage the textiles trade, but we gave him the position of a leader, managing director, or CEO. Morita employed Ohga, who was a music aficionado: he had studied music in Munich and Berlin.

Coaching and leadership does not focus on your trade; it is irrespective of whether you are a musician or a textile expert. Coaching and leadership looks at you; it is always person-centred: both coaching and leadership let people do and learn as they are.

I learnt coaching to share my ideas and conviction about developing young people, future managers, and leaders, in order to exploit my profound international, intercultural, and leadership experience with my peers—executives and decision makers—to enable them to discover that work is not all stress and it can create a contentment for life that we easily overlook or do not consider even for 1 minute. We are sold on the idea that if you do something you love you thrive. I am convinced, irrespective of what you do—professionally or privately—a conscious effort to create an environment where others can work without being intimidated or humiliated, can create the same effect. I am also convinced that a particular kind of personal behaviour, which can be inculcated through coaching, can create the same effect that you would have achieved by doing that which you love to do the most.

What is this particular kind of personal behaviour? I will demonstrate to you in the following discussion. I wanted to convey through coaching that it is possible to discover that there is more to work than the unending demand for urgent reactions, hectic meetings, airport lounges, etc. Some of my friends educated in reputed, prestigious universities in India, UK, and USA were in positions with well-known corporations doing a wonderful job in one area while demonstrating complete unawareness in others. I will not talk about incompetence on their part because they were far from incompetent. These executives were sincere in their work, and toward their manager and staff. Since I had the privilege to know them closely it was easy to talk to them about their concerns. If one missed out creating a proper environment in their company, then he thought it was the responsibility of individual managers not his own. If another one overlooked talking to his managers regularly outside of the boardroom, he thought they were being paid well and should understand everything by themselves. As soon as I started coaching executives, I encountered the same phenomenon: CEOs or other C level executives and managers with similar responsibilities doing honest work being bogged down for years with small irritating issues. I was convinced that the amount of effort most of them put in every day could get better results by reducing the amount of time they spent extinguishing small fires, playing firefighters, and fixing things. I knew that with self-reflection through coaching conducted with someone who has had a large exposure to international business, they would gain insight into what is going on with them. In *Tricky Coaching* (2012, p. 13) Korotov et al. suggest, 'There are two particularly interesting features of a career as an executive coach. First, entrance to this professional field is not possible without a substantial amount of previous work and life experience, and second, it is (consequently) a very attractive career transition option for individuals at a midlife and mid-career point.' Even though I rely on my previous work experience, I limit this reliance to life experience and personal interaction because I think if I had relied on my previous work experience in textiles and the fashion trade and offered 'fashion or textile coaching' alone, then it would not be coaching; further, it could infringe in the area of management consultancy.

I was convinced that through coaching my clients would experience how to lead a more contented approach to their work. This would affect their personal life which in turn would make them more alert and interested in their work. It is a chain that is interdependent, like a circular structure where one affects the other directly. Through coaching they would notice what they were tolerating, or that they were living with compromises they did not need to put up with. These were my own ideas that I had developed working with thousands of people in numerous countries in the world. I also thought about the question, why could they not look at it themselves?

Recently, a successful young entrepreneur from Gujrat, India, who is in the process of setting up his European operations in London, said that he wanted my opinion on certain decisions. I wanted to know why he wanted to hear my views, as I am not from his industry. What he told me validates my point: he said, 'when we business people seek out new potential partners, as I am doing here in London, we have our interests strongly influencing our decisions because we want things to take a form within a time frame. We may sometimes be willing to accept mediocre qualities in others, or even see in others only what we wish to see because we want to finalise steps, reach goals. Talking to someone, like you, who has no personal interest in our business but is at the same time a business professional could throw light on the blind spots or bring in new perspectives to make us aware of the pitfalls of our goals.' Most of us look at our own issues ourselves and we tend to legitimise them and accept them as they are.

There is also the problem of the speed with which they habitually have to react to the work challenges and succumb to their hectic routine. Try to imagine this sentence, 'we have no time to work at our work'. I had used this sentence often with those partners who chronically delayed their delivery of goods. I think that every manager should dedicate time and resources to developing future managers, leaders, and staff wherever they can, but the circular problem, of course, is who has the time? My discussion should not be understood as criticism of executives; this is the state for many: this is not new to anyone in the business world.

Whether it was a small start-up company or a large international corporation, the leadership influences how people work together.

2.1 What Is Coaching?

In a broad descriptive sense, coaching is about learning, teaching, and an inspirational-style of behaviour that is non-judgemental and supportive. In more specific terms it is about intrinsic learning, getting new perspectives on habitual situations, events, and perceptions. It is about building self-confidence and gaining self-esteem through coaching. This learning is not that of a conventional student, a participant of a seminar or from a self-help manual—aspiring to gain access to knowledge—to acquire some skill that is common to all; the difference of degree of knowledge acquired does not influence the life of the learner significantly. The degree of difference in knowledge about oneself, or better still, the confidence to attempt more than one would normally because of coaching, significantly affects the client's life and those near her.

Coaching is not the same as conventional teaching, instructing, training or any form of teaching we have known that delivers knowledge of specific skills common to all. To demonstrate this difference, I would like to give an example of conventional teaching and learning where the degree of difference is minimal between what I learn and what someone else does. Imagine I learn to drive a car; firstly, the instructor will not treat me any differently than he has his other students. Secondly, the car will not behave any differently with me than it does with others. In contrast, a coach will treat every client as an individual and adapt his methods according to the needs of the client. Going back to the example of learning to drive a car: it is most likely that through this learning and teaching interaction, I drive a car like 95 % of other car drivers. The remaining 5 % I have reserved for the outliers with 2.5 % on each side of a normal distribution curve. Driving a car will affect my life so that I can reach my destinations easily, but whether I drive a car extremely well, well, or just average will not affect my life much, unless I were an incompetent driver and belong in the 2.5 % that endanger others on the road. On the other hand, if I were a Formula 1 racing driver and had acquired specific skills for the sake of competition, I would then belong on the other side of the normal distribution in 2.5 % of all drivers. (These figures are fictive to demonstrate uniformity of learning of common skills for those in the 95 %.) This uniformity does not exist in coaching; every client learns according to her own capabilities. While it is not the case that a driving instructor could not implement coaching methods for the 95 %, it is not necessary in motor skills and driving instructors to do a good job as it is without additional methods of self-realisation. Motor skills are based on practice; the more you practice the better you get. Coaching is different: by learning through self-reflection, you have the option to encounter and react to your issues in your own environment within your own capabilities with greater ease.

I have mentioned above that coaching is on the one hand about teaching and learning and on the other about inspirational behaviour. Let me address the teaching and learning relationship of coaching first. This relationship is of a professional coach and his client where the client learns by talking to the coach, who ideally enables her to look at her own issues with a different perspective by questioning her using a specific method. The intention of the coach is to enable her to gain more self-confidence and self-esteem: instil a growth mindset. The concept of 'growth mindset' I refer to is explained in *Mindset* (2012) by Carol Dweck, Lewis and Virginia Eaton Professor of psychology at Stanford University. Dweck is known for her research on self-theories. Coaching should enable the client to better understand her own views, perspective, and capabilities, relevant to her own environment. This should lead to reducing the level of self-doubt or self-criticism and consequently increase her efficiency and performance with greater ease in her daily routine. This is valid for both the personal and professional areas of one's life. When we talk about teaching in the above scenario, it is more symbolic, even then we are assuming that the coach has some knowledge to impart otherwise the relationship would take the form of any normal conversation between two people. The knowledge that a coach possesses is that of a method, and not any other particular skill. It is not similar to the knowledge of teaching how to, for example, drive a car. Coaching as a profession is a person-centred conversational method with its sole aim to provide benefit to the client. It nudges the client to self-realisation and to gain insights to achieve all the attributes that have been discussed above to improve her life.

In the second scenario, where I said that coaching is about inspirational behaviour, the question, what is coaching, differs because the role of teacher has the power of sanctions as well as the pitfall of complacency; both can undermine the potential of dependent people. The coaching method in this scenario is dependent on one's behaviour. The purpose of coaching or inspirational behaviour that manifests coaching methodology is identical: to encourage learning of one's own capabilities, instil a growth mindset, and instate self-confidence and self-esteem. The difference is, one is practised as a profession where both components of complacency and sanctions are absent and the other is the result of one's behaviour.

Let me give you a few examples to demonstrate what I mean. Managers have the authority to hire or fire people, to allocate pleasant or unpleasant tasks, permit or refuse benefits to an employee for whatever reasons. Parents, for example can be complacent or punishing toward their own children, ask them to remain in their room or not care what they do, withdraw pleasure-giving activities or ignore damaging habits or pamper them excessively. Partners can be complacent or nagging, ask for excessive tenderness, or deny it to sanction undesired behaviour, and so on.

If we stay for a while with managers and dissect the word, in simple words, it would mean managers *manage*. We manage something that could become unmanageable or go out of control: financial management, crisis management, or what have you. Coaching is not about control; it is letting the client develop, grow, realise their potential and learn—is inspirational behaviour. Coaching should ideally be compared with leadership and inspiring people and not with management, but that is a small thought I have because we talk about management without ever thinking that we are talking about exerting control.

Going back to my discussion above, there are numerous examples to demonstrate what causes us to be contented or discontented and limit our efforts to a minimum or exceed our limits and go the extra mile. The balance between extremes is the function of the coaching method whose aim is to enable healthy learning and promote an environment of trust and confidence building. A manager who neither sanctions nor is complacent with his employees and who is more interested in them learning new skills and discovering their own potential, promotes an atmosphere of trust, self-esteem, and growth. The result is he has better results with lesser effort in his work. Parents who do not rigorously sanction or are not complacent toward their children, raise self-confident people. The result is a satisfied and self-confident family. Partners who show understanding for shortcomings or appreciate the talents of the other, support each other, develop deeper and contented relationships. The result is a better life and stable relationships.

None of this is new, so why do we need coaching? We need coaching because of the simple question: how many people practise this knowledge? Under the expression 'coaching' an awareness about a method is being spread on what kind of behaviour leads to better relationships, better efficiency, better performance, and a contentment in one's life. Those who do not know why things go wrong in their work or personal life, who do not know how things could be as they wish them to be, seek out a coach as a form of professional help. Those who have managers, parents, and partners who are practising this method will know what it is when I am talking about being fortunate. With the introduction of coaching, it is possible to teach those who affect the lives of others how to enhance their skills and to interact for superior and lasting results.

In this book, my focus will be mainly on the first scenario, where coaching is a profession but I will narrate some examples from the other scenario too. Let me give you an example of an instinct a human being possesses: to learn something without any external interference, instructions or advice. It is also an example of how a person who is interested in seeing a human learn something stays out of the process of learning. Sir John Whitmore, one of the pioneers of coaching, in his book *Coaching for Performance* (2009, p. 10) asks: 'how did you learn to walk? Did your mother instruct you? We all have a built-in, natural learning capability that is actually disrupted by instructions.' During coaching, a coach trusts this very natural capability of a human being to learn in his own interest, even when we discuss adults and not just infants. It is this disruption through giving instructions that a coach avoids and lets his clients learn at their own pace, relying on their own capabilities.

Even though the natural instinct to learn is present in all human beings, unless impaired due to some illness, not all children will learn to walk exactly within, say 397 days. Each human being takes her own time. A coach begins coaching when both sides—the client and the coach—have been able to identify what the client wants to improve in whichever area of her life. Based on that a coach uses coaching methodology to encourage the client to critically question her own questions, own thinking, and discuss her issues in an environment of confidentiality. The insights that the client gains through this process are new to her and this makes coaching a learning process or better still a discovering process for the client: gaining insights and developing new perspectives.

How do I know this? In any coaching meeting, within the first 20 minutes, my client experiences an 'Aha!' effect. In my experience, the client will most likely say something similar to, 'I never thought about it like this'. If that is not so, then the coach has not begun to understand the client or the confidentiality has not yet been established, which is essential for coaching. Coaching provokes you into thinking about new ways and triggers learning through reflection. The 'Aha!' effect is the determinant stimulus that will lead you to consider new options and this experience for the client is normally fascinating.

In professional coaching, a client thinks independently in order to create her own options, thoughts, and solutions. The dependence of a client on her coach is limited only to his method and his skill to stay out of the process of thinking and solution finding; to be present as a nudge or a catalyst. This should not be underestimated; it is not easy to stay out of the way or refrain from giving instructions. Not giving instructions is a very difficult job, because we all love to do it naturally. I agree with Whitmore (2009, p. 11), when he says, 'It may be harder to give up instructing than to learn coaching'. As soon as the learning process for a client is dependent on instructions, assessments, instruments or advice, the coaching process ceases to exist. When we talk about coaching it is not about any extrinsic skill that is taught and which people can see you implementing physically—it is a psychological process. Timothy Gallwey was one of the first people to discuss coaching as the 'Inner Game', and his book *The Inner Game of Tennis* (1974; 2015) inspires coaches today. Gallwey was a national tennis player and through his observations developed a very effective concept of performance coaching. On his website Gallwey explains, 'There is always an inner game being played in your mind no matter what outer game you are playing. How aware you are of this game can make the difference between success and failure in the outer game.' My concept of coaching is based on similar ideas: irrespective of what your occupation or business may be, there is an inner game going on internally and it is private. You may talk to a coach to help you to examine, revisit, or rethink your inner game at any time. This is the reason that I am convinced that coaching has to do with insights, self-reflection, and perceptions and not with the 'outer game', or of any particular businesses or skills. It has nothing to do with the 'do this to achieve that' way of thinking. It is not related to physical action. Coaching is purely a reflective exercise to develop self-awareness.

If that is so, why do we have so many titles for coaches? Let me give you my explanation for this situation. For example, if you decide to coach advocates, that may be your choice of a group of people you prefer to work with, hence you selected to coach solely this group of people. Coaching methodology does not change with the group of people you are coaching. Your decisions may have rested on the fact that you may have been a judge, an advocate, or a professional where you interacted with advocates and feel comfortable with them. If you propose to be a 'Law Coach' is it possible that people think that you may be implying that you will coach people on their legal issues? If that were so, would you not be treading or going near the profession of an advocate? Would this also not imply that you would advise your coaching clients on matters concerning the law? If you are advising or training people for any skill or competency you may not be coaching in the true sense of coaching as discussed above but training or advising.

Let me give you my own example from my personal experience. I had been in the corporate world for almost 35 years. Had I decided to market my coaching as business coaching, would I not be implying that I will teach you how to do business? I think a management consultant or a business-specific adviser may be better placed for this job. By choosing to be an 'executive coach', I have consciously chosen to coach my peers, irrespective of their industry. I coach, I do not advise on how to develop business strategies. What is wrong with that? Business strategies are business-specific while coaching is not. I am sure you will agree that the business strategy for selling beers and alcohol may be different to that for selling life insurance or automobiles. Coaching an executive from any of these or other industries does not depend on the products they sell. As a coach I am not restricted to a business; I can coach executives from any industry or business, and at any time I can choose to coach private people too, because I am working on the psychological level, which is coaching. Whereas if I was an expert on life insurance and chose to call myself a 'life insurance coach' I may be creating confusion because I am really offering my expertise in life insurances. Similarly, if I call myself a psychological coach, ask yourself what am I really offering that a psychologist with years of education cannot do? Coaching is a psychological interaction between two people: the coach and his client. The client may entail a single person or a group of people.

Instructional learning or teaching based on 'how to' steps is not coaching. As soon as you receive instructions you have to remember all of them and to constantly pay attention to them simultaneously. Recall how it was when you learnt driving for the first time (if you did learn to drive). Most likely, the instructor said, now press the accelerator, no not too much, you may cause an accident. No, that is too little it will kill the engine and now the clutch, and so on. Further, you constantly have to demonstrate that each instruction was followed. If you are unable to do so or slip even once you will most likely indulge in self-criticism and with it stop the process of learning that is discussed in coaching. With instruction, the coach himself becomes a prisoner of his instructions because he needs to be vigilant that he is giving them in the right sequence and that the client is following them in the identical sequence too: you cannot accelerate and then press the clutch. Instructions inherently bring with them certain evaluation processes to measure how well you have understood them, and as a consequence, it also brings criticism, which heightens client stress. This is contrary to the concept of coaching.

Despite all the discussions on coaching in various books, papers, and magazines, I am of the opinion that coaching is a service that needs no adjectives or additives that show expertise in any particular profession except coaching methodology. I am excluding your personal choice of group of people you coach, as discussed above. Its methods and all its tools are in the method of questioning in order to trigger healthy critical thinking in the client's mind. I think this view of coaching as a method serves almost any profession willing to take advantage of it: a management consultant can use it as well as a medical doctor, a parent as well as a teacher. Since it is a conversational method, it is natural that a coach stands to take advantage from the knowledge of the subjects of psychology and philosophy. There are other subjects that come into play in coaching, which I will discuss later, but not in such a predominant manner that coaching should be renamed to something such as 'psychological coaching'. Coaching as a method is psychological and this tautology is superfluous. However, what is this method? This is what this book is going to discuss too.

To conclude the discussion on what coaching is, I once again refer to Whitmore as a symbol of support in what I think coaching is. Whitmore (2009, p. 18) writes that 'coaching is not merely a technique to be wheeled out and rigidly applied in certain prescribed circumstances. It is a way of managing, a way of treating people, a way of thinking, a way of being.' This is my argument about the two scenarios of coaching: the professional one and the one that involves the behaviour of people in any setting.

2.2 The Origins of Coaching

In the beginning of the book, I addressed the confusion that surrounds coaching in Germany. To throw light on this topic, it is imperative to look at the documented facts and demonstrate that coaching is not an ambiguous concept nor are its origins unknown. Even though there is broad agreement in the books mentioned in the Introduction (see Chap. 1) that coaching comes from sports, this claim is recent and there are reasons behind it, but if we go back in time, we will discover that there is more to it than just sports. Anthony M. Grant, coaching psychologist at the University of Sydney in Australia, gives us ample evidence in his research publication, *Workplace, Executive and Life Coaching: An Annotated Bibliography from the Behavioural Science and Business Literature* (2011) that the first mention of coaching goes back to a discussion article published in 1937. At that time, even if we had baseball coaches and other sports coaches, no one discussed personal coaching or that it originated with sports. Grant's work shows the progression of discussion of coaching in time, right through until the date when different people started becoming claimants for creating coaching. Let me give you a few examples from his work mentioned above, to demonstrate the progression and to reveal how the concept of coaching has been discussed for a very long time:

> Gorby, C. B. (1937), 'A report of a profit-sharing plan in existence in the Hosking Manufacturing Company, Detroit, since 1923. [.] ... In consequence costs have been reduced, labor turnover is almost non-existent, and older employees assume the task of **coaching** others in the importance of spoiled work.'; Lewis, P. B. (1947), 'The foundation of training at DuPont is training through example all along the line. Next in importance comes **coaching** on-the-job, which is really just good supervision ...'; or Mold, H. P. (1951), 'This is a case study presentation of a training program for executives of a pulp and paper mill in the south. It is based on the work simplification approach to problem-solving. [.] ... The author's general conclusion is that the problem of executive development is a problem in (1) counseling, (2) **coaching** of each executive by his superior, and (3) training

in human behavior. It is a problem of getting the individual executive to understand his own needs for acceptance, his fear, and his aggressions [. . .].'; or Walter Mahler (1964), 'Although good **coaching** is basic to managerial productivity, most organizations have difficulty getting their managers to be **effective coaches**. The author's research provides numerous insights into this problem.'

Another article, published in the *Training & Development Journal* (1983, p. 30), 'Coaching: A Tool for Success', by Lynne Tyson and Herman Birnbrauer, who were both, at the time of publication of the article, vice president and president of the Institute of Business and Industry Inc., highlights how, 'coaching has been defined as individually helping a subordinate to improve job performance. Coaching is always directed toward helping individuals develop a particular environment and, as a result of the personal development, improve performance.' Later in the same article Tyson and Birnbrauer discuss the pitfalls of coaching which were directed at measuring performance and they mention that no standards were laid down. In the same article, they also discuss possible guidelines for coaching.

In the Introduction (see Chap. 1) I also addressed the whimsical use of the word 'coach' that has led to hesitancy on the part of both clients and coaches to take advantage of this concept and I discussed how many have complained that no one knows where coaching comes from or what coaching is. With the work of Anthony M. Grant, it is safe to say that these claims are false or at least the claimants are not aware of Grant's work. It provides evidence that the concept of coaching was being discussed in terms of personal development for a long time: coaching did not emerge from one single person or all of a sudden or solely from sports.

The emergence of coaching schools since the 1970s did not solely originate with sports; there is one more side to it. As a young student in Delhi, India, in the 1970s, the word coach was familiar to me, because I could see the billboards and pamphlets of people and private institutes offering coaching to prepare aspiring students for entrance or final examinations of reputed institutions and universities. Later on, in the 2000s, when I first encountered professional coaching and wanted to learn it, I wondered why there was a difference in understanding of this word in India and in the USA. Vikki G. Brock, a Master-Coach, has conducted extensive research on the history of coaching, which she has published in *The Sourcebook of Coaching History* (Second Edn. 2014). Brock writes (p. 134), 'In their 1989 article "Coaching and the Art of Management", Robert Evered and Jim Selman tell us that the word "coach" was first used to a person in the 1840s. It was at Oxford University where the word "coach" was used colloquially to refer to a private tutor, not associated with the university, who prepared a student for an examination'. All these references—from 1840, 1937, those in sports and contemporary references—all have one thing in common: they align coaching with helping people. Coaching is about teaching and learning—irrespective which period or context is being discussed—it is about teaching and learning. According to Brock, the first use of the word coach (to mean a carriage) in the English language appeared in the 1500s. For those familiar with historical images it was mostly a horse-drawn carriage, a vehicle used to transport people (who could afford one). This mention has nothing in common with my pursuit of coaching as a helping profession.

Brock (2014, p. 6) makes another important point about the origins of coaching, when she notes:

> the roots of coaching reach deep into the soil of human history. They push far beneath the appearance of the human potential movement in the 1960s. They extend far below the advent of management consulting and industrial organisations. They burrow past the introduction of vocational guidance, adult education, 12-step programmes, and human resources and they reach past the birth of psychology and psychiatry. In short, coaching is far, far older than the roots from which it descended. Examples of those who practiced a form of coaching stretch back into antiquity. Thousands of years before the appearance of what we now call life coaches, and before the emergence of business coaches in the corporate world, the practice of coaching—that is assisting individuals in reaching their personal goals—was a familiar human activity.

If that were the case then the coaching method also existed earlier, much earlier than the claims that it stems from sports and we could perhaps agree that it was not called coaching.

I also recall that during an online course on *Inspiring Leadership Through Emotional Intelligence* with Professor Richard E. Boyatzis of Case Western Reserve University, USA, the question or the crux of the course was who is inspiring and how a leader inspires. In my business experience, and I would like to add in my own family, I have seen that inspirational behaviour of a person has the identical outcome to that of a coaching method: people do more than they thought they could. People take on more responsibility for their actions in a professional environment. At home, children are willing to accept the ideas of a parent without any tension or crying 'generational gap!' Relationships among family members are much more stable, trusting, and supportive than they are without this behaviour.

If I were to ask you how does this happen—is it due to inspirational behaviour or coaching method? I think it would be difficult to draw a line. In my opinion, they are the same. Let us give credit to all the people named above for the origins of coaching and still ask, were there no inspiring people before we started talking about coaching originating with sports or elsewhere? If you agree with me that there were, then the next natural question could be, were they perhaps not using coaching methods or a particular behaviour that inspired others to follow them? All this probably had only one drawback—inspirational behaviour or coaching methods had not been documented in order to be able to teach it to others and spread it around for the common good of more people. Try this small exercise to validate what I have said: ask someone or even yourself to be inspirational so that people have more confidence in you, in your actions, and trust you. This exercise you can do anywhere at home or in work. It is more than likely you will ask a counter question: how can I be inspirational? For the next step forget the inspirational part and try to implement the coaching method and see the outcomes, and then ask yourself whether you inspired anyone. If the answer is yes, then both inspirational behaviour and the coaching method are children of the same mother: identical twins. Brock refers to Socrates as the first coach and indeed this is a very significant reference, which I agree with. Whitmore expresses similar thoughts in his book *Coaching for Performance* (2009, p. 10): 'The idea was not new: Socrates had voiced the same concept some 2000 years earlier, but somehow his philosophy got lost in the rush of materialistic reductionism of the last two centuries.'

Both Brock and Whitmore give Socrates[1] credit for 'voicing' or using the concept of coaching. As a matter of fact, a Socratic dialogue is an appropriate example of how a coach conducts his conversation with his client. The works of Plato and also the Socratic works of Xenophon illustrate this method very well. A word of caution here: coaching is not a dialectic method where two people hold different points of view and each defends hers to weaken the other's, which is the essence of the Socratic dialogue. In coaching, the point of view of the client is the sole focus of the conversation. If a coach holds a point of view it is best that he keeps it to himself. There is an old saying which should serve as a gentle reminder to every coach: 'Keep your own counsel'. There should be no attempt to weaken the point of view of the client. The whole exercise has one single aim: to stimulate healthy critical self-reflection. There may be times when a coach sees the necessity to give an answer so as not to appear completely rigid and inflexible; however, the purpose of both the questions and answers is to stimulate healthy critical thinking. When a coach is able to stimulate critical thinking, he is implementing a conversational method. This method opens the way for explorations—now even for a step further: critical explorations by the client. The client encounters her own questions, now posed by the coach, and begins to reflect on them from a different perspective. In my experience, this process enables the client to rethink her issues without any external advice or interventions. The coach can see the evidence of this rethinking process instantly when the client begins to evaluate and begins to give an unsolicited report that she perceives a change in intensity of her feelings toward her issues. The change in intensity manifests itself in expressions such as, 'I never thought about my problems like this before' or 'the issue I wanted to discuss with you seems so far away and irrelevant to me now,' or 'I would rather discuss other areas that seem more important to me now'.

Fortunately, the observations and the effort to document the work of coaching pioneers has made us realise that certain aspects of human behaviour lead people to learn better, perform better, and become better people. The only thing not done earlier is to name the effects of certain behaviour as a 'coaching method'. In the Introduction (see Chap. 1) I discuss how coaching does not come from or belong to management consulting, as claimed by one of the books in the list mentioned. It is possible for a management consultant to implement coaching methods to enhance his services but the claim would be false if someone said coaching originates or is a paradigm of management consultancy. There was also the question I had wanted to find out, which is whether a psychologist can coach people. Psychology is the result

[1]A Greek philosopher between 469 and 369 BC credited as being the founder of western philosophy.

of empirical findings of human behaviour. The behaviour of humans did not follow psychology—it is the other way around. Psychology seeks to understand, explain, and predict human behaviour. A psychologist is capable of coaching, as a matter of fact, it would enhance the work of a psychologist to include the coaching method in their work—as we learn in coaching classes. That is the reason to say that we do not need to discuss whether psychologists can do the work of a coach: we need both.

How did coaching reach a point where people began to learn and practice it as a profession? The profession of modern coaching began much later than the discussion on coaching. While most of us quote Timothy Gallwey because of his book *The Inner Game of Tennis* (1974) to underline that coaching comes from sports, if you look closely at what he writes in the book, it is the coaching method that Gallwey implemented in sports not the other way around. He articulated and documented something many people have done in different ways to enhance their performance for a very long time. This thought of mine is confirmed by Professor Beattie,[2] who in the foreword for the 2015 edition of *The Inner Game of Tennis* writes, 'If you read this book with the sole idea of becoming a winner, I suspect that Gallwey himself would be more than a little disappointed by your sense of purpose.' *The Inner Game* talks about coaching people to play tennis and confirms that coaching someone is about the inner game of the mind and not about learning how to play tennis.

Even though Gallwey dedicates one full chapter to the 'Ground Strokes' in a discussion of Grips, Footwork, Serve, and Power in tennis, which might, at first glance, seem like instructions, a closer examination reveals that Gallwey stays true to the principles of coaching: he is discussing how to teach and how to learn. His concern is not how to learn the best grip or the ideal footwork, his concern is clearly to understand how your student—in coaching, your client—understands you. His concern is the inner game that goes on when instructions are being given by someone: how much of it is really going to help the listener to transform it into performance enhancing learning? How does one interpret ideal grip? How will the client perceive the right feeling for herself? The instruction runs the risk of being too rigid so that it may stifle discovery of an ideal style best suited for the client. He quotes Cyrano de Bergerac as a metaphor from fencing to convey this concept: 'Hold the foil as a bird, not too loosely that it can fly away, not so tightly that you squeeze the life out of it' (1974; 2015, p. 45), and goes on to say even that is not sufficient because the personal experience of his student is understanding for them what creates the ideal grip. This is exactly what I mean when I say that coaching is about gaining insights and not about instruction that, to borrow from Gallwey, 'obey' a set of how-to manuals. The problem is that a coach could represent an authoritative figure and his instructions may become something the client feels compelled to obey. Are these instructions then executable too? This is the main difference between a coach and other helping professions, or we can expand this discussion further and say: to any method of interaction and the coaching method, a

[2]Professor of Psychology at Edge Hill University, UK.

coach is focused on what the client is discovering and not what the coach himself knows or says. As a matter of fact, the coach needs to pay attention to all he says so that it is clearly also serving the purpose for the client to discover new ideas and learning. That is the reason for me to say that coaching is person-centred and not associated with a business skill. Gallwey's book discusses the inner game of learning, as the title says, and exactly as I have said earlier—it is about intrinsic learning. It is about how people learn if you leave them the freedom to discover through insight; it becomes an extremely tedious process of learning if someone continues to give instructions. Coaching is about the inner game, irrespective whether you use it in business, in relationships, or raising children. Personal coaching focuses on human behaviour and development and human perceptions in general, which is an extremely wide area when you compare it to a single sport. To begin this discussion, I think it is imperative to go to its beginnings and then come to discuss why coaching is a conversational method.

When we say that coaching has existed for thousands of years, it would be fair to say that, perhaps for many years, the method was used differently by people but no one did not or could not specify which particular behaviours of a coach, trainer, parent, manager, or a caregiver had made an enormous difference in the outcome of the respondent. Which particular behaviour has taken the form of coaching? The credit goes to Gallwey for observing (empirically), documenting and implementing what he can implement in his own behaviour to bring better results from the respondent: that is what became associated with coaching.

According to Gallwey, after his method of coaching tennis became popular, he moved on to the business world: 'into applying the Inner Game methods of change to corporate work' (p. 115). While I agree that the concept of coaching was defined in the realm of sports, coaching did not originate in sports. What is the difference? Coaching methodology has existed for a very long time but not under the name of coaching. If it were not so, why do we go to coaching schools and institutes to learn coaching and not to tennis courts? In the same chapter, Gallwey (p. 12) goes on, 'many others who now practice in the business arena cut our teeth in sports; coaching in sports has changed little overall. It remains at least a decade behind the methodology of coaching that is virtually universal in business today.'

If coaching comes from sports, why did it stagnate while it continues to develop in the business world? Because coaching is not about sports but about human capabilities to learn and to teach to adapt our behaviour to get better results than we would without it. So the prompt answer almost all of us give or nod in agreement that 'coaching comes from sports', should be revisited and corrected. With due credit to Gallwey, we ought perhaps to consider that coaching methodology did not come from sports (although Gallwey is the first person who specified how a coaching method can bring about very significant improvement and satisfaction of the learner even in sports); instead, we should refocus the discussion on the origins of coaching from sports to human capability, and to a certain awareness of one's own behaviour that a few people have successfully used in order to bring about a change in the outcome of another's performance.

2.2.1 Coaching Is About the Human Capability to Learn

Around 1971, at the same time that Gallwey was writing his 'Inner Game', training seminars called Erhard Seminar Training (EST) for human potential movements and intensive communications and self-development workshops set a stone rolling and seem to have influenced others to create new coaching concepts. Werner Erhard's workshops were offered over 2 weekends and focused on self-help programmes. Even though these seminars did not mention anything about coaching and were not intended to be coaching events, EST deserves a mention as that was one of the defining movements that also contributed to the development of modern coaching methodology. Thomas J. Leonard was the first employee of EST and he went on to create coaching schools that were not related to sports but to self-improvement and development. Jane Renton, a British journalist, conducted extensive research into coaching, which is published in her book *Coaching and Mentoring* (2009). Renton writes (p. 89), 'If anyone deserves the title of "the father of personal coaching" it is Thomas Leonard, who nevertheless sometimes displayed the dysfunctional tendencies that coaching is intended to iron out.' Renton goes on to say,

> Leonard's genius lay in being the first to dissect the various coaching methodologies, theories and principles and rework them into accessible training modules that could be marketed globally. He launched TeleClass.com in 1998, a virtual university with over 20,000 students offering more than 100 classes a week, delivered via conference call. Two years later he and Dave Buck launched CoachVille, which became the world's largest online community of coaches.

I learnt my coaching from Coach U; it is one of the many schools created by Leonard and later bought over by Sandy Vilas.[3] The claim that Leonard is the father of coaching was not only made by Jane Renton but Coach U claims that he is recognised as the founder of professional coaching. 'In 1992, the original curriculum for Coach U was authored by Thomas J. Leonard, the person recognised as the founder of the coaching profession' (*The Coach U Personal and Corporate Coach Training Handbook*, 2005, p. ix). In the *Handbook*, Sandy Vilas, the owner and CEO of CoachInc.com (which is a holding company for the two companies, Coach U and Corporate Coach U) explains that she first took a course from the late Thomas J. Leonard in 1989 (2005, p. xi). Leonard had prepared all the documents for this *Handbook*, which had originally been compiled by the Coach U faculty. Leonard started training coaches in the early 1980s and is internationally recognised as the father of coaching. Pamela Richarde, one of the team members that co-created the International Coach Federation (ICF) with Leonard, was my co-instructor, along with Jennifer Corbin, the president of Coach U and Corporate

[3] Sandy Vilas bought **Coach U, Inc**. from Thomas Leonard. Later, Corporate Coach U was created: both companies are owned by Sandy Vilas: information provided for the purpose of this book by Ann Thatcher, client services of Coach U & Corporate Coach.

Coach U. Both Richarde and Corbin have been coaching for more than 25 years. According to a statement about their history on the ICF website, 'Professional Coach Thomas Leonard started ICF in 1995 as a non-profit organisation for fellow coaches to support each other and grow the profession.' This development was published and was spread widely, for example, through newspaper reports. On the 13th July 2003, for example, the *New York Times* published an article on coaching that discussed Leonard's achievements:

> Life coaching has its roots in the early 1980s, when Thomas J. Leonard, of Phoenix, established a financial planning business and realized that people seeking advice on how to manage their fortunes seemed to be equally interested in discussing life options outside the financial realm. Heeding his entrepreneurial instincts, Mr. Leonard changed his practice to 'life planning'. By the late 1980s, he was teaching others how to coach. In 1992, he founded Coach University, based in Steamboat Springs, Colo., the first formal coach training program. Two years later, Mr. Leonard, who died last February, founded the International Coach Federation, a professional association of personal and business coaches to certify the graduates from his school.

Coaching is defined in *The Coach U Personal and Corporate Coach Training Handbook* (2005, p. 10) as follows:

> Coaching is a catalyzing relationship that accelerates the process of great performance; it's of individuals' and/or of organisations' identifying purpose and living out of that purpose. When people are actively seeking meaning and solutions, they value partnership and support that assists them in accomplishing their goals and objectives. Historically that kind of support has come from friends, parents, therapists, consultants and advisers. Coaching has drawn ideas and techniques from many different kinds of support relationships and historical theories to create, formalize and distil the best practices for masterful coaching.

In my coaching practice, I encountered many aspects of this definition of coaching, but there were others that did not work at all with my clients. This may be due to the cultural differences across the countries, or perhaps due to the zeitgeist; what is important is that the period from 1988 up to the early 1990s was the time when coaching was being taught in the USA for the first time. Is it possible that there were still remnants of the common spiritual practice of searching for one true self from the 1970s from hippie-ism and the anti-establishment movement, which I personally observed in its full force in popular music and daily international news while I was at school in Delhi in India? During this time there was another movement in the USA of defining the 'I', egocentric, to take more care of the self and with it was the birth of self-help and training seminars, as mentioned earlier with reference to EST. There was also an abundance of books on these topics. This phenomenon is seen, for example, in the titles of Thomas J. Leonard's books; indeed, the definition in *The Coach U Personal and Corporate Coach Training Handbook* aligns with his other books. For example, in *The 28 Laws of Attraction: Stop Chasing Success and Let It Chase You* (2007), Leonard discusses organising various areas of one's life; advises not to neglect or tolerate things as they are but to correct them. The focus of the book is to propagate the idea that spiritual and emotional health makes you attractive and begins to attract success. In another book titled, *Working Wisdom: Top 10 Lists for Improving Your Business* (1997), Leonard gives a list of how to improve your business. The book presents seven areas of business improvement: Sales & Marketing, Entrepreneurship, Customer Service, etc. It gives concrete steps and techniques, as I mentioned above, it is a self-help guide: what you should do to create a good business. Some examples of the chapters are 'Things to Say or Do When a Customer says No', 'Techniques to Double-Close a Sale', 'Ways to Attract Business' (pp. 20–25). Leonard wrote two more books: *The Portable Coach: 28 Surefire Strategies for Business and Personal Success* (1998) and *Becoming a Coach*[4]*: The Coach U Approach* (1999). This book was self-published by Leonard and later rewritten and published by Jennifer Corbin.

Besides Leonard, Sir John Whitmore is instrumental in spreading coaching methodology. He went to Gallwey to learn the Inner Game and imported it to the UK and with it to Europe. He admits in his book *Coaching for Performance* (2009, p. 12), 'Many years ago I sought out Gallwey, was trained by him, and founded the Inner Game in Britain.' Whitmore used this concept for a long time in the domain of sports: tennis, skiing, and golf, as he says (2009, p. 12): 'We ran Inner Tennis courses, Inner Skiing holidays; many golfers freed up their swing with Inner Golf. It was not long before our sporting clients began to ask us if we could apply the same methods to the prevailing issues in their companies.'

Alongside coaching, the model of GROW, which was developed by Whitmore and Graham Alexander in the 1980s, was taught for performance enhancement and self-development. This model is still propagated by popular companies in the UK.

I borrow an illustration from Vikki Brock, my fellow student at Coach U, from a much earlier batch of 1996, to show you these relationships discussed above—from *The Sourcebook of Coaching History* (Second Edn. 2014, p. 176) (Fig. 2.1):

There is another phenomenon that needs to be mentioned in order to conclude why the origins of coaching have relevance for our discussion. You, as a coach, or as a client, may encounter or often read in books or hear people say that they have been coaching all their life. You may be tempted to think that they may have discovered some Holy Grail or have secrets that only they have privileged access to. As discussed before it is in fact possible that while some people have been coaching all their life, the question for a potential client is more about the reliability of the method the claimants have been implementing. If clients, due to an awareness of the origins of modern coaching, know that the method stems from the pioneers mentioned above, the client has access to their literature and also the possibility of critical examination whether her coach is really coaching according to a methodical coaching process or an idiosyncratic interpretation that he is calling coaching because it is fashionable to call it so.

[4]This information was provided to me by Ann Thatcher Client Services at Coach U and Corporate Coach U in an email dated 26 Feb. 2016.

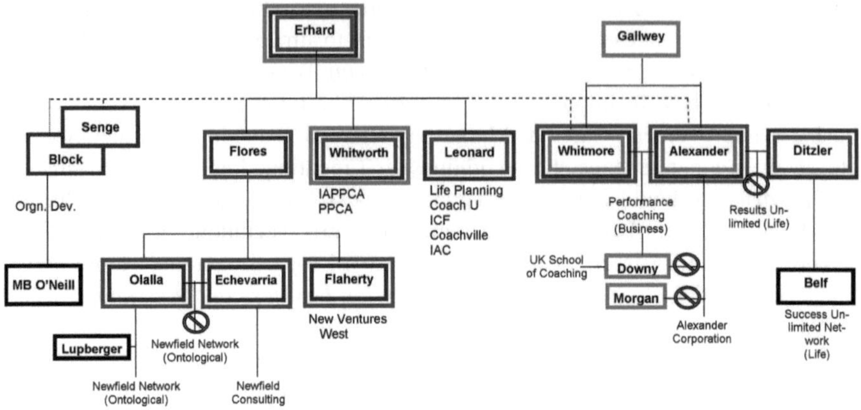

Fig. 2.1 Werner Erhard and Tim Gallwey Relationships (from Brock (Second Edn. 2014), *Sourcebook of Coaching History*) http://coachinghistory.com/wp-content/uploads/2012/05/Lineage-Charts-02-24-2008-SOCH-Color-Figure-26.jpg

When I started learning coaching all the participants in my course were told on the very first day that it is very likely that after we begin the course that all of us may say, 'I have been coaching all my life' (see also: *The Coach U Personal and Corporate Coach Training Handbook*, 2005, p. 10). On the face of it, coaching seems very simple because it is like talking to someone. This may lead some to think that they have been doing it all their life. A similar precautionary note was given when I started my studies in psychology in 2013. The cautionary note said that we may tend to say we knew it all the time: there is nothing new in psychology. You may encounter many extraordinary people who have the capabilities that some psychologists demonstrate after their studies. However, the intelligence that is worthy of praise does not make them a psychologist: a person who has learnt psychology methodically. Such claims, in many cases, are known as hindsight wisdom. There is more to coaching than the feeling of having 'done it all my life': there is a method to it. Why is a method so important if a person is claiming that she has been doing it all her life? We should be wary of descriptive or propositional knowledge and distinguish whether the claimant possesses procedural knowledge that allows for predictable outcomes through implementation of knowledge. This procedure is taught through a method. Knowing that Paris is the capital of France does not automatically make the owner of the information an expert in French culture or render him with the fluency in the French language.

I think that the knowledge and awareness of the facts discussed above should contribute to reducing speculations and ambiguity about coaches and coaching, and about the origins of coaching. It should serve to clarify that the concept of coaching was observed empirically within the realm of sports, and it was the method of coaching that was discovered. It would be reductive to say coaching comes from sports.

2.3 Creating a Personal Coaching Style

At the time Leonard created and taught his coaching methods, it is evident from his books and the coaching I learnt, that aspects of spirituality, defined techniques, and steps were propagated as part of how to achieve a successful, better life from coaching. Leonard's coaching methods were probably working very well at that time in the USA, otherwise he would not have been able to claim such success in coaching as mentioned above. I found that in 2010, with all the technological changes we had experienced up to then, coaching needed some changes and tweaking in order to be appropriate and effective for my clients, and I needed to adapt many original coaching teachings to contemporary demands. One reason is that since the conception of coaching we have one phenomenon which very few coaches address: when we talk about coaching for managers, we are today facing and serving a knowledge-based society in a modern economy as it has not existed before. People working at different levels in a corporate scenario, anywhere in the world, are extremely busy; they have access to more information than they need; almost every person I encounter is under a time constraint. There has been a very clear shift from the old paradigm where someone told you how to live your life with a prevailing wisdom for all—a step-wise guide with general techniques that everyone could apply. Recall that people visited rigorous EST seminars over 2 weekends. The present scenario is more individualistic and focused on personal choices. Nowadays, people want to live and work differently.

To demonstrate what I mean, let me take you on a journey into the fashion world. It is not very far back to 1987, to when I was still working in the fashion industry, when there was a mad rush to find trends that almost everyone would buy. Not that we do not look for trends anymore or do not always buy what others do; nevertheless, there is a stark difference between that time and now. Let me give you an example. In 1987 there was a trend that men wore silk shirts. You could go to Hong Kong and produce a million shirts in six colours in P. R. China and be certain that they would all be sold within a short time. How do I know it? I did it myself in one of my companies. Every second man on the road in Germany wore a silk shirt to work and at home. Companies thrived on such trends and very quickly made millions of Deutschemarks. This mass trend chasing has ceased to exist in fashion; you cannot make a million shirts and hope to sell them within a period of one fashion season (8–10 weeks). The concept of trend selling, which spread like bushfire in 1987, has been reduced to a bonfire today. The reason is that people have become more individualistic in their choices and personalise their expression in many areas of their life. That is true of working life too; otherwise the modern concept of flexible working hours or the home office could not exist.

In the area of intercultural communications, Geert Hofstede[5] propagated the idea that there exists individualism and collectivism in different societies. His concept is still debated controversially by many; whether I coach a person in China, India,

[5]Gerard (Geert) Hendrik Hofstede, a Dutch social psychologist, developed cultural dimensions theory.

USA or Europe, she is still a manager, irrespective of her societal background (as defined by Hofstede: individualist or collectivistic), clients are extremely individualist. G. Koptelzwea, J. Roth et al., authors of the book *Interkulturelle Kompetenz-Handbuch fuer die Erwachsenenbildung* (2011, p. 76) (*Intercultural Competence—a Handbook for Adult Education*) discuss this topic under cultural grammar. This is a departure from the beginnings of coaching. Some changes had to be made from the old concepts where the clients would find their purpose or work on goals. Coaching today is extremely individualistic to every client.

Today my concept of coaching has evolved and taken on a new form based on the facts mentioned above and has evolved into something contemporary that executives accept willingly and look forward to meeting me as their coach. The most important point I want to keep in the forefront of my discussion about coaching is that the origins are still from the course I undertook with the institute mentioned above; I did not go out and reinvent its origins as many are struggling to do nowadays.

In order to discuss the evolution or adaptation of coaching, it is necessary to address what I originally learnt. Let me list a few salient features I learnt from the curriculum created by Leonard and taught by CoachU.

1. Concept of toleration.
2. Concept of goals for success.
3. A coach listens to the client actively: active listening.

These are a very few examples I have taken from the course because these are the aspects I have adapted into my own coaching methods. Another aspect taught at CoachU, but which does not appear in their handbooks, also deserves a mention here: it was considered appropriate to use assessments, typological or ideological tools, in the coaching setting. These are popular, and some are commercial tests that, for example, determine what type of a person the client is. I do not use them; I find them counterproductive for coaching. The complete course is very detailed, supported with exemplary handbooks: three in all. I do not intend to discuss the whole course or disclose how it was conducted. My aim is to focus on the areas I have adapted from CoachU in order to make my coaching more suited to contemporary life, and also to discuss why I have done so. I will address some aspects below and others later on, where appropriate, and as relevant topics arise in my discussion throughout the book.

Let me pick up a topic at random in order to begin. A client is asked to check whether he is tolerating some aspects of his life, so that he may correct them. I think this was an excellent teaching. I think there was a treasure of knowledge that was imparted in this part of the course and I still use most of this knowledge without using the exercises too. The reason is that, while learning coaching, I simultaneously asked myself whether I would be willing to indulge in all the exercises and complete lists regularly (as a client was asked to do), would I have the time to complete them? I found it a very tedious task and thought that if I, as a coach, were to offer such identical methodology to a manager like me, he may reject such an additional workload in his already overloaded schedule. Nevertheless, I did not want to make changes to the programme based on my opinions; after all, they could be prejudiced and wrong. Over the last 5 years I have tested it frequently in real practice and I found that managers are averse to too many written exercises and lists. As per my own findings, most CEOs and managers spend between 80 and 90 % of their day responding to urgent events and business needs that, so to say, 'pop up', and they have little time to sit back and reflect on what is going on in their own life. In practice, busy managers just did not complete these exercises and still worse, because of these tasks they found themselves explaining to me as their coach why they had not completed them. If a manager finds himself in a situation where he needs to explain to his coach why the assignments were not completed, I am certain that he will experience additional emotional burdens rather than relief from coaching, and probably find a way to avoid his coach in the future. I found that the amount of work the lists and exercises brought with them for the clients was overwhelming for them. I removed them from my coaching and replaced them with focused discussions that are attuned to the needs of executives and managers.

People do not come to coaching with goals, as I discovered soon after I started my coaching practice. I must admit that I came to coaching from the business world with a certain prejudice against goal setting. Goal setting sometimes has damaging effects in businesses because many people tend to set goals for the sake of setting goals. My observation was that the higher the people were placed in a company, or the more reputed the managers were, the more absurd their goals became. In Goals Gone Wild (2009) by M. H. Bazerman et al., the authors narrate many cases that make the reader think twice about the benefits of goals. For example, the case of 'Lee Iacocca' (p. 7) confirmed my observation on goal setting. Even though the case is not from coaching, it has some commonalities: it is about goals and about managers.

> In the late 1960s, the Ford Motor Company was losing market share to foreign competitors that were selling small, fuel-efficient cars. CEO Lee Iacocca announced the specific, challenging goal of producing a new car that would be 'under £2000 and under $2000' and would be available for purchase in 1970. This goal, coupled with a tight deadline, meant that many levels of management signed off on unperformed safety checks to expedite the development of the car—the Ford Pinto. One omitted safety check concerned the fuel tank, which was located behind the rear axle in less than 10 inches of crush space. Lawsuits later revealed what Ford should have corrected in its design process: The Pinto could ignite on impact. Investigations revealed that after Ford finally discovered the hazard, executives remained committed to their goal and instead of repairing the faulty design, calculated that the costs of lawsuits associated with Pinto fires (which involved 53 deaths and many injuries) would be less than the cost of fixing the design. In this case, the specific, challenging goals were met (speed to market, fuel efficiency, and cost) at the expense of other important features that were not specified (safety, ethical behavior, and company reputation).

Iacocca was a much celebrated manager due to his success with Ford Mustang. He went on to set a goal to make a car that proved to be dangerous. I am aware that many websites and coaches value goal setting as the most crucial part of coaching. I

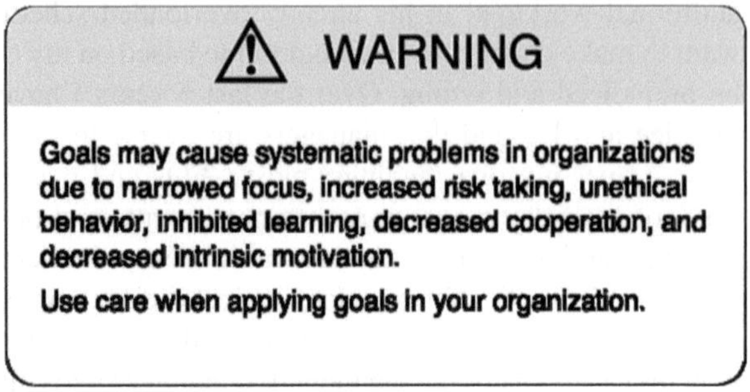

Fig. 2.2 Label (from Bazerman, Goals Gone Wild (2009), p. 14)

personally found it restrictive and reductive. The conclusion of Goals Gone Wild (2009, p. 14) is as follows:

> For decades, scholars have prescribed goal setting as an all-purpose remedy for employee motivation. Rather than dispensing goal setting as a benign, over-the-counter treatment for students of management, experts need to conceptualize goal setting as a prescription-strength medication that requires careful dosing, consideration of harmful side effects, and close supervision. Given the sway of goal setting on intellectual pursuits in management, we call for a more self-critical and less self-congratulatory approach to the study of goal setting.

I agree with their recommendation in the study above that goal setting should bear a warning label (Fig. 2.2). It should not be considered as a cure for all the problems we face.

How did goal setting sneak in to coaching? Alfred Adler, an Austrian psychologist, first mentioned the importance of goals at the beginning of the twentieth century. Brock demonstrates these relationships in *The Sourcebook of Coaching History* (Second Edn. 2014, pp. 141–142). Brock explains,

> I have grouped coaching's pioneers, some of whom became coaches and some of whom did not, into three generational categories, depending on the roles they played in the emergence of coaching. The first group, the Originators, include those individuals who either created or promoted the principal theories and tools adopted by modern coaches—even if those theories and tools were not originally intended for coaching.

Brock has diligently explained the relationships (which do not form part of this discussion); my focus is to show you the origins of goals and goal setting and how it may have come to be aligned with coaching (Fig. 2.3).

Since the demise of behaviourism as the dominant theory for personal development, new concepts evolved in psychology during the 1950s and 1960s, such as, needs, goals, and goal-directed behaviour in social learning theory and social cognitive theory, etc. These concepts are important; they all contribute to about ten theoretical perspectives in human development. Ever since the social environment has moved on, psychology and other disciplines have given us more knowledge about human development; why are we still stuck with the rusty and linear idea that goal achieving is coaching? Goal setting is

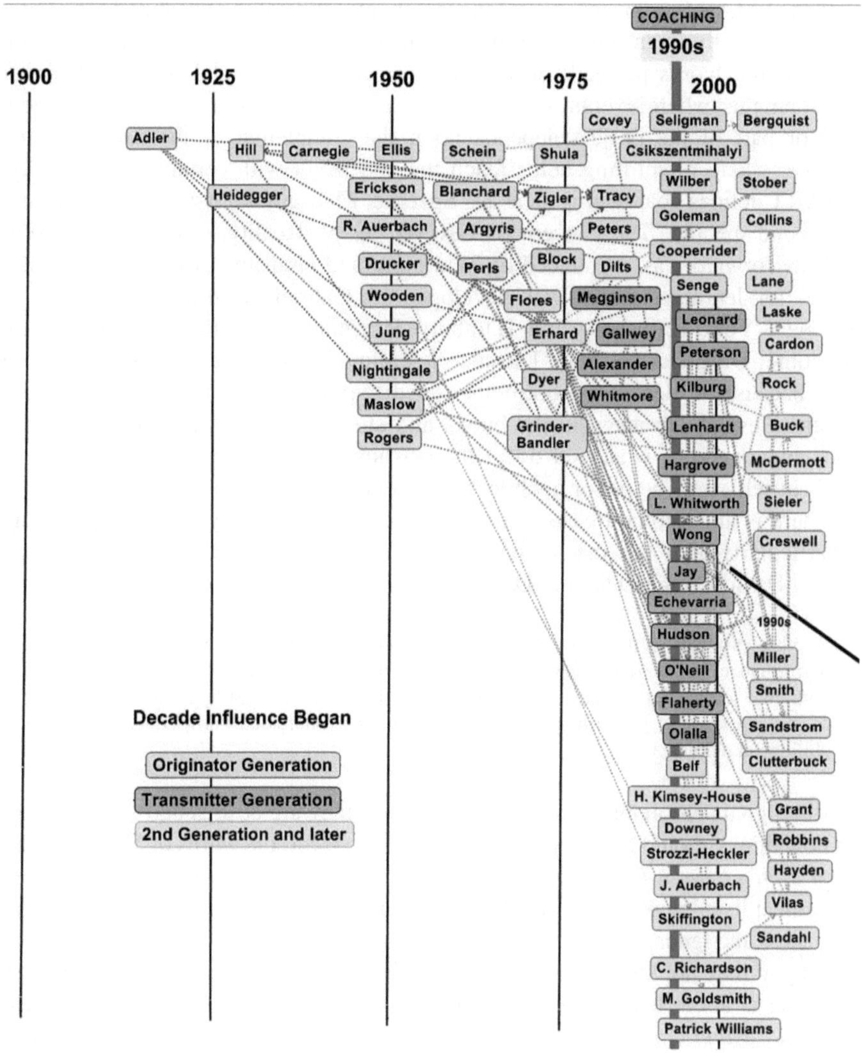

Fig. 2.3 Coaching Influences Timeline by Generation (from Brock (Second Edn. 2014), *Sourcebook of Coaching History*) http://coachinghistory.com/wp-content/uploads/2012/05/www.coachinghistory.com-Figure-22.jpg

problem-solving and coaching is not always problem-solving—it is more often than not about learning through insights. Goal setting cannot be discussed in isolation, ignoring other influences of social environment, personal emotions, personal obligations, and all other aspects that go into making a person's life. While setting goals may contribute to achieving some simple linear or unitary targets, they alone are not the answer.

The **SMART** concept from management studies is attributed to Peter F. Drucker,[6] the man who, according to *Business Week*, invented management. Goal setting works perfectly well in project management and other such linear environments where events are sequential and the success of every subsequent step or part of the project depends upon the completion of the previous step in time, where monitoring helps reach the end result with certain predictability. **SMART** defines goal-setting steps as, **S**pecific, **M**easurable, **A**ssignable, **R**ealistic and **T**ime-specific. The concept of **GROW**: **G**oal, **R**eality, **O**bstacles and **W**ill or **W**ay forward was introduced by Whitmore and Graham Alexander. A similar model for learning, which was developed by Gabriele Oettingen, professor at the New York University and Hamburg University, is called **WOOP**: **W**ish, **O**utcome, **O**bstacle and **P**lan. Distance learning and self-study is a very difficult task because it demands enormous self-discipline from the aspiring student to return every day anew to the books and studies. There is no one to monitor your attendance or what you do in the privacy of your own four walls. Setting goals in self-study helps for a while. I am sceptical about it in coaching.

There is an ongoing discussion on whether goals have any effect in coaching. I particularly like the discussions in *Beyond Goals* (2013), edited by Susan David, David Clutterbuck, and David Megginson. They write (p. 11),

> Another problem is the type of goal people try to set. We can distinguish between performance and learning goals. Performance goals are the ones we usually associate with goal setting, for instance, I will increase my results on the test by 30 percent by end of the quarter … [.] Learning goals generally refer to increased knowledge, skills and abilities in defined areas …'.

I find goals problematic in coaching because they are desires and wishes based on how things should be as a final outcome. I also recall the words of Viktor Frankl from *Man's Search for Meaning* (2004, p. xx): 'Don't aim at success—the more you aim at it and make it a target, the more you are going to miss it.' If you only aim at success and ignore your capabilities, and your goal is success, then you may miss it and you may not know that goal setting was too singular. As I discussed earlier, coaching is about learning, or as Gallwey says, your 'Inner Goal'. Susan David et al. in *Beyond Goals* (2013, Back Cover) say that there are two types of goals: 'performance and learning goals'. When clients come to me for coaching, they identify the areas they would like to discuss with me but they do not come with definite goals. I agree with the conclusion of *Beyond Goals* where everything under SMART is not very smart in coaching:

---

[6]An Austrian born (1909–2005), American author, professor and management consultant. A self-styled 'social ecologist'. According to *Business Week* he was 'the man who invented management'.

> The presence of goals in coaching and mentoring programmes has gone largely unquestioned, yet evidence is growing that the standard prescription of SMART, challenging goals is not always appropriate—and even potentially dangerous—in the context of a complex and rapidly changing world.

In *Beyond Goals*, Anthony M. Grant (see Sect. 2.2), proposes that goals should not become dominant in coaching. I agree with this concept and his idea that as long as goals are subordinate to coaching they have a scope of being useful. The main idea of this discussion is that while I do not consider goals to be the determining factors in coaching they could play a small side role if a client needs to work on a defined goal, and I keep an open mindset to the needs of the clients. All in all, however, goal setting alone is not coaching.

There is one aspect though, that works sometimes. In an online course, *Inspiring Leadership Through Emotional Intelligence*, which was conducted by Richard Boyatzis, I was introduced to the concepts of Positive Emotional Attractor (PEA) and the Negative Emotional Attractor (NEA). The concepts are, that if you ask people about their goals in longer time frames, for example, you ask people how they see themselves in 7 years, they react in a relaxed manner and are willing to talk about their goals. The other part about his concept, which is fascinating, is that leaders who are inspirational can trigger PEA. I have applied this very often in coaching and people love to talk about it. Their narrative, however, has a touch of dream-like freedom. They use words such as, 'perhaps', 'would like to', 'maybe'. The most important aspect of my observation was that they did not feel threatened talking about things so far away over a longer timescale. As soon as you talk about 15 years they refuse to talk. The moment you ask them about a goal that is closer, e.g. 4 weeks, 4 months, or 1 year clients are visibly apprehensive of giving answers with ease. If as a coach I push them to create some goals, they will come out with some but it would seem as if they are getting rid of the subject by naming something for the sake of naming it. PEA is a great verbal exercise, but only in some circumstances. At Professor Boyatzis's suggestion, at first, I implemented this concept, but I found that not everybody is open to it. People have other demands from coaching. My scepticism toward goals, I admit, has accompanied me from my business world experience. I will introduce you later to a few real world examples that will show you that people at higher levels in business tend to define unrealistic and fantastic goals; as if to say, the higher the absurdity of a goal demonstrates the higher determination of the executive.

My concern with goals is that they narrow the sight of a client and the purpose of coaching is in exactly the opposite direction: to expand their perception. Goals in coaching become counterproductive if they are seen as an 'omni-cure'. If in coaching there were ten levels to define what is most important, then conversations and reflective listening would be number one and two while goal setting would be number ten: the lowest, reserved solely for subordinated goals only if I perceived that a client wished to achieve a goal but was not certain how to do so.

References

Bazerman, M. H., Galinsky, A. D., Ordóñez, D., & Schweitzer, M. E. (2009). Goals gone wild: The systematic side effects of over-prescribing goal setting. *Academy of Management Executive*. doi:10.5465/AMP.2009.37007999.

Brock, V. G. (2014). *The sourcebook of coaching history,* 2nd ed. CreateSpace.

Clutterbuck, D. S., & Megginson, D. (2013). *Beyond goals effective strategies for coaching and mentoring*. Surrey, BC: Gower Publishing.

Dweck, C. (2012). *Mindset: How you can fulfil your potential*. London: Constable & Robinson.

Frankl, V. (2004). *Man's search for meaning*. London: Ebury Publishing.

Gallwey, W. T. (1974; revised 2015). *The inner game of tennis: The ultimate guide to the mental side of peak performance*. London: Pan Books. http://www.performanceconsultants.com/tim-gallwey. Accessed 24 Feb 2016.

Gallwey, W. T. (2009). *Coaching for performance*. London: Nicholas Brealey.

Grant, A. M. (2011). *Workplace, executive and life coaching: An annotated bibliography. Behavioural science and business literature*. Coaching Psychology Unit, University of Sydney, Australia.

Koptelzewa, G., Roth, J., Sterzenbach, G., & Tuschinsky, C. (2011). *Interkulturelle Kompetenz-Handbuch fuer die Erwachsenenbildung*. Ilmenau: Educational Consulting GmbH. English Edition: Koeck, C., & Roth, J. (2009). *Culture communication skills*. (P. Andersen, Trans.). Ilmenau: Educational Consulting GmbH.

Leonard, T. J. (1997). *Working wisdom: Top 10 lists for improving your business*. Texas, QLD: Bard Press.

Leonard, T. J. (1998). *The portable coach: 28 surefire strategies for business and personal success*. New York: Scribner.

Leonard, T. J. (1999). *The coach approach: The Coach U approach*. Coach U.

Leonard, T. J. (2005). *The Coach U personal and corporate coach training handbook*. New Jersey: Wiley.

Leonard, T. J. (2007). *The 28 laws of attraction: Stop chasing success and let it chase you*. New York: Scribner.

Renton, J. (2009). *Coaching and mentoring: What they are and how to make the most of them*. London: Profile Books. http://www.erhardseminarstraining.com/. Accessed 14 Mar 2016.

Tyson, L., & Birnbrauer, H. (1983). Coaching: A tool for success. *Training and Development Journal, 37*(9), 30–34.

Whitmore, J. (2009). *Coaching for performance*. London: Nicholas Brealey.

Online Sources

Boyatzis, R. *Inspiring leadership through emotional leadership*. Online course materials. www.coursera.org. Accessed 25 Jun 2013.

Boyatzis, R. *Inspiring leadership through emotional leadership*. Online course materials. www.coursera.org. (Week 4 Module 4.2). Accessed 25 Jun 2013.

Byrne, J. A., & Gerdes, L. (2005). *The man who invented management*. http://www.bloomberg.com/news/articles/2005-11-27/the-man-who-invented-management. Accessed 10 Oct 2012.

Peter Drucker's Life and Legacy, The Drucker Institute. http://www.druckerinstitute.com/peter-druckers-life-and-legacy/. Accessed 12 Oct 2012.

The Fallacy of Sustainable Change 3

3.1 Illusion of Sustainability

When a coach offers a sustainable change to his clients, he is promising a change that will sustain itself for a long time, if not forever. The etymology of the noun 'sustainable' derives in Latin *sustinēre*, from the prefix *sus-* and *tenēre* to hold. Even if most promises do not specify that they mean positive changes, they offer great, if not superlative, success. My observations have been that people are averse to such superlative promises, simply because they are unable to decipher what sustainable and change, as expressions, possibly bring with them. Once I asked an experienced coach in Munich—Cornelia Weber-Fuerst—'what do you think of when I say, I offer you sustainable change through my coaching?' Her spontaneous response was, 'is this not a paradox?' I wanted to know why she thought that it was a paradox. Besides being an experienced coach she is a very well-read person; she said change is not permanent, change changes. I agree with her and think of the Buddhist teachings: they say that the only thing that is constant is change: change will change that is why it is a change. As discussed earlier and I will do so later, coaching can trigger a change and the change is due to learning and it is dependent on the method and the acceptance of the method by the learner not the coach. I would be willing to accept and also offer sustainable learning: a learning that stays with you and if you are interested in learning becoming a level to make it as your next higher base for your further learning, too. But I do not subscribe to the idea of sustainable change. I think we are primed when we hear the word 'sustainable'. Is it possible that because we accept the concept of sustainable development as the right answer for urgent environmental issues to stop further damage to the environment that we automatically accept that there could be something as sustainable change in our lives because the word sustainable is already accepted by us as the right solution for the environment? Change that holds forever would be static forever; how is that possible?

Here is another extremely problematic aspect that is evident in such promises: it assumes that anyone willing to be coached can be changed externally and

A. Kohli, *Effective Coaching, and the Fallacy of Sustainable Change*, Management for Professionals, DOI 10.1007/978-3-319-39735-1_3

sustainably. Ignoring the fact that people do not just behave the way they do because of who they are, there are also constraints that emerge from the environment of every individual that demands a certain amount of compliance. The environment of any person is not identical with the environment of another person and cannot be treated as a constant factor in sustainable change. The interaction of a person with his environment creates a very unique situation for that client as an individual. Disregarding all these factors and implying that there are some very clever people with some tools and tricks that a client does not know and are privy solely to a coach is not credible. To me it is also extremely problematic for the fact that such a promise sounds manipulative: a coach can manipulate a change? For very significant reasons, I prefer to rely on teachings of developmental psychology to address the issues of change to argue that it is a fallacy to offer sustainable change through coaching. Here is a paradox for you: a phenomenon of change works in the development of human beings without any hindrance and it does so from gametes to zygotes in the womb of the mother until the death of the being, because nature is at play and has a plan in which no one dares intervene or manipulate this change. Even here change is just our interpretation of what change is; our need is more important and the need is to develop into something better, something final. Have you ever watched the excitement of future parents looking at the sonographic images of a child in the womb? They are not talking about change, even though the change is happening at a very great speed from single cell to foetus to embryo to a fully developed human being—have you ever seen a mother jump in the air to exclaim, my foetus has changed sustainably to an embryo! They are thrilled how a child is developing into a healthy human being. Can a coach offer such a sustainable change?

Let us leave the womb of a mother and go to developmental psychology. It is one subject that has looked very closely at change and yet it has not decided to call itself 'Change Psychology'. It has observed and studied the effects and implications of change for human beings. Developmental psychology has evolved since the beginning of the last century; methodical observations of changes in a child dates back to 1781 with Dietrich Tiedemann, a German philosopher and professor of philosophy at the university of Marburg, Germany. Tiedemann recorded his observations about his son Friedrich, which he published in 1787 as *Beobachtungen über die Entwickelung der Seelenfähigkeiten bei Kindern* (1897) (*Tiedemann's Record of child-life*).[1] The mention of this historical record goes to show that we have been interested in understanding change in relation to human development for a long time—it is not a new phenomenon—just as we were interested in understanding certain aspects of our behaviour to discover the concept of coaching. The focus of coaching is development and not change. Going to the level of change is reductive as we reach down to a unitary level of tinkering with smaller things in a human being.

[1]It is the French translation and commentary by Bernard Perez with notes, by F. Louis Soldan.

Developmental psychology began with observing infants then children, later on it included adolescents; in modern times, as we know it now, it studies development and changes from birth and throughout the lifespan of a human being.

When a child begins to talk, for example, there is a visible change in the child. The most important aspect of this change to keep in mind is that it is irreversible. The child will not regress into the previous stage of making incomprehensible sounds and wilfully refuse to talk. This development will stay and it has a very important aspect to it; one which is also very relevant in the context of coaching. The change in the capability of the child has created a new level: from making sounds to talking, hence created independence for the child to express herself and her needs. This development also affects the caregivers, as they will now interact on a much broader scale with the child about her wishes, likes, dislikes, joys, and so on, as they could not earlier. It is important to consider that a change does not bring development in isolation: it affects the person who underwent it and also her social environment. For the time being, I wish to focus only on the positive change although the same is true for negative change too. The change that occurred is one level higher than the previous one, implying that it is also positive, an advancement, and desirable. It has also prepared a premise to build the next change based on the last one. This is also the concept of development: one level builds on the last one and so on. For example, the next level could be the capability of conversing, narrating, or singing. Whatever the level may be, the changes take place gradually to create a further change. Sudden changes due to life-changing events, for example, serious illness, loss of a loved one, or change of country of residence, etc., are disruptive. Even though they deserve to be called change, in the context of coaching, a coach will most likely not be able to create any disruptive change for a person or an environment.

While the developments in childhood and young age are significant, visible, irreversible, and sustainable, in adulthood, for the majority of people, we face more challenges than changes, which may emerge due to tensions between our innate needs and the demands from our social environment or our desires, and the collision of the previous factors with our own limitations. If a coach is offering to change a client sustainably but fails to specify what he will change, or promises success whose outcome he has not defined clearly, I fear it is no different to a promise of a fortune teller who claims to predict and change your future to great heights. Some examples of ambiguous and nonsensical promises are 'unleash your potential' or 'achieve new heights': a client should ask a simple question: how? Another example is 'get the best out of you.' How? The next question would be—how do I know after achieving my best that there is not more to it in me?

Even if I am a strong proponent of implementing coaching methods in raising children too, I think most will agree that coaching is mostly offered to adults. They either tend to make changes based on their own informed or ill-informed choices; however good or bad, they are either voluntary or are obliged to accept situations that cause changes because of certain circumstances. In any case, an adult may decide to reverse her decisions at any time depending on the perception of her situation. How can a coach ensure that an adult does not reverse her decision to sustain the success or change that he promised? She may perhaps discover new ideas soon after gaining new insights on her habitual situation. As a coach I would offer sustainable change if I could guarantee the sequence of all probable events that I can cause due to my coaching. I can predict only one aspect; you will discover something new about yourself through insights and self-reflection. You may like it so much that you want to adopt some changes. What emerges due to those changes will be your own decision. Even then, the change you make may not be permanent, irreversible, or sustainable because you grow old and your priorities shift.

3.2 Do Clients Want to Change?

Change is the manifestation of difference between two states: the previous one and the one achieved through some acts or forced event. When we see a change in appearance or behaviour we understand that something is different. Change leads to development and into something new. In coaching, it only happens intrinsically and it is only triggered by insights and understanding of one's own environment and limitations. I have not come across anyone who wants to change his personality or overhaul her behaviour. I concede there are a few clients who want to amend or better still understand why they continue to do something they think is wrong or how they can improve some areas in their life. It is very far from change. Change is the privileged subjective conscious experience of a client. Only a client can claim whether she has experienced a change. The people interacting with the client may also notice change if it is visible and becomes obvious in her behaviour. Coaching is a very personal experience for every client and any coach following a proper method can only trigger this process: it is the 'explorative conversational method with its sole purpose to facilitate self-reflection'.

The philosophical concept of Qualia is ideal to explain this concept. The answer to the question that an American philosopher, Thomas Nagel, poses in his paper in *The Philosophical Review*, titled, 'What is it to be like a bat?' (1974). Only a bat knows how it feels to be one. How does it feel to change: only the client knows. Despite the fact that a bat is not a human being, the example of a bat is used to demonstrate that feelings, emotions, perceptions and also thoughts are a privileged area where only the owner has access; no one from the outside can know how it feels to be a bat. I first encountered Nagel while studying psychology; this example shows even if you could scientifically observe a bat, or in our case our client, you would never have complete access to how they are feeling or what they are thinking.

A few years ago, I would sit with my son, David, to see the video games he was playing. Most young boys are attracted to video games and I am against both extremes: allow them as non-authoritative or ban them as the last authority. I am for self-discovery but guided self-discovery without interference of a personal experience. I wanted to know whether the games he was playing were appropriate for his age and psyche. Being young, he was very much faster than I was. He won a few times and loved it when I lost. Once he asked me, laughing, 'Papa, how does it feel to lose?' I said, 'wait a while and I will tell you'. The next time I got the better of him and won a game, I said, 'this is how it feels to lose. Do you know it now?' He remembers this even today and learnt from it that we cannot know how a person feels when he is intimidated, happy, humiliated, or even changed.

Change is a personal experience based on our own value systems. Every person experiences the same event with a different intensity. It is important that the client gains an insight and if the insight into his own situation calls her to change she will do it effectively. Coaching can bring about a change for a client only if she is willing to accept it and integrate it into her life. If the sustainable change I offer through coaching is not an independent factor but dependent on the will of the client, how can I offer it as a definite outcome of coaching? If you like to call quitting smoking a change in a person you may be right, but it is very reductive and out of context in regard to coaching. If you are looking for visible changes in your partner, you may be surprised: it may very often depend on your own behaviour and your own expectations.

Coaching as a profession could enjoy the prospects of existing for long into the future if we decide to drop superlative promises: the idea of changing people; optimising people; making people efficient, or any other external intervention based on the fallacy that we can change people permanently.

From September 2010 onward, I coached 165 clients. I can assure you that not one client had specified exactly what she wanted to change. Before beginning their coaching with me, all clients had filled out a pre-coaching questionnaire to specify what they had wanted to discuss with me. The areas they specified in the questionnaire were not always what they finally discussed with me during coaching. They started with certain topics but very soon realised that those topics were mostly about outcomes of some circumstances they did not want to see in their life and not something they wanted to see changed.

I have addressed the fallacy of change in this book also because during the numerous interviews and coaching sessions with clients, I received unsolicited reports from them about what had changed in their work or life due to coaching. They shared their experiences openly and with a certain happiness because they wanted me to know that coaching was working. I am careful not to offer to change my clients and do not offer my services with the argument that sustainable change is possible through coaching, yet I constantly noticed that there was not a single client who did not experience a successful positive change. An improvement in the life of a client through coaching is the greatest moment for a coach. Even though the clients enjoyed the improvements and changes due to coaching, they did not want to hear before they began the sessions that someone could change them.

I would like to share with you some comments from my clients to show you why I do not promise sustainable change through my coaching:

1. 'The most important thing in coaching that I experienced with you was that you did not force me to change.'
2. 'I was relieved to see that I could still be my own self and not change to someone I do not want to be.'

3. 'The best thing I experienced in my coaching was that I did not have to fit a stencil or a schema of a success scheme.'
4. 'I was afraid that you were going to set some time lines for me to meet some goals, I do not have the time for such games.'

This one is very interesting from a lady who is a very successful manager, she said, 'I was apprehensive that you might want me to be Steve Jobs or Bill Gates.' I was curious and I asked, 'What makes you think that I could do that?' She said, 'the first few coaches I was recommended by colleagues had ideological statements from Steve Jobs or similar superheroes of their industry, such as, "I do not come to work to be loved by people". I thought if a person is going to change me into a Steve Jobs I may have difficulties.'

People are individuals and it is absolutely wrong to think everyone wants to change to become super successful or into a superlative international manager. Now, I promise my clients at the beginning of coaching that I will not change them or imagine that they come to coaching to achieve a set of goals. If all coaches knew that 'change' is a scary word for many potential clients, they would probably 'change' the way they offer their coaching. My clients are all, without exceptions, sane, mature women and men who are all experts in their fields; they are well-educated and high performers with earnings far above the national average in their respective countries. The amount of information and 'we will fix you' promises landing on their tables and on their mobile handsets is without doubt not easily manageable. Imagine in such a scenario, I go to them and say, 'I am going to change you'. It is a fallacy in coaching to think that someone wants to change. The other fallacy I want to remind you of is that someone thinks she could change someone else.

Normally it never happens but if it does and if my clients talk about the word change, it is mostly at the beginning of our coaching relationship. I think up to now only a few clients asked me because they were apprehensive that coaching may change something they do not know about. Mostly it is a simple question, what will you change? My favourite statement for my clients is that 'you will not start wearing red coloured shirts with green ties and yellow socks to bed after coaching'. All my clients: women and men, find it reassuring that there is no 'Besserwisser', a wonderful word in the German language for an omniscient smart alec telling these high calibre experts how to do what they do better: they do not need to learn that from anyone outside of their company.

There is one phenomenon which you have probably encountered yourself. There are some clients who want to know how to change others. Perhaps that is the reason why a social scientist called coaching 'remedying the suffering of employees'. To substantiate this let me begin by quoting a couple of lines from an email that a courageous young entrepreneur from Kathmandu, Nepal sent me during our discussion: 'Yes . . . it helps to begin with new freshness . . . but now, I want to ask you a question, there are certain people who can't and won't look through others' perspective ... so in that case, is there any way out?' I have deliberately chosen to quote a statement from Nepal. I could easily have chosen one from Austria or any other country for that matter. I wanted to save you from an automatic answer, yes that is true in industrialised countries. You may be surprised that most of the issues a coach faces are similar in many countries. I have encountered such a question and attitude to change others just about everywhere I have worked: Austria, Germany, S. Korea, China, Japan, Hong Kong, India, Sierra Leone, Italy, the Maghreb region, some countries on the Arabian Peninsula, the UK, the USA and a few other countries. Could one say that coaching, the issues faced by coaching clients, and the method of coaching is generalisable? I have too little information to make such a weighty claim and it would be fair to say that I never looked for it earlier. Irrespective, whether society is affluent, developing, or deprived, this question was placed to me not only as a coach but also when I was a manager where I experienced that the main conflicts among colleagues were 'she needs to change' and 'he needs to change'. Very often, the change people want to see is in others.

You may yourself have encountered marriage or partnerships going bad. Have you heard about one partner complaining he does not do this and he needs to change? She does not help in the household and needs to change. This is nothing new; people do it all the time. It is always the other who does not understand our point of view. How can we offer to change them? Coaching can change certain aspects in a client's life but giving a promise of sustainable change would not be a credible offer.

3.2.1 Case Study: 'Chris'

I discussed the possibility of sustainable change with a client named 'Chris'. Chris is a Chief Technical Officer of a shipbuilding company, in Germany, who is still in a coaching relationship with me. (I have changed the name of the person and the business of the company.) Since I was contemplating this subject I chose to ask him about change during my last coaching meeting with him, in March 2016. I have recorded our conversation below to demonstrate the issue of sustainability from a coaching client's perspective.

'What do you think of change through coaching?'

'You know, I like the idea that you do not offer to change me'.

'What do you like about that?'

'I would not know what to expect. I am happy as I am. Why would I go to someone and say change me? Into what?'

'Would you say that coaching changes nothing?' I asked, because I was concerned that the client should certainly feel the difference between the states before and after being coached.

'May I give you some examples to show you what happens through coaching, at least for me?' Chris offered.

'Sure, I am curious about that,' I said.

'I have this guy in logistics and he seemed glum to me so the last few years I would avoid him completely. Whenever I needed a detailed report on shipping costs of components, to prepare for my meetings, I would go and ask him for it. He never had the time for it and felt very stressed about me asking for it.'

'How did you discover that he never had the time for you?'

'That is what I wanted to tell you. I had assumed that he never had the time for me,' he said.

'So how did you discover that it was your assumption?'

'After beginning coaching with you, I have realised that I am not the only one who does not have time in our company. I had also overlooked that we have hired experts in particular fields so that there are people who contribute to making the company what we aspire it to be and we do not even think of them as such. We look at them as resistance. Whenever we go to see them it is with a premeditated idea that it is going to be an encounter. After the second coaching meeting with you, one day, I just got up and went to him and said, "Bernd, I have a meeting in two hours and I need a complete run down for the last year." He said, "sure no problems. I will bring it down to your office." I thought, what has happened to him? I realised nothing happened to him, it was my behaviour that was straightforward and professional.'

'You got your report in time then?'

'Yes, he came down within 30 minutes and the report was perfect. He even asked me if I wanted him to be present at the meeting for clarifications. I have never thought of it in the last 26 years.'

'So you have changed because of coaching?' I provoked purposely.

'I have not changed, look at me, I am still the same person. I have slowed down and started looking at people differently,' he said.

'That is a change, is it not?'

'No, that is not a change in me or my person; people might say he has changed his behaviour but I am the same person who I was. I wear the same clothes, eat the same food, and have not decided to change my home or anything else. I am more comfortable with this way of working,' he said.

'If people will say he has changed his behaviour, what holds you back in calling it a change?' I asked.

'Arun, I had this in me all the time; you do not think if I did not have the capability to think that there is another way I would have learnt it from a coach? How many seminars have our managers organised for team building and teamwork in the last 15 years? Twenty-three of them, and how many teams were made and improved? None! You cannot change people if they do not have it in them.'

He was a bit irritated at my insistence but that was OK with me because I wanted a top executive with experience to share his thoughts. I deliberately took him a bit further in this discussion.

'What else would you say happens if you have it in yourself?' I asked.

'I had three meetings 2 weeks back planned for a Monday morning and they were all extremely important. A subsidiary of Daimler wanted to see my plant; these guys are important. Five senior managers from a Chinese company wanted to discuss some order details and the finance guys wanted my attention and all of them between 09:00 and 11:00 am. Before coaching I would have come to the office at 07:00 am and worked my way through, moved meetings and jumped from one to the other. Anyone other than these people who talked to me on such a day would be in for a rough response. You know what I did? . . . I asked Walter, "take care of the Chinese delegation, take them around with you." I gave him four other colleagues who would have accompanied me for such meetings anyway. I told him to take them to a good Chinese restaurant for lunch, after they are satisfied with their inspections so that they feel welcome, and then get them back to the airport safely and in time. Walter glowed in the face. I thought at that moment, these experts have been with me and I was creating stress for myself. Do you know what happened?' he said.

'Tell me,' I said. I was really very curious now.

'Walter is 31-years-old and has been with us for more than 4 years. I did not know that he was good at presentations. I had never asked him to do any such thing but he started making presentations for the Chinese partners. He took our regular templates that everybody uses and started changing them and I was amazed,' he said.

'Why was that?' I asked.

'He offered to present the whole event 4 days before the arrival of the delegation from China so that I knew what was going on. He said he wanted my consent and if I wanted changes he could integrate them. These presentations I used to make at home on the weekend to the chagrin of my wife. It was a pleasure to see Walter completely immersed in his presentations. It was something very important to him.'

'What about the other two meetings?' I asked.

'I am not a finance person anyway. Earlier I would sit through these meetings but somebody else did the talking. This time I thought if I am just going to sit around why not sit with the people that are strategically important for the company: the Daimler guys.'

'So you did change,' I insisted again.

'I tried out new things because you showed me to slow down and think. I have created pillars around me and spread the weight of my responsibilities on many of them.'

'That is why you employ people don't you?' I asked.

'Logically, yes. I am leaving for a 3-week holiday to Vietnam and I have no worries about what could go wrong,' he said.

'What worries should you have?' I asked.

'Normally, I would be worried as if I was the only person out of the 1777 people we have working for us.'

I tried once more—'so you did change?' I said, because I wanted to provoke him to answer that he had changed. Surprisingly his response was not one of irritation.

He said, 'I like your question; what is happening due to coaching around you: personally and professionally. I like it because you never ask me what has changed. If you ask me what has changed I could not give you an answer. Naturally, things change around me but I am changing them, coaching is not changing me it is helping me to do it. It is giving me a chance to reflect and I like that. I like to come and take a moment to reflect on all these meetings and how I would have handled them earlier.'

'If you had been coached 25 years back would you have made the same changes? I know it is not a fair question but this is just an academic exercise, not coaching,' I said.

'I do not think so. Twenty-five years ago, I was 27 years-old. I would have done everything myself. I probably would not have engaged a coach. Like I said, if I did not have it in me, you could not have brought about this way of looking at it. Simply said, you cannot make a pig sing. He does not have the concept of singing in him. You could not have instructed me to do something I could not do,' he said.

How does a coach imagine that he could offer a sustainable change when he does not know if the client wishes it?

This discussion ended soon after and my conclusion was that you cannot offer to change people unless they wish to do it themselves. I think what happens is that if you trigger new ideas and allow people to think for themselves and find ways to encounter their limitations through their own insight, you will be more effective at coaching your clients. This is the discovery Gallwey made about the 'Inner Game'.

Let me give you one more example of how you cannot coach someone to change, even if they know the outcome is what they want. Often people just desire the outcome and not the effort or the struggle that goes into achieving it. Outcomes from our efforts are what we call a change.

In 2012–2013 I engaged an advertisement company in Munich to create my brochures and website content. The entrepreneur, Heidi, with her five employees (I am changing the names), while going through the executive testimonials, said she would love to work with such large corporations. She wanted to know how I started my business of coaching and started working with these reputed companies.

Heidi asked me, 'how did you market coaching because I think it is so tough.'

I asked her what she meant with marketing coaching.

She said, 'I want to know how you caught your big fish, large corporations; there must be some secret way.'

I told her, 'it is a tedious process because people are extremely hesitant and I have to find innovative methods in order to approach and talk only to the top executives.'

'You talk only to top executives?'

'No, I would talk to anyone, but the decision makers understand and decide about implementing coaching sooner than the people further down the hierarchy,' I explained.

'I never thought of it like this; we get stuck in so many phases before we can reach a decision maker.' I could see she was contemplating that this could be a new way. She asked, 'and you do not ask personnel managers or the HR department?'

I said, 'sure I do, but my focus is to talk straight to the CEO.'

'I would like to know how to do it. Do you make a cold call? Could you coach me for that?' She had many questions she wanted answered immediately and jumped straight to how much it would cost her to learn how to reach CEOs.

'Oh no, cold calls are not me; I think it is more than 30 years since I made a cold call to sell apparel to large companies,' I told her.

'How do you do it?' She insisted and continued, 'it is extremely difficult to find new customers for advertising assignments and I would like to know from you because I think you are selling a service that is more difficult to market.'

'Every year it is a new battle plan; it looks attractive when it is done but you need to work on it regularly,' I told her and gave her some details. All this is not coaching but a simple exchange of opinions.

She asked, 'could you coach me for that?'

I said, 'I do not coach for a particular marketing plan or strategy, because I do not think that is coaching. That would be consultancy.'

'But you could help me to go on the path you selected for yourself?' She looked worried that I would refuse it.

'I can help you, but be aware that it is a lot of hard work.'

She agreed. We came to a point where I told her that she needed to hire a marketing company who has access to the customers she wants. Within the next 5 weeks she identified five companies who offered this service and sent the details to me. After due diligence: how they worked, how they approached the customers, briefed their staff, if there was a dedicated team or was it a call centre—there were many other details, such as with whom they had worked and how long they had been in the business, telephonic interviews with them, and so on. From these, I found two of them that could fit her demands, because they were working with large corporations exactly for the same type of assignments.

The sales managers of these two companies came down from Mannheim, a town near Frankfurt, and made their presentations. After this I stepped out of this honorary assignment.

After a few weeks she called to update me and said, 'I opted for an exit clause and stopped the project after 4 weeks.'

> 'What happened, was it not worth it?' I asked.
>
> She said, 'I had received very good leads with large corporations, but the amount of work involved was not my beer.'
>
> I wanted to know, 'what was the most difficult part of it?'
>
> She said, 'I had to follow-up on all the leads every day; additional work of at least five to six hours. I do not have the time for that.'

When I was learning hypnotherapy in Munich there was one lesson our instructor gave us: 'you cannot hypnotise people to more than their integrity allows them to do'. I am talking about hypnosis because that is a state of awareness when a person is in a trance. Even in that state people do not do anything that is not their beer, or cup of tea. Our instructor had said, 'do not imagine that you could hypnotise 50 people and send them to rob banks and get rich. People come out of a hypnotic trance if it goes against their values.' I have never tested this but I think he may be right otherwise we would have more crime in our cities committed by hypnotised innocents.

Heidi was not in a trance and very present and knew what she wanted: more customers. She did not want the tedious work that comes with it. She was willing to pay someone to get her customers and she would do the creative work for them.

She would have agreed to pay me too for coaching, but the meaning of coaching for her in this case would have been: OK tell me what to do to get what I want. This is not how coaching works and it is up to a coach to educate the client about it. You cannot change people to do what they do not want to do.

So how do you promise a sustainable change?

The problem is not just sustainability, however, but because humans are involved in the process. Humans are dynamic in nature: they move to other countries, change partners, and jobs. They lament the loss of a dear one. All these factors and many more can influence the behaviour and the decisions of a person, which may, in a short time, alter their most earnest resolutions to change. George Kelly, an influential psychologist known for his work in cognitive perspective in personality theory, stated the following on human nature: 'the person's outlook on life is transitory, insofar as it is rarely the same as it was yesterday or will be tomorrow. In attempting to anticipate and control the future events, one's view of reality is constantly being tested' [quoted in Hjelle and Ziegler (1992), p. 399]. People change their minds about what is important for them depending on their current stimulations, situations, environments, or possibilities. Stating that they can bring about a change that is sustainable in human behaviour is a very big promise for a coach to make.

3.2.2 Case Study: A Joint Venture

Let me give you an example of what I have discussed in the previous section about human nature and its unpredictability. The example is of a joint venture. This should be interesting for companies working across different cultures and countries. Many executives I coach often encounter one issue: how to harmonise processes across countries. There are other simplistic questions, such as why can the others not work as they wish them to. In this real example, retrospectively, I can say that I used an effective coaching method without knowing it then. Does that mean that I was coaching even before I learnt coaching? No, that would be incorrect because a coaching method is very detailed and one should learn it properly instead of relying on personal opinions. I would have completed the process much faster if I had learnt the coaching method before this coaching. Would I have done it much more effectively if I had known the coaching method? In hindsight everything seems easier but this is not the case when I look at my notes and memos from the years 2000–2003.

From 2000 I was working in Italy in a picturesque village called Crespi d'Adda, a small village between Milano and the town of Bergamo, with Legler SpA., a company listed at the Milano Stock Exchange, which manufactured denim, corduroy, some other fabrics, and finished jeans. Let me tell you a bit about this beautiful village and the company. This village is under UNSECO protection as a world heritage site, and so was one of our factories there. We were not permitted to touch any external parts of the factory; that made the surroundings exceptional. Even today when you visit the UNSECO website, the first images that you see are of the factory of Legler SpA in Crespi d'Adda. This factory was started as 'Cotonificio Crespi' in the year 1878. There was a saying in that area that almost every family in the surrounding areas had spent over 108 years on average in the company. We had more than 3500 employees and six factories; its output was about 72 million metres of fabric for the fashion industry. It was a brand name to reckon with and was known internationally as the world leader in denim and other fabrics. Besides five factories in Italy, we had a manufacturing plant near the city of Lahore in Pakistan, employing about 1470 people. This was a joint venture with our Pakistani partners who held about 37 % of the shareholding. This company had been making a consistent loss of a few million US$ every year for 9 years, ever since its inception. After a few months of working in Italy I was invited to join the board of directors with one additional responsibility: the management of Legler-Nafees Denim Mills Limited, which was listed in the Karachi Stock Exchange. One day Faisal Sharif (the name is fictive), the shareholder of the Pakistani company, a young suave, Oxford educated man of 32 years, came to me and said he was shutting down the operations because he saw no sense in it.

> I asked him, 'would you be interested in continuing if you could turn the company around?'
>
> 'Who would not?' he asked justifiably. Further he said, 'I had invested in this company in order to make it a leading producer of denim fabrics and jeans, but despite all the promised Italian expertise, I have been making losses for the last 9 years. I would certainly

be more than interested in turning around the company but I do not know how to do it with our Italian partners.'

I told him, 'I could help you but there would be one precondition: you agree to work as per the plan we work out and not divert in any manner for the next 9 months.' I also told him, 'according to my plan, you should get restless by the fourth month and ask for doubling of the production capacity.'

He said, 'I would be thrilled to come out of the losses—forget doubling the capacity.' As Daniel Kahneman said in his book, *Thinking Fast and Slow* (2013), we humans are unable to predict our emotions, reactions, and behaviour in most situations. This I am saying in hindsight, even I did not know it then.

Despite his plight I asked him, 'agree with me, verbally, that you will not stand in front of me and argue the benefits of doubling the capacity when things start moving.'

He agreed with me.

I added, 'I also need to agree with you that if asked I will refuse any increase in capacity until I have seen the complete year go through. If you do choose to increase your capacity despite my reservations I can also tell you that the company will suffer a damage that would not be reversible.'

His only answer was, 'OK'. He was curious now and challenged; I could see it in his facial expressions. This I learnt, years later in my coaching, that a coach challenges the perceptions of his client in a manner that it becomes fascinating for his client to try out new methods and approaches to old and new situations alike.

We started making small changes and he attracted massive orders. Previously his company had accepted orders to make shorts for US$2.95 from Swiss companies. Within 2 months he was talking about eight million units at US$8.95 with customers from the UK and other countries. Looking at the momentum, he invited his brother, who was a creative man, to return to Pakistan from the UK and work with him.

His first question was, 'what do you want me to do?'

I told him, 'start going to the office everyday and remove these people from their responsibilities.' I gave him a list of directors and other people who were expensive to the company and made no difference whether they were present or not.

His reaction did not surprise me, he asked, 'do you want me to go to the office every day?'

'Yes, sir I do,' I said.

He and his family belonged to the rich class and they normally like to be served rather than work. Finally, he agreed to work as I told him to.

Since I spoke the language of both countries: Italian and Punjabi, along with a smattering of Urdu, I was able to experience first-hand the disgruntlements of both sides. The shareholders in Pakistan thought that the Italians considered them as lesser humans; I know from experience that they were justified in their feelings. The Italian managers thought the partners in Pakistan were not capable of doing it; they were justified in their feelings too. Each side was convinced that the other did not know how things were done in Pakistan and Italy respectively. The Italians thought they were right in demanding the work ethics they were used to and without a thought condemned everyone in Pakistan who did not conform to their ideas. They were of the opinion that they needed to update the Pakistani operations constantly and regularly sent experts to Pakistan for installations, quality, or management issues and the people that they sent were always Italian or at least Europeans. I always wondered why we went to set up an operation in Pakistan if we had wanted the Italians to do the job all the year around. We had hired very expensive technicians and stationed them in Lahore, living in expensive hotels. The CEO had been hired from Switzerland and stationed in Lahore. These experts, when in Pakistan, struggled with the weather, food, culture and their perceived superiority. On the Pakistani side they expected that if the experts had come, the responsibility of performance was unconditionally transferred to them and with it to the Italian partners. If things did not work out or if goods came late from Lahore, the managers would have an explanation, which was more of a template response for every misgiving: 'this is how your experts taught us'. This is the ugly side of ethnocentricity and this happens in many companies who have operations in different countries. The staff working with people in other countries have little or no patience for cultural differences and the management is too busy, if not reactive, to find lasting and appropriate solutions to harmonise both teams. We give these situations very fancy names, such as 'distance management', whereas in many cases we should call ourselves 'distant from management'. Intercultural coaches can help iron out many creases and bring about the necessary awareness about the cultural differences and teach skills on both ends that help achieve exceptional results.

The people in Pakistan, I realised, were practically waiting to see the foreign staff fail. Strange as it may be, their success and feeling of achievement lay in the failing of their own processes. This does not happen solely in companies, but also in personal relationships, marriages, and wherever two parties or persons interact at inferior levels. Some relations reach a level of interaction where the sense of success lies in the failure of the relationship. As if someone is waiting just to prove his point and say, 'see I told you this can never work.' This was one sentence I had heard from many managers before the Pakistani operations had turned around.

I did simple maths in a board meeting and asked everybody the reason for going to Pakistan 9 years before. Everyone said because of the advantages of the cost of goods. Then why, I asked, do we have four people who contribute 0.57 cents per pair of jeans? In this business where hundreds of thousands of pairs, if not millions, can be ordered in one single order by larger corporations, a price difference of 0.5 cents can be a game changer. Is spending 0.57 cents not a sure way of creating a loss? The Swiss manager and the Italian technicians were relieved of their responsibilities and the costs brought down. There were many subtle changes that were made very swiftly. I asked people from Pakistan to be trained in Italy and Germany for a period of 3 weeks here and 2 weeks there, to get to grips with certain techniques in washing and sand blasting and all the other details necessary to produce good quality products. The Pakistani shareholders had agreed to do as I said, and within a period of 6 months, the company made its first profits in Pakistan. Not because I have a magic wand. The trick was that both sides understood the capacity of the other and what the limitations and expectations were. The focus was no more on allegations but on what needed to be done. The Italians let the Pakistani partner work as best they could. The magic, in retrospect, lay in letting others work.

Let us go back to my relationship with Faisal Sharif. After 4 months on the dot, he was standing in front of me and said, 'I need to double our capacity.'

In a casual conversation strolling on our factory premises in Crespi d'Adda, I reminded him, 'I had agreed with you that you will not ask for doubling your capacity until the end of the year, until we have both examined the numbers and results.'

'Yes, but we have Matalan as our customer now and they sell eight million pairs a year. What if they ask us if we can make five million pairs, should we say no? We are now beginning to talk business with major players in the world because of the name Legler. They know we have the capacity and the know-how. We have been waiting for this for so many years.' I could see he was eager about the prospect of jumping right into this opportunity with both feet. I think Matalan was a very large wholesaler in the UK at the time.

'How would you like to encounter this situation if you do not want to say no? I also know that if you take on a large order you will damage your company and the name of Legler, if we do not deliver what we commit,' I argued.

I narrated to him the story of the giant electronic manufacturer, Sony Corporation, in Japan, that I had read in 1986. I had been impressed by the ideas of Akio Morita, one of the founders of that company. He had narrated how the company began, how it became big and most importantly what he did not do. In his book *Made in Japan* (1986, p. 92) he narrates a few events from his sales meetings and says, 'I was happy to be offered some tempting deal, but I was cautious and more than once I turned down what looked like a chance to make big profits. The buyers thought I was crazy . . . time has shown that I made the right decision.' Akio Morita had turned down an order of 100,000 transistors. The purchasing officer of his client had said, 'We will take one hundred thousand units'. He thought that would be a very large order. 'One hundred thousand Units! I was stunned' (p. 93). Despite the tempting large number, he turned it down because he had a vision for his company to become a brand name not an Original Equipment Manufacturer, supplier, who puts the customer's brand name on his own innovations. He knew where he wanted his company to go. He did not compromise his vision or his company's potential because of a temptation. Many years later his decision proved him right. I know from my own experience that in business, it is not always about large numbers and orders, it is more about what we have thought out for the future of our company and the direction we want to give it as a leader.

My effort was to make him realise that Legler-Nafees should consider the new situation as an opportunity to define and follow mid and long-term perspectives on developing the business and not jump at every new temptation. That was my idea of business. I was part of a group of very self-confident people who had invested money and were now looking in the face of an opportunity they had wished for years. In such situations you can make efforts to convince others as we say in English: you can take the horse to the water but you cannot make him drink. The thirst is a very private issue with the horse as temptation of profit is with the investor.

Despite all the examples, Faisal Sharif insisted, 'No, we will outsource it and it will work and we shall exploit this opportunity.' I knew that he wanted to expand his business; he wanted to cash in on the opportunity. Finally, after I convinced him that the numbers played against him, we agreed to delay the expansion for a while. He did not take on orders for the sake of filling up his books with numbers. In the following months the number of high yield orders grew constantly. They did not go back to the Swiss discounter to sell shorts for US$ 2.95 per unit. Pakistani operations began to do what they were conceived to do: grow and make profits for the investors. After they became profitable both sides asked me 'how did you do it?' I told them, in Italy and in Pakistan—and it is what I tell my coaching clients now—it is not I who did anything, it was you. My efforts would have been useless if both the Italian and the Pakistani partners had not realised that they stood to gain by doing what we agreed. My response was that they did everything because they understood for the first time what they were really capable of doing, and that it was also right for both to accept the constraints of the joint venture. I was convincing because they could see evidence of this explanation in their profits, which brought new self-confidence to both sides.

It is not an easy job, this intercultural part in business, but with proper methods and focus on the benefit to others, focus on the capability of others, it is not a difficult one either. Notice I am not saying it is not rocket science because with all the modern machines and good software it is perhaps easier to build a rocket these days than to talk sincerely with people who do not look and talk like you. In leadership and coaching efficacy depends on one single factor: if a leader or a coach is focused on the people first, their capabilities second, and after combines everything to bring in what is to be done, then it works well. Both the leaders and coaches inspire others because of their focus on others and because others feel appreciated for what they are. This is a very natural consequence of leadership and coaching. I am not using any adjective good, bad, or excellent. Leadership and coaching, without adjectives, are sufficient terms to define a particular behaviour without adjectives. They produce the desired result only if they consider others first: let people grow according to their own circumstances. In my opinion, there is no bad leadership or bad coaching; if it is bad, who have you led or who has grown? If there is no growth, there was no coaching or leadership.

Going back to the discussion of goals—how does it help to make large goals which sound magnificent but are unachievable because the people who are going to be affected by the goals are not considered as important as the goals? How often have I seen this attitude in business? In Legler SpA, when I had just about started working, my predecessor, Leonardo (I have given him a fictive name), was sitting with Dr. Enrico (the name is fictive), the president, and drawing figures on the board and the bottom line was—we have to make three million pairs more next year and we will be profitable. It is not difficult to add up numbers and subtract the expenses and say how much more we need to manufacture. He had planned on calling the Tunisian suppliers and the Pakistani partners to tell them this was the plan. I asked a couple of questions: 'who is investing for this new expansion?' Leonardo said, 'the Pakistanis.' I asked, 'have you reached an agreement with them?' He said, 'no, they will do it because in the end they will make money.' I said, 'Leonardo, Faisal has been making a loss for the last 9 years. I think we should make goals and plans after we know the complete logistics, etc.' He stopped short and said, 'I did not think of it.' They dropped the goal. Goals and plans are often made very quickly, particularly by people who are self-confident. As I said earlier, it seems to me that the absurdity of a goal has a linear correlation with the self-confidence of a manager: the higher the self-confidence of a manager the more absurd is a goal. Three million pairs of jeans—we can do it, we are Legler. This kind of attitude borders on arrogance and is a precursor for massive failures. They forget that the logistics of goal achieving is not based on their self-confidence but on the ground realities of how everything will be realised in the minutest details. If you go into the minute details the nature of the undertaking changes. It moves from being a goal to becoming a plan. A plan is no more a wish, a daydream of a manager, but a detailed step-wise project.

Legler SpA had been demanding 10 % commission for all sales of Legler-Nafees because we in Italy were convinced our name added value to the products in Pakistan and we were the owners of the technology. To add to it there was 1.5 % additional royalty on the annual turnover in Pakistan. All this and many more services had created an enormous debt Legler-Nafees owed to Legler. I thought that the gentlemen in Italy were indulging in adult monopoly, spending hours on discussions on how much the debt was. As soon as I was appointed to the board, I shot the ten down to 1.5 % with the argument that no fashion business that I knew of, anywhere in the world, made more than 6 % profit. How do you expect the partners in Pakistan to pay 10 % + 1.5 %?

The commercial manager in Italy, a Swiss gentleman, whose name is Bruno Schilling, had worked for our company for more than 38 years, and he came to me to ask why we had not done this smart thing earlier. He smiled because that was not a direct question placed to me. He meant Legler when he said 'we'. He knew I was too new to answer 9 year old decisions. When people see that someone is making changes that are directly helping their cause—that there is someone who is looking at them as they are and not throwing numbers in their face to prove their own importance—they get inspired to follow that person. This is valid for any relationship; raising children, relationships with your spouse, your partner or anyone dependent on your behaviour. If we strangle them, metaphorically speaking, or restrict them, how can you expect a good relationship? A coach does exactly this, he lets people reflect, and make changes on their own terms within their own capabilities. These concepts are new and after having tried out the patriarchal, authoritative, the anti-authoritarian and the liberal kind of leadership styles, today we need to act with coaching methodology if we want to achieve good results and performance from knowledge-based self-confident executives.

The purpose of this case study was to demonstrate that you can bring about a change but only if the respondent is willing to change. Now let me address the sustainability of this case.

Everybody was planning for future budgets and there were different types of threats I could hear on both sides: we will not let the Italians interfere any more and everything else that goes to protect one's interest. The majority shareholders of Legler SpA on the Italian side decided to sell off their stake in Legler-Nafees Limited and cashed out. The stock was sold for a few million euros and Legler SpA withdrew the right they had given to Legler-Nafees Limited to use their reputed and desirable brand name.

So much for the sustainability of change.

Faisal Sharif had been visibly thrilled at his management skills and so were the shareholders at the turnaround of their 9 year loss maker. You would expect both to celebrate and pat each other on the shoulders, congratulate each other, and reaffirm and say, see we were right about our venture in Pakistan. That was not so. Whenever a change happens it inherently brings with it new opportunities and new self-confidence for the stakeholders. It also ushers in new ways to look at old perceptions and structures. There is a rejuvenated will to take more risks and believe in one's own capabilities. You can never know how the change will play out on the client and that is perfectly acceptable. As a coach you have not taken over the life of someone. You do your work and let the client relish the outcome. I as a coach can never predict how someone will be affected by the coaching experience, even positively; I cannot know how they will react to change caused through coaching. Leger could have continued but they decided to stop everything in its tracks and that was the result of a dramatic positive change. You may predict that a change can be achieved; you can never predict whether the outcome of the change will sustain itself.

We can continue to discuss the reasons why the Italian shareholders sold their shares, but to what end? It was their decision and they had the right to do what they wanted. However, I had wanted to know the reasons: just for academic curiosity. I was told in a meeting with the president of the group (not by the Italian shareholders), just in one short statement, 'they hold the accounts of Legler-Nafees Limited in the books in Pakistan and they write their accounts with pencils. Do you think we will ever see a share of profits?' Loss aversion, I thought. We kept working with them as long as they were loss makers. We put in so much effort to keep their debts alive in our books and discussed it with them in every meeting for years. We sold out as soon as we started making money. What a paradox. I was leaving for China to set up my own company so I left with one lesson: do what you think is right, not for changing someone, because what he will do due to the change is his prerogative. I will never have access to his future actions because this is his privileged decision. There is no sustainable change, because change is just the outcome of actions of a human being and an outcome cannot hold itself on its own: change cannot sustain itself.

3.2.3 Case Study: 'Mark'

Mark was a 51-year-old CEO; I have used a fictive name. He had worked extremely hard for the past 27 years to reach his present position, yet he was working under the impression that he was not an important person for the company. During the first two sessions of coaching, he repeated very often, 'If they do not want me in the company I would be willing to leave and look for another job. I think with my capabilities I will find adequate work.' From Mark's description, I speculated that his immediate superior was what we sometimes refer to as a toxic person. His superior wanted to show the managers that he was a tough guy and people had to take him seriously. Once, while this superior was being introduced to a new manager, he said to him, jokingly, 'tell me who is bothering you and I will kill him. I have the power to do that.' This may have been harmless fun in his eyes but Mark told me that it left the other managers shocked. I was reminded of Dick Fuld,[2] and his aggressive speech about the short sellers of Lehman Brothers' stocks on the stock markets in which he said he would 'rip out their heart and eat it'.

I had the advantage of receiving reports about Mark's superior through various people within his company over a period of more than 16 months, which is why my speculation on his behaviour may have been closer to fact. Every time he called a manager on the phone, the conversation began by pointing out what was not going right: it was a simple blame game. The focus of every conversation was intimidation from a higher position.

Mark was extremely frustrated with his superior and interpreted the behaviour directed at him as though he were being pushed out of the company. He was leading one of the most successful business units in a large multinational company with many thousands of employees in Germany. Relying on his own interpretation of what his boss thought of him, Mark also added that his colleagues did not think much of him. His working hours were longer than those of anyone else in the company. If he went home early, it would have been 9:00 pm. His wife complained that he was neglecting his health, family, and friends. When he was on holiday, his official mobile telephone was always switched on to receive the onslaught of abusive calls from his boss. He reported that he came back from his holidays with a feeling as if he had never left work. At this stage some might tend to jump to the cliché of 'Work-Life Balance'. I do not think much of this cliché in coaching and will address it later in the book (See Sect. 9.6).

After the third coaching session, he was able to discover that his colleagues thought very highly of him. I had compiled a tailor-made questionnaire that was sent to his colleagues, which was designed both to address his constant fear of leaving the company and to determine whether he was really doing something to invite such treatment. One of the questions in the inventory of 72 quantitative and nine qualitative items was, 'What would change for you if Mark left the company tomorrow?' The answer to this particular question was an open format and everyone could give three answers to it in their own words. This format was chosen deliberately to let others say what they thought without forcing them into a choice from the prepared answers. I asked 18 people and these are the results:

- Three people said they would also leave the company if Mark left.
- Almost all respondents said that Mark's order, discipline, and his polite behaviour had given the whole company a distinct character and if he left it would disappear.

[2]Richard Fuld was the CEO of Lehman Brothers at the time of its collapse in 2008.

- All respondents thought it was not good.
- Seven respondents disclosed that people would miss Mark: as a person who they looked up to; a person they could confide in; someone who gave them personal support.
- Five respondents gasped at the question and asked me during the interviews, 'Is he leaving the company? He has made this company what it is, how can he leave?'

These results brought Mark close to tears. It took him a few days to digest the findings. In our next meeting, 4 weeks later, he reported that over the past 4 weeks almost everyone, spare one who was leaving the company for retirement, went to him to express their support and to ask if they could take on some work that would relieve him a little, so that he could go home earlier. He could not get over this discovery and kept on repeating, 'I cannot believe this, and I thought I was just another cog in the works.'

Mark had overlooked the basic facts: he had started working in this company 27 years before, when there were just a handful of people there. He had helped to create the company: the one his boss was managing. I asked him what had changed for him. He said he could not say exactly but he was no longer concerned about what his boss said or how he behaved. He was now confident that he had done a good job, not just because he thought so, but because the respondents to the questionnaire told him.

Is this evidence of the assumption that Mark was 'living by his own perception' of what people thought of him? Before his coaching sessions and before he discovered what his colleagues thought of him, Mark was constantly interpreting the toxic behaviour of another person as his own deficiency: that he was worthless. After coaching, he began to think his interpretation had been completely wrong. Mark was living from his own perception and through coaching he had changed his opinion of how things were. He had cultivated a belief about his own capabilities based on the toxic behaviour of his boss: he was of the opinion that the abusive language was directed at him because of his worthlessness and it did not seem to him that the real cause was a deficiency with his boss.

A few weeks later, at a dinner meeting with Christian, who was co-CEO of the company along with Mark, he told me that Mark had undergone a metamorphosis because of coaching. He had never seen such a dramatic change in anyone before. I was curious and asked him to tell me more. He told me that previously he would have been extremely agitated before, during, and after a teleconference with his boss. Every participant of the telephone conference would have noticed Mark's nervousness and they kept away from him for a while after it. This, in my opinion, could have contributed to making Mark feel that something was wrong with him; he may have taken this as a reason why people distanced themselves from him. I do not know for sure but why not speculate and wait to see if it was right to do so? What was the difference in Mark after the coaching? I asked Christian. He said there was a very stark difference: now he listened to his boss quietly; he found that the first ten minutes were toxic, but if he let him play his hardball game, he very soon ran out of steam. After ten minutes of monologue from his boss Mark would place forward his monthly reports and projections for the future in a very calm manner. When he asked straight questions, to his surprise, he found his boss struggling for words. This made his colleagues admire him and they wanted to know more about his way of handling his boss. He was known as a very polite person but now he was being admired for his calm disposition too.

There is a very important lesson for coaching in this case: coaching does not work in a linear fashion. Many people claim that the client will decide what he wants to achieve and a coach will set a goal for him and support him in achieving that goal. What would have happened if a coach had achieved the goal of making him look for another job? Coaching, if conducted methodically, is very effective in bringing about a perspective shift in the client. The first thing that happens due to coaching is that the way a client thinks is enhanced. You notice I am avoiding the word change. This enhancement impacts the whole person and not their skill or a single selected part of the person's concerns. Coaching is much more advanced than many older forms of counselling. That is the reason why it also impacts areas the client had not discussed or even considered. In Mark's case, coaching impacted the way he developed new coping strategies vis-à-vis his boss. Due to the new coping strategies, he won new admirers. Due to the new admirers, he developed a new level of self-confidence and this is what he changed on his own terms. This is a change brought about in a client on many dimensions due to coaching.

I did not suggest any of this: Mark was still carrying his official mobile with him on holidays but the difference was that it was switched off. He switched it on when he thought it appropriate to talk to his managers. He was accustomed to receiving a call from his boss exactly on the day he left on holiday, usually when he was in a taxi with his wife on his way to the airport. Previous to coaching, he would have responded and then received a string of urgent new assignments, which he had to accomplish during his holiday. By the time he boarded the plane he was agitated due to extreme stress. Now, he stopped taking calls until he was ready for them, and he explained to me that he was not the only one working in the organisation. I did not find this attitude arrogant or aggressive, especially if you consider that he then said: the work my boss assigns to me is in any case going to be done by an expert dedicated for that purpose and I would only call her to do it. Why can't someone, who is not on holiday, call that person instead of me?

After the coaching sessions were over he invited me to a dinner along with his wife and the occasion provided further confirmation that he had profited greatly from changing his perception of his working life. As a matter of fact, it was his wife who told me that it was great to have her husband back in her life after so many years. She told me she had consoled herself over the last many years that the hard work would be over someday and he would be able to participate in normal social activities along with her more frequently. He had started to return home at 7:00 pm. Old habits die hard, but he thought it was an improvement from 9:00 pm to 7:00 pm. He did not do that every day but he also did not return every day exhausted at 10:00 pm. His past work routine had left them no scope for any conversation or social activity in the evenings, now it was possible more often.

Mark's case also validates the first assumption that 'people act in their own interest'. His is an important one, which I will refer to in the section that deals with basic assumptions of human nature in a coaching context (See Sect. 8.2). His case study also provides evidence that sustainable change through coaching is a fallacy.

I met Mark 7 months after his coaching mandate had been completed. This meeting is part of a regular follow-up with subsequent single coaching sessions. As soon as we met, I asked him 'what was your reason for meeting me today?' He said, 'I have this funny feeling inside of me.' He went on to tell me that due to coaching he had understood that his boss was the way he was. It was not his own fault but now there was a feeling that he was getting into an area of looking down on his boss. I asked, 'can you put a name on it?' He said, 'I think I may be becoming arrogant toward him.' 'What makes you think so?' I asked. 'I have begun to somehow laugh at him; I am happy that I am not doing it openly as yet, so I wanted to meet you first because I think this is not me. I do not ridicule people.'

The lesson for me was, when people change some aspects of their life a coach cannot promise that those aspects will create a sustainable change. A positive change, in my opinion, brings new self-confidence with it. There may also be an element of increased risk-taking due to the new self-confidence. I do not think that Mark can sustain the realisation he experienced after coaching: that the behaviour of his boss was not his own fault. I think that he will create new circumstances based on the insights he gained through coaching and primarily because he is feeling more secure. Change was just the initial result of coaching. How can someone claim to sustain that and worse still, who would want to stay at a realisation permanently and not let it evolve further? People would very naturally use that realisation to construct a new dimension, or as the psychologist George Kelly in his book *A Theory of Personality The Psychology of Personal Constructs* (1963) said, new 'constructs' for themselves. That is why the promise of sustainable change in coaching is a fallacy.

References

Kelly, G. (1963). *A theory of personality*. New York: Norton Paperback.

Morita, A., Reingold, M., & Shimomura, M. (1986). *Made in Japan*. New York: Nal Penguin.

Nagel, T. (1974). What is it like to be a Bat? *The Philosophical Review, 83*(4), 435–450.

Online Sources

Crespi d'Adda homepage. http://www.crespidadda.it/bibliografia-crespi-dadda. Accessed 10 Mar 2016.

Richard Fuld. https://www.youtube.com/watch?v=GZCmWkQuyPc. Accessed 12 Mar 2012.

UNESCO Ufer, Chr. (Hrsg.). (1897). *Entwickelung der Seelenfaehigkeit bei Kindern*. Altenburg: Druck und Verlag von Oskar Bonde. http://whc.unesco.org/en/list/730. Accessed 10 Mar 2016.

4 Personal Business Experience

In 2008, I took up the position of Managing Director of Sympatex Technologies Asia Limited, a company well-known in Germany for its copolymer membrane developed by the AkzoNobel Group in 1986 in Wuppertal. We had an office in Beijing and its Asian head office in Hong Kong. Before I left for Hong Kong, I was told by managers in Germany that Hong Kong Chinese people are very aggressive. Little did they know that I had been working with Hong Kong companies since 1986. After 14 months the CEO of the German head office came to see me in Hong Kong. His first question was, 'have they all come back from a holiday?' I wanted to know the reason for his question. He said they all seemed so calm and were working in a relaxed manner. People in Hong Kong are very hard-working and not aggressive, in the manner some had painted them.

His observation also triggered a curiosity in me. I had been working there for some months already and the environment had become habitual for me; perhaps I had stopped noticing these aspects of our office. I think this happens to most executives: everything around them becomes normal after a while. When they engage a coach and talk to him they discover new perspectives, just as I had stopped noticing that my colleagues were very calm and productive. I had forgotten the fact that there were no more squabbles that affected the work of the company.

This was the first time I had wanted to research consciously to determine what I had done differently so that people in the same company became more productive and with almost no overt aggression. A small note of my personal opinion: total absence of overt aggression may be Utopia; some stress and tension is always needed for competitive behaviour.

The CEO had wanted to know the secret so that he could implement it in the office in Germany. He said it would be a dream for him to have this working environment. For this and other reasons he offered me a new attractive contract to move to Germany to take on additional responsibility of COO worldwide, while at the same time keeping the old job of managing director of an Asian company. In January 2010, I moved my family to Munich for this reason and was preparing to jet between Hong Kong and Munich every 15 days.

A. Kohli, *Effective Coaching, and the Fallacy of Sustainable Change*, Management for Professionals, DOI 10.1007/978-3-319-39735-1_4

My response to his question of how this can be achieved was more of a discussion. Let me give a gist of it all. I told him you cannot come to your office with a template of how you would like people to be, that does not work and creates only frustration with colleagues. Your own behaviour can influence others very significantly. They will emulate you, if they think you are doing something that they appreciate. The appreciation comes mostly when people notice you doing good for others. As a leader you have to demonstrate that you are not favouring anyone over others, working in a non-partisan manner, and are fair to all. This sounds very simple but I have thought about this for some time because I practised this not just in my companies for years but at home too. If you do not show that you practice non-favouritism or non-partisanship, people will rush to you for every small thing such as: 'he said that to me and she did that to me.' It creates a kindergarten in an adult company. How do I know it? When I entered Legler SpA I saw this behaviour of adults working in a small division. If you choose to be a 'fixer', a person who will fix every one's ailments, you are the only person of authority who will address everything. The downside of addressing everything yourself is that discontentment of everyone in the company is with you. Your own discontentment will be so enormous that you may notice yourself complaining: 'I do so much for others, I do not know why they are so ungrateful.' In my opinion these people also tend to compare themselves to silverback gorillas and call themselves 'alpha males'. The tragic part is that most of the time they are extremely ineffective in their work because the majority of their time is spent in proving themselves to be someone of extraordinary qualities who can fix everything.

If you practice non-partisan working, your reports will emulate you and they will practice it too. According to my experience, in a company hierarchy, the more instances for decision-making you create, the more people react quickly to issues of work without confusion. What does that mean? Imagine you are the CEO and you have under you the following team: IT manager, the technical manager, the finance manager, the purchase manager, the sales manager and let us add a marketing manager. All these managers have somewhere between 10 to 75 people working for them. If you are non-partisan all the managers will not come to you for every small issue; they will make decisions themselves. If you are tempted to say, is that not what they are employed to do? You would be right. In practice, the top executive very often jumps in and tries to tell them how to do it better. How do I know it? I have seen it in many companies and in many countries. If the top executive has more confidence in his reports all the issues will be resolved at this instance and leave him time to do his work: to lead the company.

In my coaching practice I saw that those who reported back after becoming aware of such concepts said that they have lesser work and more reliability from their reports and more time for themselves.

A second way to create massive confusion is by telling people that you are responsible to Ms. A for disciplinary purposes and to Ms. B for operative purposes. This is not an uncommon practice that leaves people directionless. They do not understand the hierarchical structures and the two people responsible for one person do not know who is leading the person in this diarchy. I saw that in Hong Kong and in Italy and removed it very quickly. Trudy Ng (I am changing the names) was a very accomplished technician and had been in Sympatex since the first day. Someone in Germany told me she was responsible to me for disciplinary issues but will report for operative issues to Ms.— in Germany. I am convinced that it cannot work in most situations, and I think it is even more difficult over continents and cultures. I let it run for 8 weeks; later on, the financial department asked me why Trudy was spending so much money on her travels. I said, for her operative work. Why do you not ask Ms.—because she is giving her the work? The lady responsible said, 'I do not know the travel costs in Asia.' Sometimes you have to let people play their fantasy for a while, till they realise the absurdity of creating systems that will drive straight into the wall. I am convinced that diarchy is one way of creating an 'authority free', 'non-productive system' with very high certainty of poor results, not to talk about absence of leadership. I had already discussed the disadvantages of such a system with everybody concerned on every possible platform in Germany weeks before. I think we often pick up new concepts from articles in magazines and forget that the people or circumstances may not be suitable for it. I ended the system and with it ended the confusion. Subsequently Trudy had to talk to me for everything and in the interaction I had the opportunity to address all the aggression too. She had been a grey eminence that no one dared touch before me. People in a company and even in a family like to follow a clear hierarchical structure. If you disturb it, they lose direction. In companies some may also abuse this confusion to their personal advantage.

I told the CEO that you need to demonstrate to them the limits a company system will tolerate in personal behaviour. You have to show them that you will care about their capabilities and then ask them to do particular work, not set goals with complete disregard to the feasibility and tell them, 'now go for it.' When I landed up in the office everyone had had an affiliation to one group or an ideology. For the previous 5 years or so there had been many different CEOs and no one had stayed long enough to cultivate a proper Sympatex culture. My predecessor was a sales director in Munich, in Paris, and interim CEO of Hong Kong. There was a feeling that there was no one who took care of the people in Hong Kong. No hierarchical structures or authority. People had complained as they do so very often in such set-ups: 'we are the step children of the company.' This kind of feeling leads to everyone scrambling to protect their personal interests first. Since there was no one with the responsibility of leadership present, as in the case of Hong Kong, the only reaction left for the executives in Germany was to believe whatever was told to them by every individual in Hong Kong. Whoever came first must be telling the truth—that was the common attitude. No one was actively leading people or giving them the feeling of belonging. Every person, without exception, working there thought that another person was the root cause and evil of all and had to be fired. This situation had to be removed and I did it in many small steps but with one thing in common in all steps: I let them realise what desirable behaviour is. How do you do that? Conversation. Today I would say through a conversational coaching method.

There was a small team in Beijing in P. R. China with a general manager and his employees. We were spending about US$44,000 for rent and salaries per month. The people working there were excellent people. I recall two people distinctly: Michael Xu, the sales manager, and Jenny Qiu, office administration and finances. I closed down the Beijing office within 6 months of my arrival. They had never made any profits but met all their goals every year. The CFO in Germany had agreed that they always reached their goals. In the year 2007 they had achieved their goal by selling to Shanghai Baosteel Group Corporation, a company of a size that a whole town is named after Baosteel. The goals had been achieved by paying sales commissions and discounts of about 34 % on their orders. This is the absurdity of goals; you can continue to discuss that the goals were achieved and maintain loss-making business units and completely ignore that the purpose of an undertaking is not setting goals but making profits and ensuring growth for the company and its people.

I was surprised at what Michael and Jenny had said to me while we were winding up the operations there. Michael came and thanked me and said he was grateful for the honesty and for treating them as equals with respect. I thought what does that mean, treating people with respect? I did not bow down to greet them, or put my hand over their shoulder, as a sign of closeness, while talking to them. I did not follow any of these clichés. I had talked to them as normal people, as I would with anyone. What was the difference they had seen? He said that no one before me had treated them like real people. The previous CEOs wanted to be picked up at the airport and dropped directly to the hotel and the next day they looked at the reports and told them what they were not achieving and all that they wanted to see them do. The interaction was very poor and limited to directives and authoritative instructions. He had thanked me for closing the company. I was surprised because no one thanks anyone for losing a job. He said that he could see for a long time that the company would have failed and had wondered that no one was seeing it in Germany or Hong Kong. I asked him why did he not look for a new job if he knew that the company would fail anyway in China? He said, he was convinced that the product was great and hoped that someone would come and either do the right thing and improve the state of their company in Beijing or shut it down. He said it was a great honour for him personally to be related to a German brand and he had hoped that he could continue. That was the reason he had not looked for a job earlier. He offered me his help even though he was not working with us anymore. Even today, 7 years later, I hear from him sometimes. Jenny was the wife of a Colonel in the People's Army; she did not need to work to earn her livelihood. When she was leaving the company, she had wanted to know a couple of things. She asked me, 'why did you chose to stay in the hotel where you stayed?' I replied, because I thought the hotel was reasonable and clean. She said, in the whole history of Sympatex Beijing, she had not seen a manager who came from Sympatex who had not asked for the hotel across the road: The Swiss Hotel. 'Why did you not take that?' I said because it is three or four times more expensive and a company that is not making any profit is unable to support such extravagances. She asked further, 'I also noted that you did not fly first class: why not?' 'The same reason, Jenny; the company is not profitable and for a 2 hours' flight from Hong Kong it is a waste of money,' I explained. The lesson was that people are listening to what you are saying and comparing it to what you are doing to see if your words are congruent with your actions. If I say the company is not making any money but at the same time I display extravagant expenses, is it possible that in such situations people feel as if they have been fooled or feel that their intelligence is being undermined by telling them that there is no money but enough can be found for extravagant spending on one single person? Could it have something to do with silent humiliation: giving a feeling of excluding some from the riches that I may relish because of my position? I am not propagating communism. Executives deserve to earn more and receive perquisites but not when companies are down on their belly. If I continue with my extravagant behaviour, I become incredulous for them and they will disrespect me. They accepted the closure of a company not as an affront to their person but as a natural consequence of the company results. They felt respected because they did not see themselves being misled or humiliated: everything I did was coherent with what I was saying. I also asked them how long they would need to find a job and if we could do anything to support their search. You could say this is all normal. I have not seen this practice in many companies. I discovered, in the companies where I worked, if people are working to their bare minimum—just what is needed, the nine to five routine—then it is the first evidence thereof that they do not see any sense in contributing to that company's development. The reason lies mostly with the leadership not with the people working there. A common complaint by many managers working across cultures and countries is that they are different, they are unreliable, they are aggressive—the list of complaints is unending. Your sincere behaviour toward others is what leadership is made of; it can have the same effect that coaching can: trigger self-motivated higher performance as long as people know they are being told to do something which you would also do yourself. This is part of the realisation and only when people realise themselves that there is something that they appreciate will they follow you or will want to perform more or respect you as in the case in Beijing with my colleagues there.

Let us fly back to Hong Kong and look at the mess there. In the first 5 days it was impossible to hold a meeting because of overt aggression toward each other. The technical head, Trudy Ng, was important for the technical inspections of our products in China, Indonesia, S. Korea and elsewhere in Asia. According to the German executives she was indispensable. Erhard (I am changing the names) who was an expert on lamination, and stationed in Ningbo in P. R. China was also indispensable. Nancy Wu, an accounts person was indispensable. The sales team was as important, but all seemed to be at loggerheads with each other. On the one hand, they were humiliating each other at every opportunity they got, on the other, extracting exorbitant raises from the executives. Between 2007 and 2008, the year of financial meltdown in the New York Stock Exchange, collapse of Lehman Brothers, and the subprime scandals and derivatives that took Iceland's national finances down, Sympatex Technologies handed out about a 68 % raise to an accountant and between 58 % and 76 % to a few others. That was before I took over. You could say perhaps they deserved it. I asked the CFO in Germany why was that done; was there any contractual commitment?

The CEO and CFO looked at me and said, 'we do not know that.'

'Why don't we check this up? It seems strange to me because we are not making any money there and I have not seen any exceptional performance in any particular area. You receive a monthly report don't you? That should reflect these massive changes,' I asked.

'Yes, let us ask Marcel Duchamp,' they said. He was the director in Paris and sales director in Germany and had been the interim CEO of Asian headquarters.

Two days later I received the answer, 'if we had not given the raise these people would have left the company. Now you must reduce it to …', the CFO said.

'With what reasoning should we reduce it? And why is it that we do not feel threatened any more that they may leave the company?' I asked.

'You must tell them that we are not making any money and they have to accept it,' he said.

'But we have never made money there for so many years because the company was conceived as a service centre for German operations,' I said.

Managers think the others are not watching all this. Michael Xu in Beijing knew that this was not how Sympatex would become a great company in China. Why does the C level executive not see what a sales manager can? Why did they not talk to their colleagues in China and Hong Kong? What I heard was a very common response from many managers: 'no, you have to convince them and they have to accept it,' the CFO said.

Why do we do such silly things with our own people? Give such massive raises and then wake up to mistakes only to embarrass them by saying now we will withdraw your benefits? Whenever there is no direct authority or a structured hierarchy a company is vulnerable to all sorts of threats from the employees; paradoxically, they also begin to be perceived as indispensable. As a matter of fact, people are perceived as indispensable because those at the top are incapable of gauging their importance. It is just a fear reaction, not management; let us not even mention the word leadership in this context.

I did not change things overnight. Within the first 30 days, I demonstrated to them non-partisanship and null favouritism and I showed that each member of the company was equally valuable. I had practised this even in my family. Once, in Italy, our daughter Anna came to me and asked, 'papa, I am your favourite child, aren't I?' 'Yes, you are our favourite daughter and David is our favourite son.' This was a conscious effort to remove any distinction or favouritism. They were both equal; this is also what I practised in my business environment. This is what worked in Hong Kong. It is sufficient that the colleagues see that there is no favouritism and they can resolve their matters between themselves as easily or even casually rather that running to the boss for every little issue.

I recreated or better still redefined the work environment. There was one person, Erhard, a German technician; he was about 59 years, and another very important cog in the wheel, but he was always involved in quarrels over small entries in his travel accounts. There was always a feeling that anyone could do anything and yet get away with it because all had some expertise that was vital to the company. This situation emerged because we had managers in the past who showed little intercultural competence in working with a mixed team. They said that the Chinese colleagues had to take care of everything that the German colleagues did. I asked Erhard to take care of his affairs as my Chinese colleagues did for themselves: the issue was resolved. I demonstrated zero tolerance for disrespect from either side; if someone got aggressive to another colleague, I refused to accept it and asked them to look for a better method of talking to each other. I introduced a system of six-weekly meetings. Every time a different person was to chair the meeting, formulate the agenda, ask everyone for their general grievances: be it as banal as the taste of coffee or tea in our kitchen or lighting or whatever. They were forced to talk and take into consideration the needs of each other. In the process they realised that they were not very different from one another. I did not interfere and was only a participant in such meetings. I did this for a few months and then they created their own system of discussing matters that were of common interest.

Through these meetings they realised what kind of process is required to bring about an agreement for small matters in a company where no one will be angry. They began talking about consensual decisions. I noticed that soon people began to imitate me; they talked and held meetings the way I did. Their behaviour was much calmer. I was very careful not to create an environment of fear because people do not perform well when they are fearful. In the beginning I gave a lot of attention to individual people and the work they were doing but with time I let them do their work as they could and it was excellent.

Alice Chang (I am changing the names), a young woman I had employed for customer services, asked for leave because she was expecting a child. Even though there are excellent laws to protect young mothers, in Germany most people get extremely anxious if someone is pregnant in the office, that was so at least up to 2000s. They got extremely concerned about the costs and absence of the person due to maternity leave, etc. In Hong Kong I asked that the occasion be celebrated. In China there is a custom that on the Lunar New Year the boss will hand over a red envelope with a small amount of cash as a gift to each one of his employees. It may be a HK$100 or 100Yuan. After the birth of her child, I sent a red envelope to Alice to the hospital with money as a sincere supportive gift to the young parents. No one had known about the amount, but Alice must have been very happy at the surprise. Ricky Chan who was 54-years-old and responsible for operations in Hong Kong said, 'I want to get pregnant to get a gift from the boss.' People love and rejoice when they see that someone does something good to others. They look down upon the manager who demands extravagant treatment solely for himself.

Alice returned to work too soon. As laid down in the law she could have stayed away a bit more. I asked her if she wanted more time at home. No, she had said and thanked me for the consideration.

People, I have seen, will behave reciprocatively: 'You care for others, they will reciprocate.' My understanding of respecting a host culture is to demonstrate that I have noticed what they do and value it. I am aware of it and accept it and will not question it; I may want to understand more but I will not reject it. I have seen it in many countries during my work; people want to show you what is important to them. My cultural understanding of a joyful event in the life of those around me is to partake in their joy and express my happiness. I do it, like many millions around me, by giving appropriate gifts. In China one of the most important events is the Chinese New Year; people express this by handing out a red envelope. I combined the two and it was received without any misunderstanding. This for me is showing understanding and respect to the host culture, adding on your own culture to it to make the respect even richer. What kind of impact did this one small gesture have on everyone? How did people think of each other? They all gifted Alice a red envelope; they started copying the boss. Do you get to fight with each other in such a situation?

You cannot ask people to respect the other because respect is an ambiguous word. If you are the boss define it and people will follow you, if you show that you also practise it. Start respecting people and their culture and you will see they start respecting each other. This is how you can infect people with your intellect. I believe that is the primary job of every leader: a parent, a teacher, a manager, or even a politician.

If you ask a leader, 'do your people feel humiliated by your behaviour?' the answer will be no. Not because they are aware of it—no one thinks that the behaviour of a leader can not only be intimidating but also humiliating—very often it is, and I have seen it more often than the behaviour of respect for others.

People do not forgive humiliation very quickly and that is very often the root cause for disgruntlement in companies. You can implement this thought to any conflict in any setting; a family, a society, a company, or even between countries: in any group where people collide due to the conviction that they are disrespected or humiliated there will be violent aggression, if not anarchy. In such situations people will blame the leader and the system, whatever the relevant system may be: family or a company, a country, or a society. I do not want to divulge but try to apply this concept to the present international conflicts and you will discover a similarity.

The corrective measure and the answer lies in the behaviour of the leader. Motivational lectures or logical sounding value systems or mission statements such as 'passion for excellence' do not work if the behaviour of the leader is not exemplary. As a matter of fact, such measures heighten mistrust in the leadership, if they do not result in mockery of such statements. Superficial niceties or loud joyous gestures and claims about having achieved the goals in Beijing (who cares if they caused a loss), that some managers in Sympatex used to convince each other that everything was great, does not work to improve the state of disgruntled employees. Paul Ekman, in his research with Wally Frisen, which they published in *Emotions Revealed* (2003), demonstrates how we are equipped to detect true emotions. They were making an effort to discover whether anyone can conceal their true emotions or 'create an expression that looked genuine when it was not' (pp. 213–215). They found out, empirically, that even if the expression was as short as 1/25 to 1/5 of a second, which they called micro expression, they noted that they produced nonverbal leakage about a person's true feelings.[1] This is what my colleagues had detected with their managers, including me. They had known who was genuinely interested in the benefit of the people and the company and who was not. The behaviour of the leader reveals or, to use the words of Ekman and all psychologists, 'leaks' the true emotions and intention of a leader. People compare what a leader is saying with what he is doing. That is one more reason for my conviction that instructions do not have the convincing power that insights have and that is why a coaching method is effective. We lead people to realise what they are doing and what they really want to do through insights.

In Hong Kong I had to see to it that people were stimulated to reflect on what they were doing so that they made necessary amends to their own behaviour. I had to find ways for them to understand their own behaviour using their own inner language and compare it with something as a benchmark. The benchmark would be my behaviour. They needed to realise it for themselves rather than be instructed on how to behave themselves better. I am convinced not everyone listens to advice voluntarily. Everyone understands what is right but only when they discover sense in something themselves. This is what I do in my coaching; I enable my client to discover sense in what she wants to do as compared with what she is doing.

In the case of the Sympatex impasse an easy quick fix could not be implemented. It had to begin with me and I had to display the qualities I expected of the employees. As I discussed earlier, people emulate their leader or the person carrying authority. My challenge was how to make the environment decent for everyone at work. I had the words of a great contemporary philosopher, Avishai Margalit, often resounding in my head, from his book *The Decent Society* (1998, p. 4).

> I began with a rough characterization of a decent society as a nonhumiliating one. Why characterize the decent society negatively, as nonhumiliating, rather than positively, as one that, for example, respects its members? There are three reasons for this: one moral, one logical, one cognitive. The moral reason stems from my conviction that **there is a weighty asymmetry between eradicating evil and promoting good**. It is much more urgent to **remove painful evil than to create enjoyable benefits**.

I will not discuss the other parts; the logical and the cognitive of his thoughts, as one is sufficient for my example.

The most relevant for leadership are the last two lines of the above quote: remove the evil before you distribute the benefits. How often have you seen that the response of a manager to threats from employees to leave the company is to distribute benefits? Their dissatisfaction or conflict seldom, I would say very seldom, originate because of lack of benefits. They are to be found more in how people feel they are being treated in a company. How many managers pay attention

[1] I do not want to leave unmentioned the work of psychologists Ernest Haggard and Kennet Isaacs for having discovered micro expression three years before Ekman, as mentioned in *Emotions Revealed* (2003).

to that? I will leave you guessing but I will give you a hint: the number is extremely small.

It is not as if a manager or a leader after reading this should concentrate on finding out how his employees are feeling. It is much simpler if you think it all begins with you as the manager and you are capable of infecting others with your attitude and emotions. The concept of 'Emotional Contagion', as explained by E. Hatfield, J. T. Cacioppo, & R. L. Rapson in *Emotional Contagion, Studies in Emotion & Social Interaction* (1994) comes into play; people constantly imitate hierarchical authority. This is what I demonstrated in Beijing: people notice when the person of authority is doing something they appreciate as being worthy of imitating.

The importance of hierarchy should not be underestimated. Without hierarchy it would create an unmanageable chaos in a company, if not anarchy, if everyone was to decide what he or she wanted to do. In E. M. Zitek and L. Z. Tiedens's study of hierarchies, 'The Fluency of Social Hierarchy: The Ease with which Hierarchical Relationships are Seen, Remembered, Learned, and Liked', published in the *Journal of Personality and Social Psychology* (2012), they found that hierarchy is welcomed, even if people at first show resistance or argue that hierarchy creates inequality. Zitek and Tiedens conclude that hierarchy gives a certain sense of security; people need to be able to get a sense of direction in social interactions. That is what had also been missing in Sympatex Hong Kong. Hierarchy brings with it certain dominance that is seen in the expression of the person. In the referred study, the scientists call it 'Facial Dominance'; the dominance is seen in the facial expressions of a person higher in the hierarchy. Dominance inherently brings with it a sense of authority.

My experience in the corporate world taught me that environments without properly defined authority tend to be very ineffective, if not lethargic. Examples of such ineffectiveness or lack of authority are also seen in structures where two people are responsible for a top job, or if there is no clear demarcation of responsibilities. A sort of diarchy: two CEOs in one company; their roles ambiguous. Authority can be interpreted in many ways. I would like to exclude the dictatorial, autocratic, and abusive form of authority, which is exercised solely for personal gains. That is not authority that is corruption of authority. I would like to attach authority to the responsibility for making decisions that are binding in any context.

The staff in Hong Kong understood within a very short time of my arrival that this aggression would not be tolerated, not from anyone. They also understood that it was not my ideology or eccentric behaviour but it was for the good of others. The moment people realise that any behaviour is being propagated for the common good it is easily accepted. The problem with employees begins when executives expect people to adhere to certain norms but do not conform to them themselves. If there is clear hierarchy and the defined authority is not corrupt or partisan it is easy for people to work in that environment: this is of the utmost importance in leadership. It is understood by others when the leader genuinely himself has it in him. What does that mean? Demonstrate and 'Be the change you want to see in the world', said Mahatma Gandhi and there is a whole lot to be learnt from these few words. I use them as an example. As I said, in coaching you do not give answers or instructions, just insights. I did not tell them what I thought but let them see what the facts were.

I think there are lessons in this example. Coaching executives faced with this kind of multicultural and international exposure is my contribution to enhancing the leadership of my peers. I offer an insight into what works even in very diverse professional environments using an effective coaching method.

4.1 Case Study: A Small Company

In the corporate world, as noted before, one of the biggest challenge executives face today is shortage of time. Most of them find it difficult to attend to the behaviour of colleagues that they may think is not productive or even disruptive. I have not seen many executives who talk about strategies for finding lasting resolutions that would let them and their colleagues focus on their work. Secondly, when we talk about the corporate world and the relevance of coaching, many entrepreneurs think that all the discussion is about large corporations. Very often I hear them say, this is not for us this applies to the big companies. I have chosen a few experiences from a small company that I owned and other experiences that I gathered over the years. The situations were challenging on the one hand but on the other they are so common that many will see their own situation in them. I also discuss how I resolved them, what I learnt from them, and what insights they gave me which I also use in my coaching skills.

In January 1994 after a personal tragedy, I went back to my business and pressed the 'reset' button on my professional life and started a new company. Within a matter of months I had a turnover of a few million Deutschemarks and was also able to employ five people in Dusseldorf. The designer and the sales manager, both young women, were at first very good friends and then worst enemies. All this is not my concern in my company. One said, 'If she is going to India, do not expect me to be there.' The other one was uglier in her comments and I will leave it out. The mention of it should demonstrate that people go to great lengths to manifest their dislike, but it is up to the manager how far they continue when it begins to damage a business. They were not being humiliated by me and that was ruled out as a reason for their aggression. The aggression was more of personal competition. It is relevant in this case to mention that both were exceptionally beautiful and saw competition in the other. How do I know that? I employed a young man named Thomas Goetting, who was in the final stages of his law studies in the university of Dusseldorf, to take care of legalities in contracts and conformity with customs laws for importation of our goods in various EU countries, and he told me about their 'real' struggle. He would watch them closely because they were in a different office than mine. He came to me one day and asked me how do you resolve this? 'Throw them out, both of them', he said. 'How do you look at it?' He asked me because to him I seemed untouched by their personal views of each other while he was concerned for the impact it had on their work. I said, 'Imagine in a human body, the lungs begin to complain that the heart is too loud and says, I am getting out of here. Both of them will cease to exist and the body will die. I need both of them and I have not decided as yet what I will do but I will find a way.' I had promised him.

'I think if you told them that, they will understand how important the other person is,' he said.

I told him that people in anger rarely want to listen to advice or 'wise words'; I had meant the latter sarcastically. I also told him to go and try it out and say it to them. He spent more time in their office than I did. He was their age about 26 or 27 years and he thought he might be able to talk their language. He came back after 3 days and said the designer said, 'get a heart transplant.'

I had one thing in my favour: the young women wanted to know how I achieved and sustained these exceptional numbers in my small company. The sales manager had come from a very large company, who then owned 1275 retail outlets in Germany and Austria. They had been my customers for some time, even in my previous company. I had asked her why she was interested in moving from a large company to a practically one-man show. She had said that she had never seen such a reliable and relaxed interaction as she had between my company and hers. Her company was considered ruthless if the goods were delayed by even one day. A shortfall of 5 % in quantity was sanctioned with heavy financial penalties. Her company had taken the cartons delivered by us and photographed them to serve as templates. They had circulated them to all the suppliers with the instructions that this is how they wanted their goods delivered. No single person can achieve this kind of precision alone. He needs pure dedication from the other stakeholders; he needs people who will follow his vision to the last alphabet. In coaching I see that many clients are struggling with urgent issues or issues that are close to their chest. Colleagues and managers only steal time, that is their perception of others. The moment they realise that they have not even considered relying on others but have been giving instructions, there is a kind of new awareness of the capabilities of others around them.

I used every opportunity to demonstrate to colleagues the importance of reliance on others during our several business travels to India, Bangladesh, and Hong Kong. I demonstrated to them how to respect people. I showed them how to de-focus from irrelevant things such as the outer appearance of a supplier. I did not talk about any of it but showed it through my genuine wish to meet these competent people. To them they seemed to be dressed poorly and spoke in an accent that they found funny. I talked about their skill to deliver on time and their reliability. I had a track record of 99 % punctuality and 98.95 % of ordered goods delivered with 0.01 % rejection rate. These figures spoke for themselves, but they found them baffling. They wanted to learn how to do that from all these countries. The only sentences they had heard were, 'we have burnt our fingers in … ' then came any of these countries. I do not think you burn your fingers; you shut your eyes and expect people to perform what you imagine in your mind. As I said earlier, look at your manager, your supplier as a genuine contributor to your business and not someone who you are competing with in superfluous matters. I told her on one of our business trips to Bengaluru (previously called Bangalore), it is my sincere and genuine interest for the person who is making it possible for me to sustain my business. If these men and women did not perform as they did, I was no one in the business. She probably related the importance of the designers' work for her sales. Soon after returning from India, I did not hear of the mudslinging and I could see civilised exchanges.

It is not difficult but many think respecting others is going soft and changing your language to something loving. You do not have to stand in front of suppliers as a Sanyasi, a follower of Bhagwan, to show how much you appreciate humanity and hug him or be awestruck and ecstatic at every job done well. It is sufficient to let him know in plain language and in terms of the business you give him. It is a regular exchange with respect for the other. If this sounds normal to you and you do not see anything extraordinary, then probably you have not experienced how some managers behave in other countries: often condescending and strange.

Going back to my small company, imagine the mindset and confidence of a sales manager who was certain that she could rely on 99 % punctuality for all she sold. I have known the sales side of business for more than 40 years and I can confirm, if a company can deliver quality goods, there is nothing more important to a customer and respectively to a sales person, than a punctual delivery. The travels were focused on making new products or placing new orders. The products depended on the designer and the orders on the sales manager. When each of them saw that their success depended on the work of the other they began to accept their presence. If the designer had created new products and the sales manager did not sell them well, the designer would have been labelled incompetent and vice versa. They did not change—you cannot change people—but you can influence their acceptance of realities. The influence is strongest when they realise it themselves and not by smart words.

In coaching my focus is on self-reflection and discovery of what is good for my client: no 'wise words' can influence anyone. If I had given in to their threats of 'I will leave the company if you do not fire her,' I would have to keep on looking for new people.

4.2 My Group vs. Your Group

For the sake of distributing responsibilities of work and competencies, most companies divide the organisational structures into divisions, departments, and other groups. They are a good way of managing businesses; however, they can become detrimental to effective working relationships and even battlegrounds when one or more of the executives begins to claim these areas as their territories; when they begin to protect it as if it were a question of life and death. They drag in innocent employees, who normally would not like to be involved in small bickering, into their personal wars. These circumstances are underestimated and in many companies not resolved for years. I would like to cite one more lesson from my business world experience that lets me identify the problems in companies easily. It is not as if these lessons have become templates for coaching; they provide a reference point when too many aspects of a phenomenon are visible in a company. In this respect, when coaching, it useful to refer to business experience.

Once again the example from Legler SpA. In a small division dedicated to the manufacture of jeans, we had 137 people who were divided into two groups, one side was called 'correspondenti', who corresponded with the customers and were directly under the 'direttore commerciale' (sales director) who was called Rudolph (this is a fictive name). He had been in the company for 36 years and he controlled the 'correspondenti'—one of those feared grey eminences. The other side was for production, called 'operativi' and the 'direttore operativo' (operations director), was responsible. They had been on a warpath for many years, and Rudolph was always right. The 'correspondenti' received orders from the customers and did not think it necessary to discuss them with production. They wrote it down in a ledger, an old long register. In the era of computers and networks, they wrote it down physically in a book and did not inform operations. I do not think that any executive in his right mind would have overlooked the fact that this old system was built for the sake of a small personal game by Rudolph. The two departments were two metres apart from each other. It was left to the production people to discover the orders and deliver them on time. It was as if sales were waiting to rejoice the failure of production.

I had witnessed the development of this chaos from many perspectives. I had joined the company as an outsourcer in a division that was responsible for ready-made jeans to help them resolve sourcing in Asia, and particularly in Pakistan. I sat in an office where I could see and hear all the mudslinging as it happened. Within 12 days of my arrival, I was asked if I would like to take on the responsibility of operations director. In this position I could see first-hand the audacity of this system. It was conceived to humiliate the others and they were truly humiliated. No one had dared to speak from the operations side. In the next 3 months I was asked if I would accept the position of CEO, in Italian it is called 'direttore generale', or even as some called it 'primo dirigente'. Soon after, I was invited to join the board and lead Legler-Nafees. My predecessor told me, as he called it, there was a white paper and I was being considered for even higher positions; however, I had other plans.

Going back to the sales department and the director, it is not a new phenomenon that the sales and production people are often arch enemies, metaphorically speaking. It is up to the executive to accept the rivalry or to act against it in such a manner that all stakeholders understand the futility of constant conflicts. The results of this structure were losses of a few million euros every year, just like in Legler-Nafees. The small division piled up at least a few million euros every year. Delay in the delivery of goods, and the quality of goods coming in from Tunisia, had roughly a 33 % rate of 'seconda scelta', which sounds romantic in Italian, but it means rejects, which had to be reworked in Italy. The result was that costs shot through the sky.

Within 12 weeks of taking on the responsibility as direttore generale, I asked Rudolph to leave the company. Firing people is not always the right answer; it can sometimes be a bad shortcut. But I had reasons. Before reaching this decision I had asked him to prepare a sales plan for the next year. He had submitted a handwritten three-page table. I asked him whether the sales plan was based on some observations in retail, some mathematical projections from our own financial department or most importantly, on discussions with all the clients over the last 12 months. I had wanted to know the probability of such a plan reaching its potential of realising the figures he had written down within just a few hours. Was it 85 % or 90 %? This, I explained to him, would influence how much money would be allocated to which area because every company depends on their inflow. He said, very blatantly, this is how I have made my plans for years and no one has ever questioned them. I did not want to be dragged to his magnanimous way of talking. I asked him if he knew why this division made losses for the last 9 years? He shrugged his shoulders. This was still not sufficient for me to make any decision. I asked him to bring his complete customer records to discuss who he could be talking to for the sales plan. It emerged that he had two companies he was serving and had laid out a fictive plan for 57 of them. After a discussion with the president, I decided to ask him to leave the company. No one does that in Italy; no one fires people after 36 years of service.

My decision sent shudders throughout the company right down to Pakistan and Tunisia. I had eight directors who came to me to congratulate my decision and said, this should have happened years back. I had directors from Pakistan calling me requesting me to come to Lahore to do the same for them because there were many who they called 'cobweb directors'.

The 'corrispondenti' were visibly shaken. One of the senior women colleagues tried to ask the president to help them because she feared, with Rudolph gone, I would be unfair to her. There was one lesson I learnt from her Enrico, that I do not see being used by many executives: the president said to her, 'In good or bad, Mr. Kohli is the boss. Let us wait for 12 months to see whether he is right. Is that not why we asked him to take on this important position?' I think this attitude is very necessary for the top management. When we employ people we should know why we do it. If that is true, then we should also let them work to show to us why we hired them. There are many executives who hire smart managers and then go and tell them how to work in their company. Why hire someone for innovation or to improve the financial results if you are going to tell them how to work at every step?

Let us go back to this division. The 137 people in this division were reduced to 37, the other 100 were spread out elsewhere in the company. We did not believe in firing large numbers of people in Italy—with five trade unions watching over us we displaced them to other jobs. The 'correspondenti' and 'operativi' were reinvented as 'Account Executives' and they began to understand for the first time that they were working for the same company and the same outcomes. The losses vanished and the romantic 'seconda scelta' lost its glamour and dropped from 33 % to 0.75 %. It was all being done by the same people; I noticed that no one had changed: they were still the same.

Let me take one single example of one person, but the others reacted in a similar fashion. Paula (I am changing the names), had always been polite but direct in her interaction with others. She had also been in the midst of the conflict on the 'corrispondenti' side of the aisle. She was a dedicated person who believed in delivering precise work. After the change in structure she was still gentle and dedicated to her work. Earlier she had followed how Rudolph had created groups and indoctrinated the concept of 'them vs. us'. After the restructuring (or renaming), everyone followed what the purpose of the division was. Achieving singular goals of the sales department had vanished. The hall where they had all worked in the first 12 days of my arrival (I originally named it a fish market because of the constant and aggressive chatter) was 12 weeks later renamed the meditation room: there was silence and people were working more and not quarrelling at all, just like in Hong Kong. Paula's work had not changed in intensity or quality. She now understood that conflicts between groups are created by leadership and not by individuals. It is the environment we create as managers, parents, or politicians that influences the behaviour of the stakeholders. I did not tell them what to do or give them any instructions. I let them see and realise that group interest as primary targets are counterproductive. I do not think that you can change people completlely and discuss sustainable change; what you can do is to influence their response to circumstances and events. You can change their perspective. You can change the perceived limitations: how far they may go with their habitual reactions. Coaching can inculcate self-realisation and bring about a different perspective, which may be more effective for their work, but it cannot manipulate a change in people.

The behaviour of my colleagues in Hong Kong and in Italy was the consequence of their perception of their environment; the result of what their bosses did or did not do and that of what they thought was permissible: these were limits set by the leadership. The conflicts in both cases were that all of them wanted to protect their own interests individually. When the focus of a team or a group in a company is about protecting personal interests there is no collaboration, there is survival of the fittest; it becomes the elbow society as we call it in German, 'die Ellenbogengesellschaft'. Every time someone says that our society has become an elbow society, everyone agrees: yes, it is an elbow society, terrible. There may also be an additional sentence, 'survival of the fittest', as if to confirm that it is OK, we can accept the inconsiderate behaviour of others, as if by quoting Herbert Spencer (an English philosopher influenced by the works of Charles Darwin's *On the Origin of Species*, in his (1864) *Principles of Biology*) we infer that this behaviour is also academically approved (whereas, Spencer first used it to demonstrate similarities between his own economic theories and Darwin's natural selection theory). Survival of the fittest is not OK for relationships within a company and you can influence the environment with your behaviour to make it better. I think Spencer and Darwin are readily quoted by those who do not wish to stop and consider how they could influence their peers or the company through their behaviour. Very few people mention that Charles Darwin said something about environment too. Bruce H. Lipton is a cell biologist from Stanford who used his scientific studies to address his concepts on consciousness in his book *The Biology of Beliefs* (2014, p. 20).

> Even Charles Darwin conceded, near the end of his life, that his evolutionary theory had short-changed the role of environment. In an 1876 letter to Moritz Wagner he wrote: 'In my opinion, the greatest error which I have committed has been not allowing sufficient weight to the direct action of the environments, i.e. food, climate, etc., independently of natural selection ... when I wrote origin, and for some years afterwards, I could find little good evidence of direct action of the environment; now there is a large body of evidence [...]'.

Look at the countries, companies, or families that flourish and compare them to those that do not. You will notice that those who flourish are where the leaders create environments to let businesses and people flourish. It is the same with companies and families. The focus is on 'let' and on environment. In a coaching context, compared to instruction or training, coaching lets people discover, reflect, and flourish; whereas instruction or training has to be followed by people, and they are restrictive: coaching creates an encouraging environment. You may pose the same question in a family setting or corporate culture. If the environment is not healthy you will not have healthy growth. This aspect of the responsibility of a manager is not defined or agreed in any employment contract. It should ideally be included: create and nourish an environment where people can perform their work and contribute to the growth of the company, without intimidation or humiliation.

What has coaching got to do with it?

In coaching, when CEOs and other C level executives talk to me, the first thing they realise is how little time they spend in consciously creating a healthy environment in their company. You may look at the statement of a very successful managing director, published in the first few pages of the book, where he says that as a top manager one spends too little time developing future leaders or managers. The environment is directly dependent and has its roots in the thoughts and ideas of the leader in any setting. As you saw in the example of my colleagues in Hong Kong the behaviour of a top executive is infectious. That is the reason executives need to spend more time reflecting on what they are saying before they speak. I am convinced that a coach can be extremely helpful in bringing about awareness of this aspect of leadership and can impact the results and the working atmosphere of his client's company.

We need to look at society as a benchmark to see how and with what concepts people come to work. An executive who is aware that certain thoughts are automatically brought into the company by her colleagues, because of the prevailing cliché or acceptance of concepts, such as 'elbow society', can prepare a strategy for the company in order to reduce its effect. We are creating such new environments constantly, in our family, in our company, in our friend circles and wherever we have social encounters, and there is one common denominator in all these scenarios: you. You can influence it positively with your behaviour. It is possible to influence what people do and the consequence will be according to their behaviour, but you cannot change people because you think they need to change. What you can do is to change the environment so that their behaviour can change.

4.3 Coaching as a Mindset

My focus on developing people in a company setting dates back to 1987. In coaching, I began with coaching private people who were looking for help and my practice evolved slowly into one that focuses on coaching executives. In the examples provided in the book, you will encounter examples of a warehouse worker, of managers, of people stuck in spots and looking to move on in their career, and finally also the C level executive. As I discussed earlier, I had chosen executive coaching because I feel most comfortable interacting with my peers and I know the pitfalls and the opportunities of this level of working. Secondly, the life experience that I have gathered by working in many countries and cultures permits me to coach an executive from one company but different cultures with ease. With all my coaching, although I draw on my life experience. I am mindful and stay alert that my previous profession-specific experience does not interfere in coaching, as that may tend to push it into the area of a management consultant.

All the people with whom I learnt coaching had one thing in common: they all had a desire or a question in their mind: how they could help others. They had certain compassion to contribute to the development of others. I looked back at my own history and realised that I had consciously begun helping young people in their personal development from 1987. This was without the concept or knowledge of coaching. I was instrumental in setting up and later responsible for operations, sales, IT, logistics, and other significant matters of a company. The company's name was then Sorrel Moden GmbH, and was established in the apartment where I lived in 1979 in the Mauerstrasse 24 in 40476 Dusseldorf, and was registered with the registrar of companies in Dusseldorf on 13th of January 1983. Its spin-off still exists today as the brand name for men's fashion ('Lerros'—it is Sorrel read in reverse).

As long as I can recall I have always made it a point to take time to talk to the young people working in the company—not just the office but in the warehouse too. Even though my office was two floors above I would often go down and talk to them. I wanted to know what made these people work in a warehouse. I wanted to know about their ambitions and plans—they were mostly between 18 to 24 years of age. This was not a judgemental inquisition; it was plain curiosity. I wanted to know what makes a person rise higher or why and how people decide right from the beginning of their career to stay with simple work. Some were satisfied doing monotonous and strenuous work while others saw it as a transitory phase. After one such exchange with all my colleagues in the warehouse one young woman, her name was Christine Schmidt (I am changing the names), she was I think 17 or 18 years, said she would love to learn the mechanics of foreign trade but our company offered no such programme. In Germany there was a very unique, dual education system to facilitate young people into professional life. The young were asked to attend school while being employed by a company for a very small amount as a salary. They were called 'Auszubildende' apprentices. You may say, you know what an apprentice is but in Germany the apprentice went to school and the trainer had to undergo training to get certification from the authorities. This training lasted for a few months and ended in a rigorous examination of the capabilities of the trainer by the official of the Chambers of Commerce and Industry. I thought if a young person is looking for an opportunity we should provide one and offered to create such a position in the trade in which I was a master. I went to school and learnt how to train, received a certification from the Chambers (Industrie-und Handelskammer in Dusseldorf), and trained her. She worked with me up to 1993 until I asked her to look for another job, as I wanted to make changes in my companies due to life-changing events. She went on to become a manager at a company selling luxury watches from Switzerland and I lost contact with her after 1993.

My reason for citing this small example is that a coach does not normally spring out of the earth and become a coach. Like Gallwey, a person who is observant and sees what is working for others is much better equipped to become a coach than someone who thinks that coaching is just talking to people. I can do that! While it is an interesting profession it requires compassion and the will to help others. I have a host of such examples but let me give you one more of a person who went on to become an example for even directors of the company to wonder what my mentoring had done to him.

In the year 2000 a young person approached me: Marco Cefis was 21-years-old; I am still in touch with him. At that time, I was then the 'direttore operativo', COO or operations director at Legler SpA. I have introduced you to this company earlier. Marco had returned from England after a couple of years. He had learnt to lay tiles there. He asked for an appointment with me. I was not aware what he wanted but I agreed to meet him.

When he came to me I asked the formal question that everybody does, 'what can I do for you'. He said, 'I want to learn from you.' I told him that I was not a teacher. He said 'there is word going around that you promote young people and help them in their career.' I asked him, 'why would I take upon myself to promote you?' He said, 'I am willing to learn and my family has spent over a 100 years serving this company.'

I agreed to hire him because I thought he was not from the textile trade and therefore he would not enter the company with prejudices and a mindset of knowing it all. There is nothing more damaging than such a mindset of 'I know it'.

I told him that there was only one condition he had to follow: 'you will not stop anyone in their job and ask questions or disturb others in their work for up to 6 months. You will receive small assignments from me, see me doing things, and you will try to imitate and learn from it. I will give you small jobs. After you have understood them you will execute them independently and as soon as you master one job you will get the next higher one.'

We set up a weekly feedback meeting and a measurement system to show that he had learnt something new. During these meetings he had the opportunity to criticise; he could tell me what he disliked about the work or me, while I could give him feedback on his work. This was also to be seen as an opportunity to clarify any doubts he may have raised during the week.

He said that was easy. I knew it was easier said than done. The idea was that I did not want to give him instructions like a teacher but see if he was capable of developing into a future manager. Why? He had the courage to approach the top man for operations in the company and ask him to give him a chance. He came empty-handed; I thought he must have something special in his mind about his vision of his own ambitions. At this time, I was still unaware of the concept of coaching. After 5 months he came to me one morning and said, 'when I started with you, I often asked myself, what is he doing, it does not make any sense to me, he must be crazy. Sometimes I thought I would ask you but I did not want to look silly. I decided to emulate what you were doing. I tried to understand your language in communication, the telephone calls, the tone and how you interacted with clients.' He added, 'along the way I let my own words, actions, methods and preferences play along and I have come to you to tell you that the big picture has fallen together this morning and I wanted to thank you for it.'

I cannot go into every detail of how this worked over the 6 months but I can confirm to you that each planned step was carefully crafted to one end: let him learn the way he can. With this method I had developed a new assistant manager for our company. In retrospect I had coached this young man without knowing what coaching was. The moment I learnt coaching, at first I also said I had been doing it all my life. As soon as I learnt more about coaching and its methodology, I corrected myself and said, this is exactly what I had wanted to learn.

Six months after his apprenticeship (I call it apprenticeship for lack of a better word but which director trains an apprentice today? I think more of them should). Marco went to Tunisia to oversee our production processes there. I was by then the direttore generale and member of the board with a responsibility also for our joint venture in Pakistan called Legler-Nafees Denim Mills Limited. A few months later he travelled to Pakistan and was working as assistant manager in the purchasing department.

There were two lessons and also confirmations that I drew from this and earlier experiences. If you want to develop future leaders, let them see how to lead, don't tell them the best tips and tricks or how good you are; let them discover what they think is working for them. Later on he spent some time in sales and showed qualities that managers with 36 years of experience did not even notice. He started looking at international brands to sell ready-made jeans. Travelled to Paris and Amsterdam, agreed to high value orders with brands like 'Paul & Joe'. I think they were selling the jeans we made for them for about €370 a pair, which was high-end. Our older sales managers were still chasing the discounters in Europe.

Marco was a fully fledged manager 3 years later at another company. I could see his gratitude even much later, though it may have been coincidence. In August 2006 I received an email from him in which he told me he and his wife had named their children Anna and David just like my own children. If a leader is good, he will leave behind people who want to be like him in some way. If a coach is inspirational, he will leave behind inspired clients too.

After seeing Marco working in his job, I had at least 15 other people from different departments asking me to train them, some of them were directors and others were colleagues of Marco. One senior sales manager for all of Germany and Scandinavia, I think he must have been around 38-years-old then, came to me once and asked, 'could you please train me to work in China?' I said, 'I do not train people, I am not a trainer.' I recall another young person came to me and said, 'do the same thing to me you did to Marco.' I asked him why. He said, 'I would like to be active internationally as Marco is.' There is one very important lesson here for managers and coaches: if you do good work for someone for the sake of doing good work and not to prove yourself, your reports, colleagues and everybody else will take notice and want to follow you. It will inspire the person you coached, trained, or helped and others will either want to learn or to copy it. This effect you can see anywhere.

There was a concept I read about in the 1970s that the work of the top person is reflected in the lowest paid employee of the company. Yes, indeed it is; I have seen it very often: work done with good intentions for others inspires all those around you and they, for some reason, show reverence and try to imitate such behaviour. This is the behaviour I meant when I began discussing 'What is Coaching?' (See Sect. 2.1). This is what I meant when I said a particular behaviour works just like coaching. This behaviour has one more powerful effect: it infects people to do similar good acts. I have already discussed the concept of 'Emotional Contagion' above, but a word of caution here; 'Emotional Contagion' works also when the boss is toxic. If a boss is toxic it is not a surprise that you experience the employees as unbearable too.

Going back to the people asking me to train them, I noticed the difference between Marco and a few others. Marco had wanted to learn; his focus was not on the outcome, whereas many who came to me were focused on the accolades that learning had brought Marco. There are various forms of teaching that tell us that focus on outcomes is the wrong way around: we ought to focus on how we do what we do. Some of these teachings go back to the ancient holy Hindu scripture, such as *The Bhagwat Gita*, which teaches us to do the act to your best: 'Karma', do not be focused or concerned with outcomes. It is not an easy task to understand this, especially when most coaches offer result-oriented coaching. The lines on success in the preface of *Man's Search for Meaning* (2004, p. xx), a book written by Viktor Frankl has a similar idea:

> Don't aim at success—the more you aim at it and make it a target, the more you are going to miss it. For success, like happiness, cannot be pursued; it must ensue and it only does so as the intended side-effect of one's dedication to a cause greater than oneself [.] . . . I want you to listen to what your conscious demands you to do and go on to carry it out to your best knowledge [.] . . . in the long run, I say! success will follow you precisely because you had forgotten to think of it.

Gallwey's *The Inner Game* (1974; rev. 2015) discusses the inner game of a player when she is learning something new and not her focus on success. Is this not similar to the teachings above? Focus on how you do it and not on the results; the concept of not trying to focus on the success of every stroke and every piece of footwork, as discussed by Gallwey. Even though you can educate and train people for certain skills, it is still not certain whether the skills will automatically lead to success. Success, itself, is an ambiguous word because of the fact that it has a different meaning for different people. It can be interpreted by anyone according to their own perception or wishes for their own higher aims.

Coaching, as I have experienced it, helps clients realise and reflect on their own views and perceptions and lets them create their own version of success—one which is achievable by them. I have also seen people make small adjustments to their perceptions of success during coaching. You will read more about it in the case studies ahead.

I had planned to learn coaching consciously because I thought it may be close to what I really did all my professional life: help people grow. I searched for a coaching school, learnt coaching, and changed my profession to a professional coach. During 35 years in business, mostly on the top of the ladder as CEO and at times member of the board, I have experienced using an analytical approach to problem-solving. I also realised the limitations of an analytical approach when it came to leading people. I found coaching offered an appropriate way of letting people realise, reflect, and create their own solutions. Besides applying these skills to my own companies, I also observed the practice of management with my friends, peers, suppliers, banks, customers, and everyone else I came in contact with, and when I reflected on the causes of poor quality of service and the failures within many companies. Not that coaching will offer to eliminate all ills of the world, but it will certainly mitigate many for those who choose to stop a moment and reflect.

One hobby I had developed very soon in my childhood was to predict outcomes. This is a very delicate matter and can easily derail into whimsical predictions which are based on wishful thinking rather than discerned observations. This habit goes a long way to developing intuition. This should also not be understood as black magic, it is simple logic working at a very great speed and helps in decision-making. It is a concept which I was to find reinforced years later in Gary Klein's book, *The Power of Intuition: How People make Decisions* (2003, p. 13): 'I don't think you can make effective decisions without developing your intuition.' Klein cites numerous examples to show how people who rely on their inner feelings based on their experiences develop what we call intuition and perform much better than those who do not. As per my experience, if I make a decision, and along with it I also predict the outcome of my decision, I would have a mechanism to measure whether my decision was based on correct assumptions about the expected outcome or whether it was simple overconfidence that made me make the decision. I think many decisions we make are also very private and our intentions and motivations are not always visible. The idea of this discussion is that it would help us in decision-making if we also had mechanisms to measure our own decisions.

What does this have to do with coaching or leadership? A coach and a leader, in my opinion, should be able to predict, even if not very precisely, at least a probable outcome of their decisions and their own work and behaviour, as well as that of the people they interact with.

As soon as I started studying psychology, I learnt that one of the main aims of the discipline is also to predict a person's behaviour, and this encouraged me to take it more seriously as a means of enhancing the skills I can offer through my coaching practice.

4.4 The Perception of Coaching in Business

In addition to my own corporate world experience, I interviewed 123 people, 67 of whom were CEOs, MDs, and entrepreneurs; in short, decision makers, coaches, and also others who had nothing to do with coaching. I wanted to know a few things and one of them was what do they know about a coach and coaching. My research, observations, and claims are non-theoretical and tested in real-life situations. I can say with confidence that if coaching is implemented systematically and methodically and based on knowledge acquired it is a boon for the modern knowledge executives and managers.

In Conducting Interviews with a Few Market Leaders About Coaching I created a structured interview with 39 items where the answers for some questions were in open format and some were in forced choice. These questions were aimed at CEOs, MDs, and other decision makers, such as entrepreneurs. I wanted to find out the criteria they used to decide who was a coach, who was the right coach, and how they discriminated between a coach and a trainer, a management consultant, and a psychologist, and when they implemented coaching in their company. Finally, I wanted to establish how and when they decided if they themselves needed coaching. This was also my quest when I worked in the corporate world: to find an appropriate method that could contribute to the development of managers.

There was another questionnaire I compiled to interview people who were actively coaching. This questionnaire had 19 items and all the answers were in open format; they were qualitative.

The third category of interviews was not planned, but evolved while I was studying at different schools in order to understand the new forms of coaching. In total, I held over 123 interviews:

- 67 interviews with the decision makers
- 33 interviews with coaches
- 23 interviews of a more detailed discussion, not structured interviews, with people who were learning coaching in different schools.

Let me begin with the most important part of the research: the end consumers; the decision makers. I will take you through the questions that are relevant to the present discussion instead of listing the entire questionnaire here. One of the questions I asked was, 'What, in your view, is the difference between a coach and a management consultant?' My intention was to find out if the managers thought that a management consultant could contribute to the personal development of a manager or any other person working in the company as a coach. There are other subsequent questions that I formed in order to confirm whether the managers were aware of other distinctions. I wanted to find out if the difference among the services was only my perception and my own interpretation or whether the managers were also aware of it. I also wanted to know whether there was any clarity about the concept of coaching. The answers to my questions were expected in open format. The client could choose her/his own words. Below are some examples of answers provided by a few of the market leaders questioned:

1. Vice President of HP, a market leader in computers and related hardware in Germany, said, 'Coach is a friend.'
2. An engineer at Porsche AG, a company known for its world class sports cars, said, 'Consultants make presentations.'
3. A top executive at Open Text in Munich, an international company famous for its software solutions said, 'Consultant has a clear job and a specific set of objectives.'
4. A director of the world famous pharmaceutical company called Merck KgaA said, 'Business processes are for consultants and a coach has a much more profound and a different level of relationship.'

The next question I would like to cite from my interviews was this: 'If you were to look for a coach, how would you do it?'

1. The CEO of Hexal AG, in Holzkirchen, Germany, another market leader in pharmaceutics, now at Novartis, said, 'Network; my coach should have operative experience, experience is very important.'
2. A director of Arvato Systems, The Bertelsmann Group, one of the world's largest publishing and media houses, said, 'I would look at his experience, recommendations from friends, and his age.'
3. An IT Process manager at a major automotive company near Munich called Draexlmaier Group, said, 'Networks, and recommendations.'
4. A CEO of a major fashion company in Hamburg, Germany, who wishes to remain anonymous, said, 'Only through recommendation: nothing else. How do I know who is coming to talk to my important managers?'

The last question that I would like to cite here from my interviews is this: 'What do you think of when you hear the word coach?'

1. Vice President of the world famous company, MTU, in Friedrichshafen, Germany, said, 'Personal development, team building, learning from the experience of others.'
2. A manager from Arval, a company owned by the famous French Banking Group BNP Paribas, said, 'Why have I not been coached up to now? Preparing new managers for new positions.'
3. The CEO of a major shipbuilding company in Germany, who wishes to remain anonymous, said, 'If there is a need for discussing present issues, restructuring.'

4. A world famous banker from Frankfurt, Germany, who prefers to remain anonymous said, 'We do not have time to reach out to all the managers as we should. We need coaches.'
5. A Managing Director of an international apparel company in Taipei, Taiwan said, 'When I hear the word coach I think that the bottleneck is always the CEO. If he thinks he can hire a coach to repair someone, he is dead wrong.'

I have quoted just a few from the 67 different top executives here but let me assure you that all the interviewees were clear in their answers to the questions; there was no ambiguity whatsoever. This was the first evidence I found that top executives were very well informed about the difference between various services and how to access them.

The question that remained to be answered was, were they also clear about what coaching was? This was necessary, because if they knew coaching was not any of the other services, I wondered why they were apprehensive, or at least not receptive, to coaching. This was not a part of the structured interview; this question emerged during the casual discussion that followed after the interview was over. These informal discussions revealed that they were not apprehensive of coaching; they were all apprehensive whom they could engage to coach them. They could not distinguish between a management coach, a business coach, a personal coach, and the many other versions of coach. Their answers were given in very simple terms. The following examples are some of the comments I later recorded:

1. 'Do you know who is offering what?'
2. 'How do we know what is effective?'
3. 'What is a methodical and serious coaching I could rely on?'
4. 'Can we entrust our human resources to any one calling himself a coach?'
5. 'How to navigate through superlative promises?'

The interviews were spaced out over 3 years, primarily due to the time constraints of the busy executives. The result of the interviews was that, while they did not reject coaching, it was clear that they were unsure about how to make the decision about when and how to engage a coach, and what kind of coach they should engage.

Alongside Interviewing Decision Makers, I also Talked with 33 Coaches About Coaching One of the questions I asked was 'does coaching work?' From these 33, I did not receive one single detailed answer or an explanation that seemed plausible. The common answer was 'Yes'. This was not sufficient for me and I have discussed this topic in the book and also given evidence in the case studies cited here to demonstrate that effective coaching works.

References

Ekman, P. (2003). *Emotions revealed*. New York: Holt Paperbacks.

Frankl, V. (2004). *Man's search for meaning*. Boston: Beacon.

Gallwey, W. T. (1974). *The inner game of tennis*. London: Pan Books (revised 2015).

Hatfield, E., Cacioppo, J. T., & Rapson, R. L. (1994). *Emotional contagion, studies in emotion & social interaction*. Melbourne: Cambridge University Press.

Klein, G. (2003). *The power of intuition*. New York: Currency Book.

Lipton, B. H. (2014). *The biology of belief*. New Delhi: Hay House.

Margalit, A. (1998). *The decent society*. Harvard, MA: Harvard University Press.

Zitek, E. M., & Tiedens, L. Z. (2012). The fluency of social hierarchy: The ease with which hierarchical relationships are seen, remembered, learned, and liked. *Journal of Personality and Social Psychology, 102*(1), 98–115. doi:10.1037/a0025345.

5 Effective Coaching

Coaching works if the method of coaching is implemented procedurally. This means the coach does not attempt to change his clients and, importantly, he does not give the client standard answers. With many of us the nature of answers generally is that they inherently attempt to define causality. If there is a cause, there must be something responsible for that cause: a person or a circumstance. The moment a coach identifies what is causing disgruntlement in a client, he has relieved her of all further critical self-reflection and contributed to aborting the process of personalised healthy and critical exploration or discovery of a possible coping strategy. Just like you ask a medical doctor the reason for, let us say, your light cough, he also has a response to it and can prescribe a cough syrup or whatever. Similarly, if a coach has an answer he probably also has a solution. A ready answer will not allow the client to think about her own solutions. During my arguments below you will encounter a mechanism that I have developed for measuring whether coaching works.

Let us consider for a moment why some people do not listen to their spouses, or why some children do not listen to their mothers but will accept the advice of a stranger. James W. Pennebaker in his book *Opening Up* (1997, p. 113) writes:

> Why do people tell their deepest thoughts and feelings to strangers but not to their spouses or friends? It's not that they trust the listeners, or even that the listeners are non-judgmental. Rather, according to the classic sociologist Georg Simmel, it is freedom from recrimination. If I want to talk to my airplane seatmate about my darkest secrets, I am safe in the knowledge that I will never see that person again. The knowledge is liberating. By definition, whatever I say will never affect any long-term relationship. Furthermore, if the person is judgmental, it will have no ramifications.

Imagine you were in a normal harmless conflict situation with your partner. I do not need to specify anything, almost everyone faces some differences in relationships. What does a partner say when you accept that she or he was right about something? Most of the time the response could be 'I told you; I know you; you never listen. I only tell you that for your own good.' Is that not what the helpless

A. Kohli, *Effective Coaching, and the Fallacy of Sustainable Change*, Management for Professionals, DOI 10.1007/978-3-319-39735-1_5

mothers and fathers spend their life telling their children? Yet many people may not understand why the others still do not care about their advice or listen to them. These kind of well-meant complaints and accusations are the stuff that makes people shut off their listening capacity and a precedence is set for the next time. The listener expects that the next time they receive advice, it will be accompanied with similar accusations: 'I told you and I know you very well; you never listen to me.' This is the reason why the next time they will go ahead and do what you want even if your partner, mother, father, or just anyone who is concerned about your well-being disapproves of it. You want to avoid the accusations and lamentation. Even if after a while you find out, for example, that your mother was right about your being dressed too lightly for the winter day, you will probably not admit it. It is a phenomenon that recriminations have a way of conditioning people negatively. People will try wherever possible to avoid such unpleasant discussions. B. F. Skinner,[1] famous for the behaviourist school in psychology, would have rejoiced at the idea of conditioning appearing in a book on coaching. He was opposed to the concept that people exercise free will and propagated the idea that human action is a consequence of our conditioning: reinforcements, whether negative or positive, resulted from previous experiences and formed our future behaviour. Fortunately, there is an enormous amount of knowledge in psychology that humans are capable of changing their behaviour, or even environment can play a part in changing the behaviour of a person, even if they were conditioned in a particular manner.

Going back to our discussion, recriminations can create an explosive atmosphere in relationships. They can create certain tensions at the back of the mind of the person who wants to ask her partner her opinion, and they hinder an open discussion. It comes very close to the concept of reinforced conditioning.

Consider this example: what does a parent do when they think something is right for the child? They overpower the kids with their concern, which, to the child, sounds, and feels like intimidation. If a parent, a spouse, a boss, or anyone who is emotionally close to you, or one who has the capacity to influence the emotions of others, does not give an answer but begins to explore what is right for the person asking for help or advice or just talking to you, you will see that the relationship takes on new dimensions and a sense of openness begins to prevail. Coaching slows down the thinking of a client. It does it without accusation, and that is where coaching begins to work. I use the concept of slow thinking or reflection as it is discussed by the Nobel Laureate Daniel Kahneman in his book *Thinking Fast and Slow* (2013). He discusses the merits of slowing down and coming out of the automatism that most people fall prey to. Automatism should not be seen as something negative because it serves a purpose and allows us to process or react to many demands of the day in a secure way. If that is so, why discuss the need to change it? The results you may be getting from some automatic responses, also called habits, may sometimes be hindering better results. It is nothing new; you

[1]Burrhus Frederic Skinner (1904–1990) was an American psychologist known for operant conditioning.

probably know how difficult it is to break away from a habit or habitual response. Slowing down retards your reaction and allows you time to reflect on your own decisions.

Most of my clients, as I said, are high performers, and they each have their very definite routines. These routines demand time-bound actions and reactions. They never think of stopping for a minute to slow down. When they meet with a coach, they discover many facets within themselves that they have not been exploiting. For example, some realise they have been neglecting a part of their life; others report that they have not been fair to their subordinates and begin to have casual lunch, or whatever. All of this is a slowing down process to rethink what they have been doing at a much higher pace.

Here is a short list of effective coaching methods. It is compiled from my observations in a coaching situation. It is not a prescription for every coach:

- A coach will ideally slow down your thinking and with it retard your reactive response.
- A coach will empower you to think about your own solution based on your own value system, possibilities, and capabilities.
- A coach will be adaptive and work solely on your individuality.
- A coach will enable you to experience insight about yourself.
- A coach will empower you to discover the correct source of your issues.
- A coach will be your professional confidant.
- A coach will enable you to talk about subjects of your choice: non-intrusively.
- A coach will enable you to engage in self-reflection.
- A coach will empower you to self-realisation.
- A coach is non-accusatory.
- A coach will hold everything in extreme confidentiality.

In my coaching practice I have developed a list that is a reminder of what I will not do in coaching:

- A coach will not give you a diagnosis on yourself.
- A coach will not give you a diagnosis on anyone working with you.
- A coach will not give you a diagnosis on any of your family members.
- A coach will not become party in your conflicts.
- A coach will not treat you medically: there are no interventions in coaching.
- A coach will not treat you psychologically: it is the job of a trained psychologist.
- A coach will not ask you to go through any rituals that are strange, repulsive, comical, or foreign to you.
- A coach will not give you an evaluation on your character or learning type.
- A coach will not rate your strengths or weaknesses based on the rank of your birth in your family.
- A coach is not a psychoanalyst in the sense of the school of thought based on Sigmund Freud's teachings: that remains the domain of a clinically trained psychoanalyst.

Effective Coaches Give Neither Solutions Nor Answers to Clients Not giving answers, though, is not the only reason why coaching is effective. I have a glaring case to demonstrate this claim in the example of a young woman, 42-years-old, who had worked with Nokia Siemens Networks in Germany for 15 years in marketing and event management.

5.1 Case Study: 'Anne'

Let us give her the fictive name of 'Anne'. During company restructuring, she was asked to look for a new job. Large corporations in Germany have a very social and humane response to such a situation. The company gave her, I think, 22 months of paid time to reorient herself. During this time, she received her salary, with minor reductions at the tail end. To enable a smooth transition into a new job, the company provided her with two professional coaches to help her cope with her new situation. Sixteen months passed by and nothing happened and she started to get worried about the outcome when the 22-month period ended. Her brother is a headhunter, although it was in the fast-moving consumer goods industry, but still he could not help her get a job. He suggested that she came to see me. After four meetings, she was in a job. I did not find her a job. Since this is a real case, you may read her testimonials on my website, www.arunkohli.com. She told me that she had been extremely sceptical meeting yet another coach after having met the two coaches provided by her company. She said it was her obligation to see them once every 2 or 3 weeks. I do not recall the exact intervals. She had been doing it for the last 16 months and all she had heard from them was, 'you are a very smart person'; 'I am confident you will find a good job.' She asked herself how they knew that she would find a good job, and whether they were completely blind to her psychological state when paying compliments to her or discussing the colour of her dress. What happened? Why was she able to find a job after attending my coaching sessions?

A coach, if he facilitates the process of critical self-reflection, will invariably lead the client to insight. The insight will lead the client to discover the redundancy in her actions and let her focus on the areas actually important to her. In my opinion the client finds her way back to her fictive −15 to 15 area, as depicted in the 'Mid Zone' (Fig. 5.1).

The 'Mid Zone' represents two extremes −100 and 100 of a person's mental state. If we were to discuss mental activities of any person, she normally has a tendency to create an area where she feels that she is being herself: in her element, so to say. If the mental activity goes down to −100 it would represent chronic depressive disorder and the other extreme with the value 100 would represent a constant high of someone on psychotropic drugs. Both these extremes restrict a person's ability to participate in normal social life as the majority of humanity does. Let us say this range of −15 to 15 is my range; you could choose to make it −12 to 12, or any other value to fit where the norm is in your lifestyle.

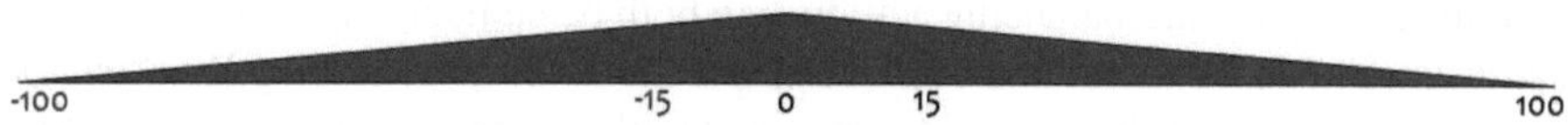

Fig. 5.1 The mid zone

To remain at zero a person is in a meditative state as experienced by anyone who practices meditation: a state of contentment without desires, without fears or concerns. You may have experienced it while doing something you love to do, such as hiking in the mountains, sailing on the sea, painting, playing music, cooking, etc. It should be distinguished—if you are someone who gets seasick, this may not be a great example. If you cook because you have to it is a bad example. If you do not like mountain hiking it may be a strenuous exercise that you may not want to do. As I mentioned if any of this is your preferred activity, better still your passion, then nothing affects you in that moment: you lose yourself, so to say. You may spend some time there; in the ancient Hindu scriptures, there is a term for a meditative state, called 'Sādhanā.'[2]It is a temporary state. If that were not so you would be living as a hermit in the Himalayas. It is similar to the concept of flow of action as discussed by Timothy Gallwey in his book *Inner Game of Tennis* (1974; revised 2015, p. 5), 'The Player seems to be immersed in the flow of action which requires his energy, yet results in greater power and accuracy.' The second mention of flow is found in research on happiness conducted by Hungarian psychologist Mihaly Csikszentmihalyi in his book *Flow* (1990, p. 4), 'I developed a theory of optimal experience based on the concept of flow—the state in which people are so involved in an activity that nothing else seems to matter.' However, when considering meditation, I prefer to stay with the traditional concept, which formed part of my upbringing.

Most of the time when people have to find solutions or answers under constraints or compulsion, as was the case with my client named Anne, they overextend themselves in one direction: they make too much effort. They may then extend the pendulum of activity slightly beyond the fictive −15 and 15. The problem with extending the range to one side is that it is very likely that it would extend on the negative side too. This is the nature of a pendulum. I know from the business and professional worlds that it is very common that professionals who work very hard also play very hard, sometimes self damaging. It does not automatically mean that they depend on artificial stimulants, but one can observe visible compensatory behaviour.

It is irrelevant which way they overextend themselves: on the negative side, not doing anything, or in the positive side, in, for example, excessive mental activities. Both are strenuous, and people seek to counterbalance one form of extreme activity with a compensatory activity. The problem with this way of working is that the

[2]A word found in Sanskrit language defining the concept. It is also found in Hinduism, Buddhism, Jainism, Sikhism, and a form of it is also found in the Chinese language to denote a state where one transcends one's ego while performing some spiritual and often also mundane tasks.

activity and the counterbalancing activity can both be damaging emotionally. It can cause extreme frustration if the duration of such an activity is too long. Working too long every day can be as frustrating as indulging in extreme compensatory activities. Coaching, in my opinion, brings a person back to the -15 to 15 of the 'Mid Zone'. I am assuming that -15 to 15 is the normal area where a person feels her own self. This is what I call slowing down from the normal hectic pace of working life. A person may then begin to think of sometimes taking a break at the zero point too. If they do that then they feel safe and secure and begin the process of finding their own solutions with renewed confidence in their own capabilities.

That is what Anne did. She had been working as a marketing manager and organising events for a giant corporation. She had decided to change her work and move away from event management but continued looking for a job only in marketing management. To a reader it may sound irrational, but who said humans are always rational? Sixteen months passed and she was still only looking for a job in marketing management. The reason that it took her very few meetings with me to get where she wanted to be is that, once she slowed down her thinking, she realised what she really wanted: coaching helped Anne to get back to her true 'Mid Zone'. She started looking for a job outside of event marketing and landed one within a few days.

Thinking about slowing down and finding the 'Mid Zone' reminds me of the story in the teachings of Buddha. He was sitting on the bank of a river when he watched a teacher trying to instruct his pupil how to tune a musical instrument. According to the story, Buddha overheard the conversation between the teacher and his student. The teacher told his student: 'if the string is too loose, the music you play will not sound anything like music. If the string is too tight, the instrument will again reproduce unpleasant sounds and not music.' This is why Buddha chose the middle path for a good and balanced life. In my coaching, I choose not to use contemporary citations on 'comfort zones' or areas, but rely on the teachings of Buddha, which are more than 2000-years-old, and time tested. The strangest thing about human behaviour is that we may redefine such wisdom in new words; however, despite the ancient teaching of Buddha, we will not adapt them to our lives but continue to struggle at extremes, even when we know it will get us nowhere. We continue to strive to achieve more than our bodily and psychological abilities allow us. It may be very healthy to experience bursts of extremes to overcome difficult hurdles for a short span of time. It may also not always be that all of us intentionally indulge in such excesses. In the case of Anne, she was forced to act under time constraints in order to maintain her living standards. I have noticed a similarity between people who are under stress: high performers; those who think that they are experts or think that they are highly educated. For these groups, the 'Mid Zone', or the pendulum becomes very small: the tolerance for errors is very small. In my opinion, maintaining a state of extreme intensity is damaging. (An extended period is anything above 2 weeks.)

5.2 Linear Thinking

Going back to the case of Anne, coaching is not effective if a coach is only paying compliments or discussing irrelevant superfluous topics with educated managers. Coaching works when a coach can nudge the client to reflect through her own knowledge. I am still in contact with Anne and even after 2 years, she is still in the job she found after meeting with me. Anne's case is also an example of how the confusion in the market about what coaching can do for clients, and who is a coach, can cause financial damage to large corporations. In their ignorance, companies are willing to pay people calling themselves coaches, without realising that their staff, the clients, receive a shoddy treatment. The job that could not be done by two coaches in 16 months, I achieved in four meetings with Anne. In this case, you do not have to be a finance expert to determine what is good for your company. Coaching is extremely effective, but not all coaches can be effective for clients. It would be prudent for decision makers to spend time getting to know the coach, whether hiring a coach personally or through a company. Take time to research coaching and coaches before engaging a coach. There are many sincere and good coaches, young and old alike, who do not need to spend 16 months coaching a person to realise that she is perhaps pursuing something she does not want.

I would like to use one more case to demonstrate that coaching is effective if a coach brings the person to her state where she feels encouraged in self-reflection; where she is able to think slow and find her own solutions. In this case, the client was a young woman, a graduate of marketing studies from a prestigious university in Germany.

5.3 Case Study: 'Victoria'

Let us call her 'Victoria'. Victoria had worked as a laboratory assistant for 14 years. Victoria had formed a pattern in her working life: she would take up employment and then resign after 2 years. When she came to me she had resigned from a well-known international pharmaceutics company near Munich and was actively looking for a new job. Guess where? She was looking for another job in pharmaceutical manufacturing. I asked her why she was working as a laboratory assistant in a pharmaceutical company when she had a graduate degree in marketing. She told me, 'it somehow happened,' she said, 'I am certain that I cannot go any higher, or earn more in a lab because I am not a researcher in pharmacy or any related discipline.' She knew the limitations but continued to be where she did not want to be. Similar to Anne she was pursuing something that she did not want to. Six months after coaching, Victoria started working as a marketing assistant. Some months later, she was employed as a marketing manager. Over the past 3 years, she had not changed her job. Victoria's problem was that she had become entangled in linear thinking. She thought that, if she started to look for a job in marketing, she would only find a job where she had to start all over again, from the lowest position. The linearity of such thinking is that one thing will follow from the previous thing.

Such a thinking process is not particular to Victoria's situation, but it is very common, because it is a protective mechanism. The only logical answer Victoria persistently got through her own thinking was to get a job with a pharmaceutical company as a laboratory assistant. It was a cyclical process—a logical fallacy for Victoria: if you try to get what you do not want, you will not attempt to get what you do want.

While at school and studying at the University in Delhi, India, I had confronted some people from dire poverty and complete hopelessness. When they received any advice or answers to their issues, I noticed that they did not act on any suggestions at all. They became static, and I wanted to know why. Were they relying on destiny or had they given up on any hope of improvement? They refused to do anything about their state because they thought that one single act or small change cannot bring about any significant change. They had a sequence of issues that needed to be corrected one after the other and they asked how could one act make a difference. I realised that they were waiting for all solutions for all perceived issues to be present simultaneously and only then they would act to resolve everything in a sequence. But, I asked myself, if it were so then would the issues not all be resolved and need no action at all?

In 1980 I arrived in Neuss, Germany, to take on a new job as Managing Director (Geschaeftsfuehrer) of an apparel company owned by an American entrepreneur from Scottsdale, Arizona, USA. In this position I had, beside my own staff, also people from other countries who belonged to this group coming to me for personal and professional issues. I was surprised to discovered that this behaviour of hopelessness had nothing to do with deprivation or poverty: people in affluent societies behave in an identical manner. Let me give you an example: a young lady in Austria had separated from her partner with whom she had two children. For 11 years she was without a romantic partner. At a family celebration I was attending in Austria she asked me what she should do to stop living as a single mother. I will not go into details but what she disclosed confirmed to me that people do think linearly. She had wanted a partner who should be tall, ideally 190 cm, blond hair, blue eyed, single, should have no children of his own, but love her children, the list was long and she saw no problem in it. The linearity was visible: if the potential partner was not tall he was struck out of the list. If he was tall and not blond, he stood no chance. If anyone had the first two attributes but was not blue eyed there he goes down the list of those rejected, and the list goes on to show that the likelihood of finding a romantic partner was left to divine intervention in such linear thinking. My question to her was, 'if you had a loving partner, what do you think, how would he behave with your children?' One single question was sufficient for her to start thinking that she was stopping herself.

I noticed it in India and I notice it now in coaching in many countries, that when the change takes place, it does so on many levels and it does not necessarily begin where you want it to. You do not begin by looking for the height of a romantic partner, as I narrated above, to find yourself not living a single mother's life. Change is never linear. A very simple analogy of your action is that of a stone dropped in a pond of water: the waves spread in 360°. Change spreads 360° not linearly. There is another aspect to change in one's life: it slides in silently. I have often noticed that when I see people stuck in a situation for a long time, it is often due to this linear thinking. A coach could help here by simple Socratic dialogue and not by setting goals, assessments, typological tests, or coaching tools to find a 190 cm blond, blue eyed, children loving romantic partner. The last lines are just a sarcastic example to show the redundancy of goals and tools and not about the lady mentioned above. Try this intellectual exercise while reading the case studies in this book. Ask yourself how many of my clients were stuck in linear thinking. You will discover this is one of the most important aspects a coach should be looking at in his client's issues.

Since we humans are adaptive beings we do not necessarily notice the small silent changes occurring everyday due to our own actions. That is also one reason why feedback forms an extremely important part of effective coaching. That is also a reason why coaching meetings should be limited in order to allow the change to take place independent of a coach and for the client to see it manifest based on her own capabilities. The manifestation is not immediate and that is why it is important to let the client experience the change and meet her later to receive a feedback on its efficacy, perhaps after 6 months.

As an answer to the question whether coaching works, I can confirm that if coaching is relieved of superlative promises and superfluous marketing tactics that are intended to attract customers but fail to deliver the promised outcomes, and if it focuses solely on assisting the client in gaining insights through critical reflection, it works very effectively.

5.4 Measuring the Effectiveness of Coaching

I have developed two mechanisms that enable me to measure the effectiveness of my coaching methods.

A client, let us call her 'Catherine', after her coaching sessions gave me some interesting feedback, which helped me to develop the first of these two mechanisms. Catherine said, 'It was a pleasure to see a coach sincerely interested in the well-being of his client.' I did not want to bask in the praise alone and wanted to understand what she meant. She explained that she had been coached previously, but the woman who coached her, while she was extremely professional, had ended each session abruptly. After all the coaching meetings were over, it was all over: Catherine never heard anything from the coach again. She said, 'I thought she was not interested to know if coaching had made any difference to me.' That was the worst memory of coaching for her and left a lasting experience. Such an experience and feedback from other clients motivated me to create a method to ensure that my clients continue to evolve after coaching. I am also genuinely interested in knowing whether and how they are evolving.

I created a qualitative system of measuring the post-coaching development period with a feedback form that all clients fill out 4 weeks after the coaching sessions are ended, because I think it is too soon to ask questions about the efficacy of coaching straight after the sessions are finished. At this time, clients could give positive feedback, even if they do not feel it appropriate. The question of social desirability (a concept in psychology) comes into play, which is, take into consideration while interviewing people that they may give answers simply to project themselves as being socially correct or better than they perceive themselves to be. Through the feedback form, I wanted to create a mechanism that was free of these constraints.

Learning from Catherine's experience, I began to call my clients following a period of around 4 months after the coaching sessions had ended. The calls lasted anywhere between 15 and 20 minutes. I have not yet come across a client who is not happy to talk about her thoughts on how she has benefitted from coaching, even several months after the coaching sessions have ended.

The second mechanism I have created measures the long-term effects of coaching. I invite my clients to a casual dinner after about 1 year to hear what they have to say about their coaching. Irrespective whether the client is a CEO of a company with 20,000 employees or the operational head of a small plant, I try to see them. Some people are extremely busy and I need to keep trying and follow through more often, as was the case with Anne. I met her again in January 2016 in Munich, more than 2 years after her coaching was completed. After our dinner, she told me: 'I should have met you much earlier.' I asked her why she thought she should have done so. She said she did not know the exact reason, but thought it was because of her coaching that she now saw things in a different way. I wanted to understand what she meant. She talked about events that were 10 or 12 years old. She said, when she dwells over her past decisions and reflects on the consequences today, she thinks that she could have done things differently if she had engaged a coach earlier.

I think that memories of past events are not a reliable source because we tend to distort them every time we recall them. This fact has been studied by many reputed social scientists and is not my personal opinion. I would like to remain critical even about my measurement methods because they are qualitative and dependent on subjective self-reports from the client. It is very easy to indulge in selective interpretations and cherry-pick whatever confirms the answers we are looking for. A coach should, as the scientific philosopher Karl Popper, in his book, *The Logic of Scientific Discovery* (1980, p. 40) explains the concept, 'falsify', and perhaps also refute the findings at first, instead of jumping to a conclusion as soon as an answer suits the one they desire.

With Anne, I wanted to know what was different in her way of looking at things now. I also asked whether the difference could not have been because of other events in her life or because of the passage of time. She said, when she needs to make a decision in a difficult situation, she slows down to think of all the aspects and the one thing that is common in all these activities is she recalls what she learnt during her coaching. It was only after coaching that she had shed the habit of vehemently trying to do what she really did not want to do, such as trying to find a job that she never wanted. Is this not a paradox? Earlier, in Chap. 3, I showed how sustainability in coaching is a fallacy, but it seems that a client, even after more than 2 years of coaching, still thinks the coaching she received continues to be helpful to her. I do not think it is a paradox. I did not promise her sustainable change; also, I had not promised her a particular change. I am certain that coaching can offer sustainable learning and that is what Anne was talking about.

The mechanism for measuring does not end with the coaching session. I make it a point to talk with my clients even a few years after their coaching. I receive unsolicited feedback; sometimes they are first-person feedback and at times also through a third person. Third person feedback emerges if someone else had recommended the client to me and that person feels that he should inform me about the effect of coaching on the client. This shows me whether coaching was effective or not. It is most encouraging to see that coaching makes an important difference in my clients' lives. This mechanism tells me how much a client values coaching.

Another client who is CEO of a very large company, during our first meeting after 1 year of his coaching asked me, 'I was wondering if, by meeting you for seven times I have experienced such a dramatic shift, does it go any higher? How high does it go?' I said I do not know because it depends on what you want. He wanted to meet me again after 6 months and he did. I asked him if he would be willing to give me a comment on coaching for my book, which I could convey to my potential readers and clients. I told him it would help others to understand what my clients thought about coaching. He laughed and said, 'It does not hurt.' I asked him what he meant. He said, 'when my boss had said, you should engage a personal coach and recommended you, I was very apprehensive of undergoing assessments and being told about the type of person I should be in order to be successful. I was apprehensive of things that I might have to do to prove myself as a successful manager to others. I was pleasantly shocked that I am still myself. I am happy that I did not have to change my person and that is what I mean, coaching does not hurt.' This statement demonstrates how threatened clients can feel when they receive promises that coaching will change them.

5.5 Optimum Length of Coaching Sessions

I offer to meet my clients for five and a maximum seven times for effective coaching. While interviewing coaches to find out how they structure their services for their clients and how long they intend to coach a person, I discovered that there are people who offer contracts in coaching that bind a client for up to 12 months and include at least 18 sessions. There are others who offer 40 hours of coaching in a contract. In my opinion, I don't think 40 hours with a client is only coaching, but must include some form of therapy, remedy, psychoanalysis or training.

In 2010 I started out by offering coaching sessions over a period of 12 meetings. I discovered that neither the client nor I had much to say after about 10 meetings. I therefore reduced the coaching sessions to 10 meetings. After a while even this seemed too long to me. I then reduced the coaching sessions to seven meetings, which were spread over 5–6 months. What I learnt from my coaching experience is that, within the first three meetings, the coach and the client have made very big strides and the client has by then understood what her challenges are. By this time, there is also a certain clarity in what she wants and she has already talked about her most important issues. She should, ideally, by then, have discovered whether she was right about her real issues; if not she should have changed her agenda. I offer my clients between five and seven meetings with the offer that they can abort their coaching at any time if they find that coaching is not working for them. I also keep the option to abort the coaching if I find that the client has underlying pathological issues or is looking for particular outcomes or techniques and tricks to outmanoeuvre others.

I think it is fair to mention that the school where I learnt coaching taught us that we should not offer too many coaching meetings. A realistic time period for coaching meetings is no more than seven. There is a very strong reason for this number. People do not necessarily come to coaching because they are in serious trouble, to resolve traumatic conflicts, or to manage stress. There are other experts who resolve these kinds of serious conflicts, such as lawyers, psychologists or experts who are very good at stress management.

Recently I asked a manager to abort his coaching after five meetings because he was a very good manager of a small plant and I noticed that he did not need to discuss anything further, and had begun to repeat himself. When I told him he could close his coaching, he was at first surprised and asked, what about our contract of seven meetings?' When I told him that he had achieved what he came for he was very happy and grateful for the sincerity.

Coaching Is a Knowledge-Based Service It can provide support to the issues that have emerged from a modern knowledge-based lifestyle. Coaches should be prepared to provide modern responses. Coaching needs to break from the old conservative method of using up long periods of time. Coaches need to adapt their services and find knowledge-based solutions, keeping the well-being and interests of the client in the forefront.

If a coach lacks methodical competency and subsequently the confidence to acquire new clients, he will find ways to keep his clients paying for his services, such as long contracts. In my opinion, long contracts have two risks: the first risk is that a coach is creating dependency in his client, which is counterproductive in coaching. Coaching aims to create insights, enhance the client's mindset, and focuses on self-development. If a client is dependent on a coach for a long time, then the part of self in self-development is certainly being neglected. The second risk is that a client tends to lose interest in coaching and the efficacy of coaching may diminish very quickly and give the whole exercise a bad reputation.

If a client needs to discuss their issues for 40 hours, a psychologist may be much better experienced for such a challenge. Coaching, we should keep in mind, is a conversational method. Much as we are in a discussion to demystify and demarcate the role of coaching, it is also the responsibility of a coach not to infringe those areas where others may be better equipped. For example, if we claim that a coach is not a management consultant, he should exercise self-restraint and leave the area of management consultancy to those experts. If a coach notices that a client needs psychological assistance, then it would be irresponsible for a coach to continue coaching merely in the interest of his earnings. Coaching should be a short-term relationship; ideally a coach should not create dependency for his clients.

A client notices within the first 20 minutes of her interaction if a coach is good for her or not and, most probably, will also notice if coaching is likely to work for her. What a client does not see coming, as I have experienced with numerous clients, is that, at an average of 4–6 months from the end of coaching sessions, a client will often make a visible shift in her environment or behaviour. The prerequisite is that it happens only after the coaching has ended. If a coaching relationship is too long a coach may deprive the client of this experience or delay it. The client begins to notice the marked difference herself when other people in her surroundings report it to her and ask what she had done to make the difference. Some do not want to believe that a person can make such a shift and will start their sentence with words such as, 'I do not know whether it is coaching, but I have seen a great improvement in the person's behaviour.'

5.6 Defining Effective Coaching

The discussion above about what is coaching and what it is not compels me to create a new definition of coaching for my own purpose and that is: **Coaching is a person-centred, non-diagnostic, explorative conversational method with its sole purpose to facilitate self-reflection that leads to insight of one's own behaviour relative to one's environment**.

My coaching methods have evolved since my original coach training from Coach U (See Sect. 2.2) combined with business experience and observing the manifest behaviour of the 'basic assumptions of human nature' in coaching sessions (See Sect. 8.2), so that I can provide effective coaching to both business and private clients. At this point, I think it is helpful to highlight the key features of effective coaching and the principles I follow in my coaching practice.

I borrow part of 'Article 1' of the constitution of the Federal Republic of Germany in the Grundgesetz für die Bundesrepublik Deutschland: '[Human dignity—Human rights—Legally binding force of basic rights]: (1) Human dignity shall be inviolable. To respect and protect it shall be the duty of all state authority' [. . .]

1. Human Dignity Is Inviolable

There are many reasons to start here. A coach may tend to become a consultant, adviser, an omniscient guru of sorts and interfere in the relationships of a client as per his personal ideas. That is wrong. Imagine I supported Mark (See Sect. 3.2.3) by telling him what to do, disregard his person and become party to his struggle. Imagine I asked Christian (See Sect. 8.3.4) to leave his friend. A coach should never cross a certain ethical line of interfering in the life of a client. Regard the client as a person of his own integrity and accept him as he is. This would also avoid the fallacy of claiming to be able to enact change in others when they perhaps do not want to change. How close can a coach go to a client without violating his dignity? Close enough to stimulate a process that leads to critical self-reflection and insight and no further.

2. Use Non-suggestive, Non-abusive Unambiguous Language During Coaching
A coach needs to pay attention so that nothing out of her personal life or experience is suggested to the client as being the ideal solution. Suggestions or implications that may not conform to his value system can influence the decision of a client. Imagine you suggest that the client should separate from her partner, or leave her employment, because you think it is the right thing to do. That is not coaching, that is knowing better than the client and it is counterproductive in the context of coaching. Foul language could suggest counterproductive ideas in the mind of a client as you will read later in a case study.

3. Confidentiality Is Not Negotiable
There are no thresholds that should allow a coach to expose the confidentiality of a client. This is extremely important. Take an example from the corporate world. There are two distinct parties who are beneficiaries. The corporation that gives me the mandate to coach its executives and the executives that I coach are two distinct entities. A coach may be tempted to please the paymaster and disclose details that were entrusted to him by the client. Konstantin Korotov et al. discuss the situation of confidentiality in a coaching situation in *Tricky Coaching, Difficult Cases in Coaching* (2012, p. 57):

> Many companies may be tempted to use the coach as their fixer to resolve their problems with an undesirable employee. Professors at reputed coaching institutes suggest: All too often the organization uses coaching as a way to deal with an executive it cannot confront directly. Moreover, coaching may be used as a disguised way of suggesting deficiencies to the coachee, or even hinting that the latter should be looking for job opportunities elsewhere. Coachees, in their turn, might also (consciously or unconsciously) try to use the coach to influence specific individuals or the organization at large.

If a coach agrees to serve his clients in this manner, this kind of collusion would be wrong and would not have anything in common with coaching, not to talk of a violation of the client's trust. It also violates the first principle listed above.

4. Do Not Diagnose a Client
Diagnosis is a domain left to those trained in their field of clinical specialism. A diagnosis carried out by a layman is as secure as a horoscope in the yellow press. A coaching client does not seek clinical interventions or remedies.

5. Do Not Coach a Client with Pathological Conditions
If you become aware that a client may be exhibiting a pathological condition, direct your client to a medical professional and abort coaching without regard for financial considerations.

6. State Clearly What a Client Can Expect from Coaching
The ambiguity of certain coaches that the client is the solution holder may lead them to be uninterested in the outcome and leave the responsibility of a successful outcome completely with the client. This would be wrong. Whether a coach

receives a payment for coaching or not, it is his responsibility to deliver the promised service with certain predictable outcomes.

7. List the Insights that a Client Has Gained

This process is best carried out with some kind of feedback from the client. After the feedback, use one or more methods to validate whether an insight has been gained or whether the client reported something that did not happen during coaching.

8. Ensure a Post-Coaching Follow-Up

It should be in the interest of a coach to follow-up the coaching sessions after they have ended in order to determine if the coaching is having a lasting effect on the client. The follow-up should be in the interests of the client and the coaching methods.

9. The Coach Does Not Have Any Answers

The coach should allow the client to find out the answers and solutions to her issues. Do not give her your proverbial glasses to read.

References

Csikszentmihalyi, M. (1990). *Flow: The psychology of optimal experience*. New York: Harper.
Gallwey, W. T. (1974; revised 2015). *The inner game of tennis*. London: Pan Books.
Kahneman, D. (2013). *Thinking, fast and slow*. New York: Farrar, Straus and Giroux.
Korotov, K., Florent-Treacy, E., Kets de Vries, M. F. R., & Bernhardt, A. (2012). *Tricky coaching, difficult cases in coaching*. London: Palgrave Macmillan.
Pennebaker, J. W. (1997). *Opening up: The healing power of expressing emotions*. New York: Guilford Press.
Popper, K. R. (1980). *The logic of scientific discovery*. London: Routledge.
Skinner, B. F. (1974; revised 1976). *About behaviorism*. New York: Random House.

Online Sources

Grundgesetz für die Bundesrepublik Deutschland. https://www.gesetze-im-internet.de/englisch_gg/index.html. English translation: Professor Christian Tomuschat and Professor David P. Currie. Revised translation: Professor Christian Tomuschat and Professor Donald P. Kommers in cooperation with the Language Service of the German Bundestag (The house of commons of the German Parliament). Accessed 3 Mar 2013.

6 Who Needs a Coach?

If you were to ask a coach, 'who really needs a coach?', he will most likely say, 'everybody!' That is not true. Coaching can be effective only for those who are not looking for a treatment, remedy, psychoanalysis, or thinking of manipulating a change in an employee or any kind of therapy. Before I go on to discuss this topic, let me tell you what I found out when I interviewed the managers and entrepreneurs (See Chap. 4). I asked two questions related to who needs a coach:

1. 'When do you think it is appropriate to engage a coach?'
2. 'Who do you think needs a coach?'

A few representative answers for the first question were:

1. 'When there are problems with people in a company.'
2. 'Anytime: it can always be done for professional exchange.'
3. 'In case of conflict.'
4. 'When my own behaviour is not getting me any results.'
5. 'For developing new managers.'
6. 'A coach is needed in case of conflicts.'

A few representative answers to the second question were:

1. 'Young leaders and managers.'
2. 'People who are stuck on one spot in their work.'
3. 'If the boss says so.'
4. 'Anyone who wants to talk to a professional sparring partner.'
5. 'Anyone who considers they need to develop themselves personally or in business.'
6. 'Top executives.'

Another common belief was that a coach will fix things.

A. Kohli, *Effective Coaching, and the Fallacy of Sustainable Change*, Management for Professionals, DOI 10.1007/978-3-319-39735-1_6

My findings are not based solely on the answers of the interviews but how my practice has evolved. I would like to contain this discussion to three groups of people who can profit immensely from effective personal coaching. I have my reasons to discuss these groups. As I have discussed earlier I feel comfortable working with my peers, other coaches may chose to address other groups.

1. Leaders, top executives, and decision makers.
2. New leaders and managers: not only young managers but also experienced operations experts moving up the ladder into leadership roles.
3. Intercultural environment: People working in environments where cultural differences may be the cause of latent tensions.

6.1 Coaching Leaders, Executives, and Decision Makers

Coaching can offer the most effective, appropriate response to the modern lifestyle of a knowledge-based high performer. In contrast to other helping professions, coaching does not have any stereotype or stigma attached to it. What is this modern lifestyle and the knowledge-based high performer? I asked my clients, how many hours do you work a day? 'From 08:00 a.m. to 8:00 p.m.', was the most common response. That is roughly 60 hours per week from Monday to Friday. About 20 % of them, mostly in manufacturing, said from 07:30 a.m. to 9:00 p.m. That is 67.5 hours per week from Monday to Friday. What about your weekends, I asked most of them. About 35 % of them said they work on Saturdays but a bit relaxed from 10:00 a.m. to 3:00 p.m. Some reported that they also use Sundays and public holidays to travel to and from business meetings so that they do not lose their office working time during a normal working week. Some expect their reports to use their holidays for this purpose too. These working hours in professional environments were not known in earlier decades. Some people may have worked such long hours even earlier but the number of managers that work such long hours demands a response to such a routine. When I asked if Sunday was a holy day, so to say, no, emails and messages continue even then. We did not have this in earlier decades and this is also working even when not in the office. This is the modern working manager's routine as far as I have come across it in my interviews with clients and friends.

Let us begin our discussion with the leaders, top executives, and decision makers. Decision makers are all those people who influence the work of others in a company, a country, or a community. They are managers, entrepreneurs, politicians, and even heads of non-profit organisations. In my experience, this group of leaders comprises two further subgroups. According to my experience the first is made up of people with high potential, ranging in age up to the age of 45. I have not met with any person with similar traits above the age of 45. The other group comprises people above the age of 45. I find their behaviour and reactions to be different to workload and stress; however, one factor is common to both groups: both experience isolation within their own company due to their workload. They have limited their exchanges with managers and reports to professional issues:

targets, achievements, or budgets. There is minimal social interaction within their surroundings, by social I mean in the sense of talking about personal matters or feelings about their environment. Many managers I met were neglecting their personal life and families. They reached home late at night. I know of some managers who see their children once a week. When they leave home it is early morning and when they go home their children are already asleep. A large number of managers who carry big responsibilities on their shoulders, such as CEOs and many C level executives, were single. Why were these high performers single? I asked some of them. 'No time, we do not go out to meet people with the purpose of getting to know anyone,' was the general answer. On further insistence, I found out that the state of being single is not desired only tolerated or accepted as 'can't do anything about it.'

Many managers work extremely hard and push themselves to their limits. This phenomenon is also visible with other professionals too. I had a client who was a young medical professional and worked like any top executive: a singular aim was to establish himself. He showed the same symptoms that result from excessive work in a top executive: after a regular working day, he got home by 8:00 p.m., then he spent 45 minutes answering emails and messages sitting in the car in front of his house. By the time he entered his home he did not have time to eat. He had developed a habit of getting something to eat quickly in front of the TV. Consequently, he fell asleep there. If he finished his work by 7:00 p.m. he would go to a restaurant, get a pizza, or something easy to prepare, and followed the same routine. Besides the fact that such behaviour is very damaging for health, the people who recounted their daily routines reported to me that it was not their desired way of life. I asked what they would like to see differently? Most of the time it was the stress that came along with their work routine. When they reflected back to how they used to live even 10 or 15 years before, they said that the lifestyle that had slowly crept in and excluded the social part was shocking even to them. They were hardly seeing people for social purposes. They did not notice the slow increase in the amount of stress over the years. Activities that switch off stress were not part of their weekly plan. According to neuroscientist Robert M. Sapolsky who has researched for over 32 years on stress and its effects on humans writes in his book, *Why Zebras Don't get Ulcers* (2004, p. 3), 'The diseases that plague us now are ones of slow accumulation of damage—heart disease, cancer, cerebrovascular disorder', and he explains that humans do not know how to switch off their stress, as animals do. He takes the examples of zebras that he has studied too and determined the level of stress hormones present in the blood of those he examined. He says when zebras are attacked by a predator, they may lose a younger member of the family or if they are lucky they may all escape the predator. In both cases: whether loss of a family member or successful escape, after a life-threatening situation has passed, zebras return to normal levels of stress hormones in their blood and they get back to the business of normal living. In contrast, at the end of a stressful day at work, people drop the car keys and start looking for other stimulants: mortgages to pay, issues with relationships to resolve, unexpected bills, notices or other letters threatening conflicts. Some people successfully continue to maintain a high level of stress until they go to bed. Some are capable of maintaining stress levels for months on end. It is a modern phenomenon caused by the constant demand to respond: to emails, chats, instant messages and other stimulants that demand instant attention.

I observed a similar form of behaviour with at least 16 high performing young managers who had one thing in common: over time they had gradually created the circumstance where they did not challenge their routines anymore and accepted them as fait accompli. They accepted their state of high stress along with long working hours as it was, as if it were a normal way of life. There was a paradox: their habits had created one place they could go to every morning and that was their office.

The amount of stress that an executive creates for herself must have very damaging effects on her health. I have done this myself: Dusseldorf to Delhi-Madras-Singapore-Hong Kong and back to Dusseldorf, all within 4 days. As if that was not enough, within 3 hours of landing in Dusseldorf, I drove 275 km at very high speed on the autobahn in order to attend a sales meeting. There are some lessons I learnt from this lifestyle and drew conclusions from it: we do not have time to live our lives. We do not have time to work in our own office. It was not uncommon to meet a colleague somewhere in Asia who complained he never had time to finish his work.

I was 37-years-old then and my wife warned me that if I chose to continue at the same pace, I may be increasing the risk of heart disease by the time I reached the age of 40. With all the knowledge available to us, we do not need to be a medical expert to predict harmful outcomes of excessive behaviour. She was right and I followed her advice; that was the last trip I had made to compete with the speed of the earth's rotation. I think all of us who indulge in such excesses also have answers ready to explain why it is necessary. Each one has his own very plausible version. I am not going to discuss whether this is right or wrong. If this gave you the impression that I am talking only about myself, let me assure you that more than 70 % of the young managers and professionals I have coached have reported similar lifestyles.

Society or other helping professions did not anticipate this fast change in our modern life and hence do not have a response for it as yet. Coaching could offer one with conversational methods and critical self-reflection. The majority of executives know a whole lot about their work and all that they do not know they can access much faster than their peers 25 years ago. This is not just my personal opinion, the recent book by Robert Colvile, *The Great Acceleration: How the World is Getting Faster, Faster* (2016), discusses exactly this problem and how little is being explored about this subject. This is because a lot is expected of them and that is why their own response systems become very short. Not just my clients but executives today are very well-educated people and require an educated, quick and plausible response to their needs, otherwise they will reject it. Coaching works at this level if the coach is well prepared to face such high performers: for example, if the coach also has a high level of knowledge, they will accept his coaching. Coaching works with this group of people if it is knowledge-based and not infested with so-called coaching tools and assessments. If for example someone learnt coaching with the famous 3-day system (See Sect. 9.8), it would not be possible to be called a knowledge-based coaching. If a coach has knowledge about how to help the executives in the subjects such as cooperation, about how ineffective cooperation can be without a perceived threat of punishment, I do not mean corporal punishment, I mean a consequential behaviour of the leaders that can dispense appropriate sanctions, and the meaning of hierarchy and authority for humans and its significance in leadership; morality and how people perceive their leaders on their moral scales; concept of 'Emotional Contagion', that your own behaviour may be infecting your reports and employees; the theories of personality, psychology, philosophy or life experience to share—then this coach can impart effective knowledge-based coaching.

What is missing with these high performers is a pause at the zero level (Fig. 5.1 The 'Mid Zone'), for a few hours. Is it possible that the more they work the more they cross their 15 on one side, let us say to 30, and to compensate, they need to go to the other extreme of 30? What resources do they have at hand to talk to someone about their wishes, their dissatisfaction, or their stresses? They could talk to their friends about it but there is a major problem with this approach. I have already discussed (See Chap. 5) the ideas of James W. Pennebaker in his book *Opening Up* (1997, p. 113). 'Why do people tell their deepest thoughts and feelings to strangers but not to their spouses or friends?' People do not like to share everything with everyone, they need a certain sense of confidentiality. Over the years, they have also created a public profile of a successful person who has everything under control. Talking about problems or feelings has no place for 'successful' people, as this could clearly disturb relationships or they would answer in line with 'social desirability'.[1] At least, this is a perception: that there could be a serious risk of loss of face.

The number of hours per week being put in by some executives reaches between 60 and 75. These are all new phenomenon; people have not lived like this before. I do not know of a manager who would share his concerns with his colleagues. I have faced CEOs from companies with a multibillion-euro turnover. When it comes to talking about how they personally feel about their life they do not have many choices—there are not many choices when it comes to sharing their personal feelings about their work. After the coaching mandate has been completed, most of my clients meet with me regularly in a cycle of 6 to 7 months. The reason is just to exchange views. Many of them arrive tense. I can see it in their face; they have particular concerns, such as that the future strategy of the company is not clear, and other concerns. Fifteen minutes in to the meeting and you can see them beginning to relax. Usually, talking with a coach comes with the promise of superlative changes. Clients, according to my experience, will not accept claims that offer superlative

[1]The concept of 'social desirability' in social sciences is a term used in research that describes the possibility of an interviewee answering questions so that he is viewed favourably by others. It can take the form of over-reporting good behavior or under-reporting, or undesirable behaviour, it would interfere in talking honestly with friends.

solutions due to the amount of workload and stress they are already exposed to. I asked some of my clients why they were suspicious about superlative claims offered in coaching. Many said that they were faced with the ground realities of issues that are simple not superlative. 'I do not want you to "bring out the best in me". There is a technician in my company who is also an honorary employees' representative, as per the German labour law. He wants all the perquisites that are given to the responsible managers: the best parking spot with his name on it, etc. and wants to be called a co-manager. I do not know what a co-manager is? What should I do with bringing the best out of me? I want to discuss with my coach how do you get around the issues of authority and hierarchy,' responded one client. For managers, a coach who doesn't offer superlative claims is more approachable.

Leadership roles come with certain self-made restrictions, or what I would call self-restraint, such as limiting how much a manager can disclose to their management team and at what stage. The idea behind this is not privacy but corporate prudence. If leaders face internal conflicts they articulate their opinions conservatively so as not to show favouritism to any side or any particular person; they need to be discreet, such as in the case of corporate changes, and other sensitive business information, as well as self-restraint mentioned above mixed with the additional workload that comes with new technologies. New technologies have given us big advantages but the downside is that technological evolutions have added to our work during hours which were once private or personal time. In 2013, I was working with a few people at the automobile giant, Volkswagen AG, at Wolfsburg, in Germany. I was told that receiving and answering emails on weekends was considered stressful: the mail servers were switched off so that the employees were not bothered at weekends. Corporations are beginning to take notice of such stressful effects of technological changes. I worked and lived through the typewriter era with carbon copies, which has given us the CC in emails, to the use of telex, to Fax, and then email. Now text and video conference add to the tools of very busy executives. I recall that in 1992 I bought my first mobile telephone. I could use it just as a simple telephone. In 1995, I had a heavy laptop that weighed 5 kg and had 80 Mb of hard disk space. There was no instant communication on both these devices, if we exclude telephony, which was too expensive to use compared to present possibilities. Email was possible on the laptop but not on the mobile handset. There were some companies using email that had just about moved from Telex to Fax in 1988. Since the year 2000, the amount of messages that one could access over a handset has grown immensely, and with it the increased amount of work and reduction in response time from days to minutes, means that the workload is continually increasing. In the years 2010 onwards the response time for a few urgent messages has been further reduced to a few seconds. I can cite a couple of studies, but I have the personal privilege of experiencing the amount of work an executive does and know that it has increased considerably compared to 20 years ago. In 1995 if I received six faxes I had a few hours to respond. In 2009, sitting in a car in P. R. China on the way to a factory, I received 80 emails within 27 minutes. To respond to just these emails I would need at least 5 hours—no one expects you to answer in 5 hours today, they need a quicker response time. Often it is not possible to manage such high communication traffic without training on what to attend to and what to leave for a while. The need and expectation of speedy response creates a very focused and stressed work day. When people are focused on work they tend to lose sight of their social needs and fall into automatism. With top executives, there is a factor that confounds this; they need to be very selective about what they say, when, and to whom. Whenever we are careful, we are automatically alert and this increases stress. These factors: speed, increased workload, along with immense alertness brings with it a certain isolation for top executives. New technology offers great opportunities, such as holding video conferences at short notice. In companies that operate in different time zones, managers step in to compensate for the time difference. Working in Hangzhou, P. R. China it was not unusual to video conference with customers in Italy or with reports in Denver, USA at midnight. All this leads to added work and the reduction of personal time. Technology makes it easier to do more in lesser time and hence increases the temptation and pressure at the same time to conclude more work at shorter notice and this leads to enormous stress for busy executives and other people exposed to such circumstances. This is the stuff that makes executives extremely focused on the work issues with little time for much else. It becomes a way of life. The downside of this focused working is loneliness. In my interviews, I found out that most CEOs and decision makers thought coaching was for others. When I asked whether they had ever considered coaching for themselves, the most common answer was 'no one asked me'. With whom do these high performers share their concerns and doubts? This is the spot where promises like 'bring out the best in you' fail to attract potential clients because they are not even being asked. It is sometimes sufficient that a busy person can vent his thoughts and talk to someone. The only problem is, with whom can they talk? With their partner? Certainly, if she or he has the will to listen to his or her professional concerns. More often than not, it will not produce the desired effect of venting thoughts. In many cases when an executive has been coached by me and goes back home to share his experience with his wife or partner about the first meeting with me, it is not unusual that I receive a feedback in the next meeting about what his wife said. For example, 'my wife said, all that your coach has told you I have been telling you for years. I told you so; see I could be a coach too.' What is wrong? Why does the executive not listen to his wife or partner? It is not what a person is saying that makes a difference, but the context in which it is being discussed. The absence of accusation and the methodology behind the important message makes a difference to how it is accepted.

You can continue to lament that your son does not eat healthy food and he will not do it. One fine morning he wants everything you have been telling him for years. You wonder what happened. A friend told him or a study in the school showed what is right for his age. There is no big secret to this. Could it be that the mother is so concerned that her insistence covers her concern and displays it more like a lament or a nag? It is the context in which the message is delivered that determines whether it is accepted. In coaching, it is important that a coach is accepted as an unthreatening, non-judgemental sounding board. Very often my clients ask me to meet them just for a casual conversation over lunch without any particular goals and just for simple discussion. At times, just talking to a coach gives them space. As I said before, a coach need not arm himself with grand promises of sustainable change. It is sometimes enough that a top executive talks through his thoughts or vents with a professional of the same level of experience. This is where an eye-level relationship earns its validity and this is where knowledge plays a big role. If the coach is not equipped with the level of knowledge his client has, it will not work.

The discussion above about executives being under additional workloads and the amount of stress that can be damaging to their health is not solely my own finding or experience. Professors of reputed universities who have researched particularly this subject have similar thoughts. For example, *Inspiring Leadership Through Emotional Intelligence* is an online course offered by Case Western Reserve University, USA. It is conducted by Richard Boyatzis, Ph.D. Professor of Organisational Behaviour, Psychology and Cognitive Sciences. In Lecture Five, Professor Boyatzis discussed executive behaviour. If you are an executive what do you think you do when you get up in the morning?

> What was the first thought that came to you? Oh my God, a beautiful day here! Probably not. You probably thought oh, I have to do that thing at work... [.] What am I going to do about that email that really annoyed me last night? We often activate the human organism when we wake up to prepare for our to-do list. But it's not a positive to-do list, usually it's a negative... [.] In professional managerial positions,... [.] ... we're actually under a degree of cognitive, perceptual and emotional impairment. For example, most of us have 180 to 270° peripheral vision. Under this onslaught of chronic stress, with occasional doses of acute stress, it goes down to 30°... [.] The same thing happens when you consider new ideas. Under this chronic stress, you're much more likely to have your first reaction to reject any new ideas... [.]. that's why people under a lot of this kind of chronic power stress, have higher incidences of viral and bacterial infection, influenza, type two diabetes, ulcers. At least three of the 87 diagnostic categories of cancer. You have a lot of problems with heart attacks, strokes sleep disorders, gastrointestinal difficulties and sexual dysfunctions. [...] Welcome to leadership.

Boyatzis discussed how stress reduces the vision of a person from 270 to 30°: what kind of reaction could we expect from a person who should be leading others? I think perhaps a stress response. The person would be occupied in finding his homeostasis rather than offering innovative solutions. What is the solution then to these conditions? One answer that strikes me from my experience is to slow things down. Slow down a response sometimes so as to allow oneself a recovery break. When people talk to a coach they are not just talking to him but during the coaching conversation also looking at their own narrative from a different perspective. While they are talking to their coach, the coach is questioning their narratives. In an effort to explain to the coach they are getting a new perspective on their own situation. It slows down the process of thinking for a while and creates an Aha! affect with the client. People need a coach who will slow down their thinking and retard their reaction, not as a cure to all diseases but as a response to the uninterrupted working stress. As a consequence of slowing down and rethinking their own point of view from a different perspective, they experience coaching as a positive change. Whereas coaching did not change them, it led them to reconsider their own views. If they like the change and its side effects they may want to continue adapting other parts of their life to this change and make it sustainable, but a coach cannot claim to manipulate it through coaching—only the client will change what he wishes.

6.2 Coaching New Leaders and Managers

Those who are moving from one level of management to a higher level are one of the most vulnerable groups in any corporate environment. A subgroup with similar vulnerabilities is composed of people who have never experienced a leadership role within a larger company. They have been very effective and reliable employees at operational level in the past and their superiors are of the opinion that they either deserve or are capable of stepping into leadership roles. One of my first clients who was within this grouping was working in a large international corporation, with over 40,000 employees worldwide, based in Germany. Within the first couple of minutes of the meeting, he broke down with tears in his eyes and said he was going to give it all up.

After a few months, when his coaching was over, he sent me a short email: 'unbelievable, it is all over.' I asked him what was over? He said, 'the crisis, as if it had never existed.' I can retrospectively report that he had not thought to evaluate what effect the transition from a mid-level manager to director would have on his person and his work. His explanation during our first meeting was, 'I do not understand, the people I am working with are the same but I am having serious difficulties coping with the demands of my work.' That was also the core of what he had wanted to discuss with me during coaching.

6.3 Case Study: 'Simon'

Let me give him a fictive name of Simon. When Simon moved from one mid-level position to the higher management position he overlooked that with the new position he would have people working as his reports who are at the level he was up to the point when he moved up. He continued to be their buddy as he was previously. What is wrong with that? Nothing at all; the problem begins to become serious when the buddy with his new responsibilities continues to do his old job and begins to fix things for his buddies: that is not management. This attitude resulted in a flood of petty jobs that came straight to his table: 87 people asking for permission to go on holiday went straight to him and not to their own manager because they had known him as a buddy from before. The demands from his bosses that had not existed earlier, because he was not responsible to them but to his one single boss, were new to him. The topmost person, the CEO, could now call him at short notice, which he did not do earlier because his previous boss would be called. Now he was his previous boss. The fascination of bigger remunerations, the perquisites and the status that go with the new position can be very tempting. The changes that the new position brings with it, in terms of quality of work—to keep the performance of the reports and their reports to a level of efficiency—are what management is made of. As a member of top management he was no more expected to complete singular tasks himself, but he was now responsible to ensure that multiple tasks similar to those he had executed earlier would be executed by many who were in his team. The transition from conducting 'hands on' operative tasks to managing other managers is often underestimated. During his coaching sessions Simon understood this concept and began to create certain virtual barriers up to where his managers could ask for his support and created an awareness for individual responsibilities for each of his reports. At a certain point he realised that people did not come anymore to him for every small issue but went to their own line manager. With this concept he himself created a mechanism to reduce his workload and increased the efficiency because there were more people interested in getting, so to say, the job done.

Many managers, at any level, are vulnerable of becoming 'fixers'. They get entangled in doing work for others. By being available to resolve everything they breakdown management structures and leave themselves open to do the work that someone else is employed to do. The episode I have recounted is old. Even today, in March 2016, I met with one client who is the CEO of a company with 1700 employees and he was discussing with me a similar problem. I asked him a straight question: 'are you making decisions for the reports of your managers; doing things for people because they think you can do it quicker?' He agreed: 'Yes, and that is now stealing too much of my time.' He asked me the question, 'do you know why we employ managers, pay them high salaries, and then begin to do things they were employed to?' I joked with him with an intention to suggest, 'perhaps we think we can fix things quicker?' 'That's it, I have become the Mr. Fixer. What have I got to do with the technical issues that a CTO can resolve?' This is just an example of what coaching can do for this kind of situation: create awareness that managers need to let people work.

Due to the changes he made in his own work, Simon decided that his job was good, and reported to me that his approach had been self-destructive. He told me once, 'nobody stops you from doing more than you are asked to do, but sometimes we need to think, why do we employ other people if we know more about everything and do it ourselves?' I wanted to know from him what he felt was the main benefit from coaching. He said, 'I thought I could not reject the demands from my old colleagues, after all, we had been close. I thought I would appear to be arrogant because I have gone higher in the hierarchy. I was wrong. Everyone knew that the situation had changed. I held one meeting with all of them to clear up this misconception. An open discussion on what I expected from them in my new position and what they expected of me. I made my case with them that I was now their boss. I did not change my personality but made it clear that I would not be able to lend a hand as I did earlier.'

Simon is still with that company and has gone a level higher since the end of his coaching sessions. He met me for seven times in 8 months and was able to resolve his perceived problem through effective coaching.

This particular group of executives are vulnerable to very disruptive change in their lives because there is no methodical training for the new role. No one told Simon that it would not be possible to interact in the same way with the people with whom he exchanged his daily tasks across his office table. This is not particular to Simon; I have seen this over many years and in my experience people are promoted to new higher positions and very few, I would say extremely few, companies spend time to make them aware of the rules of the game, so to say, and how to conduct themselves in the new position. I have not seen anyone being clearly told, 'this is expected of you from the day you take on your new position'. It is mostly 'trial and error' or 'learning by doing'—new managers make a few mistakes and learn how to conduct themselves and be more effective in their new positions. These people have mostly been in the company for some time and give the impression to the decision makers that they know everything about their job. That is mostly true, but they do not know everything about the new responsibility: about leadership. The client is convinced that he has been doing the job with his colleagues for some time and he does not need to change his behaviour in his new position. Then comes a rude awakening. For the person making this step there is a paradox: on the one hand, he is moving up; he wants to improve his status and earnings, on the other hand this is going to be a very disruptive change but he does not realise it. Since he does not know what will happen, he cannot imagine what it will do to him.

Let us take a very common example of a great sales person moving up to become a sales manager. Very few managers who move a person from a lower level to one higher think about one fact: that the person who was, for example, a great sales person had a single mandate—selling. In this position people are willing to extend a helping hand to other colleagues. Now imagine one of these colleagues has become the boss of his previous colleagues. First of all, he does not take into account that he will have a different set of colleagues who may have multiple responsibilities, as discussed above in the case of Simon. Secondly the expectations of the superiors are very different from a sales manager as compared to that of a sales person.

I mentioned above that there are very few companies who prepare a new manager for their new positions. I have been coaching managers at a large multinational corporation for many years. This is one company that is an exception to this rule. Recently a very smart manager from this company asked me to coach a person who had managed a production process for the last 12 years. Somehow, the manager knew that his colleague would head for a problem if he was not coached before taking on the new position. That is why I call this manager smart; he was taking steps to prevent mishaps instead of waiting for them to happen.

The moment I met with the client, he said, 'I have been doing this all the time and my colleagues know who I am.' After 25 minutes of coaching, he gasped and said, 'Do you know what a disaster it would have been tomorrow morning? I would have walked right in to it thinking I am the same old colleague, but now I am the boss.'

How often have you seen a great salesman become a lousy sales manager? Have you ever wondered why some managers are chronically impatient? Could it be, as discussed above, that they are not trained or equipped to handle their position, while others attribute their shortcomings to various other causes, but not their incapability in leadership?

I have clients at this level, who very frequently ask me the question, 'Why do we not learn these skills in business school? We learn strategies and financial number-crunching but nothing about how to work with people or how to move people from one level to the other.' Coaching can consistently help young managers become aware of what to expect and create coping strategies for such important moves in their professional life.

6.4 Intercultural Coaching

A young sales director in a high-tech, electronic microchip corporation near Munich, with a few billion-euro turnover, complained to me that people do not even care to greet each other in his company. While talking about the issue with him for over an hour I discovered that the practice had become part of their corporate culture. 'What do your managers at the top say about it?' I asked him. He said they were not concerned about it. I asked him whether he had personally addressed the issue with someone at board level. He explained that there were at least 14 different nationalities working there and they had all complained about this disrespectful if not humiliating atmosphere. I found his complaint strange, particularly as in German society people are extremely careful to be polite. Even if you are a total stranger on a bus and you happen to sneeze people are very likely to wish you good health. The client went on to elaborate that even when they do something extraordinary: higher sales or finalise a profitable contract, they did not expect to receive an acknowledgement from their managers. 'Why have you stopped expecting some acknowledgement?' I asked. He said, 'the top executives said we managers were all grown-up enough and we should know how to manage our emotions about success and failures.' Some managers tend to forget that their employees run the companies. I asked myself why this practice should have come about in this German company, as Germany is a disciplined society. Is it possible that on the other side of the coin called discipline the expectation of certain conformity to rules and regulations is extended beyond the mechanical processes and engineering to the area of emotional acknowledgements? I have worked for over 40 years with German companies and with people in top management. Comments like 'well done', 'great job', etc, are all part of everyday working interaction.

Once in a discussion with a manager from Boesch, a multinational giant, we were discussing 'emotional intelligence' and its importance in leadership and management. His response was what you may encounter often: 'I am free of emotions in work. I have no emotions.' This is normally found in cultures where 'power distance'[2] is high. G. Koptelzwea, J. Roth, et al, in their book *Interkulturelle*

[2]A concept from cultural dimensions theory formulated by Gerard (Geert) Hendrik Hofstede, a Dutch social psychologist.

Kompetenz-Handbuch fuer die Erwachsenenbildung (2011) (*Intercultural Competence—a Handbook for Adult Education*) discuss this topic under cultural grammar. In this concept people did not have access to their superiors. Access is permitted only by passing through various people, such as a secretary or other managers who may decide whether I may meet a superior or not. Germany has a very low power distance; there is transparency in communications but emotional issues show different behaviour, as if talking about emotions would mean coming too close for comfort.

Having lived in many cultures, I have the advantage of enjoying what is known as 'Constructive Marginalisation'[3] as discussed by Janet Marie Bennett in her essay on 'Cultural Marginality: Identity Issues in Global Leadership Training', in Joyce S. Osland, Ming Li, Ying Wang (eds.) *Advances in Global Leadership* (2014, pp. 269–270):

> The resulting sense of being between two cultures or more, living at the edges of each, but rarely at the centre, can be called cultural marginality. When these issues remain unresolved, the person is often confounded by the demands, and feels alienated in a state called encapsulated marginality. The constructive marginal resolves these questions by integrating choices from each culture of which the person is a part, choosing the appropriate frame of reference, and taking action appropriate for the context.

I can exist at the edges of any society or be fully immersed in it without condemning any of the societies I live in. That is why my comments are more of observations and not criticism of German society. I have a very high regard for my adopted home.

Many companies need to rethink their intercultural strategies and engage coaches for their leaders as well as other personnel. It is not sufficient for a company that has decided to work within other cultures or to employ people from other cultures to say, as I have experienced, 'they need to learn how we work in Germany'. This way of thinking could be one of the major factors why companies run in to difficulties in managing their ventures in other countries or with personnel from different cultures at home. I am certain that, despite all the talk of globalisation and of 24-hr reachability, there is a very big gap between how we really interact with people from other cultures. Companies talk about being intercultural but they do not act to employ and integrate interculturalism into their business models.

At the German company, Sympatex Technologies Asia Ltd, for example, in 2006–2007 they employed a German national living in Singapore to run their company in Hong Kong as the CEO. On the face of it we had gone to operate globally in Hong Kong but we needed people from our own culture to run the global operations. There is nothing wrong with sending a top person from the country of the mother company. It becomes ridiculous and absurd at the same time, when companies undertake huge expenses just to comfort themselves in the feeling that

[3]A concept created by Milton J. Bennett.

there is one of us sitting in Hong Kong to run the show. All the careful checks and mechanisms to measure the competence of a person are waved aside or wilfully ignored, and the sole criterion for the choice of the top person is his nationality. No one asks whether that 'one of us' is competent for the job, whether this choice of a compatriot may be exorbitantly expensive. These kind of arrangements cause operational costs that leave other colleagues wondering why such immense costs should be paid for one single person (as was the case before I reached Hong Kong to take over as the managing director). Every weekend for months the previous CEO had travelled to Singapore. His travel bill was twice as much as his other compensations; these personal travels are not operational costs but are accepted to satisfy the fears that in global operations we can only work with people who look similar to us. The company paid twice the amount for this one person compared to the wages bill for the entire staff. An understanding of how to operate in an intercultural environment could reduce such unnecessary costs.

I have observed major international companies trying to establish operations in foreign countries who have not been able to succeed for years and wondered whether part of the problem was a mindset or apprehension about interacting with people from other cultures. This is my own experience and I do not rely on any reports or studies as yet. I do however think it would be fascinating to find out whether intercultural studies have found out why such ventures have to bear such heavy but avoidable additional costs. There is one very serious problem I have observed in such scenarios: the investors or company begin to think of themselves as the giver; they consider the ventures in other countries or their own new subsidiaries as takers or dependents. Which is not true because the company establishing an operation in a foreign country is not doing it out of benevolence: it is a business decision. In the electronic microchip manufacturing company mentioned earlier, there is a similar attitude at many levels. They do not take care of their company employees in other countries: they are the step children, and there are no guidelines in their foreign subsidiaries similar to those they rigorously follow in the parent company. This attitude of the top management filters down to the operational levels: 'Emotional Contagion'. In the case noted above, the interaction between the German head office and the operations elsewhere became extremely strained, leading to mistrust. If a giver and taker situation arises, it is normally accompanied with a very difficult psychological phenomenon that begins to guide such relationships. Besides the phenomenon of in-group and out-group (the giver seems to be in the right by the virtue of the giver and the taker), the partner in the new country or people who will work in the new set-up seem to feel intimidated by the giver and his behaviour. Leaders of such companies need coaching and the people working across continents need some understanding of working with other cultures. I am not talking about the general form of acceptable intercultural coaching where a list of 'what to do if' skills are taught. The phenomenon of in-group/out-group can be understood in layman terms as us against them or vice versa. However, there is more credible knowledge, based on studies conducted by social scientists, to demonstrate how quickly a feeling of enmity or otherness can emerge if this phenomenon takes hold in any environment, not just the intercultural one.

The first studies conducted by Henri Tajfel, a British psychologist born in Poland, for example, in his article, ‘Cognitive Aspects of Prejudice’ in the *Journal of Social Issues* (1969), 25:4. Tajfel writes under the topic: ‘Justifying advantage as inherent superiority’ (p. 95):

> An improved group position and the resulting stronger affiliation of its members is often achieved at the cost of using the group’s capacity to put another group at a disadvantage. . . . An intensified affiliation with a group is only possible when the group is capable of supplying some satisfactory aspects of an individual’s social identity. This can be defined as the attribution by the individual to the in-group of certain characteristics from the sharing of which he derives some satisfaction; i.e., the group is an adequate reference group.

When companies undertake ventures outside of their cultural environment or employ people from other cultures they need to create a new awareness that the social identity of the company is not where they are born but who they are when they work together: create a new in-group that is inclusive for the people from different cultures. The new social identity could then underline the globalisation of the company, propagated both internally and externally: what kind of company we are.

A friend of ours was to move from the UK to Switzerland. His company provided him with pre-posting intercultural training. Examples he was given include, ‘What to do when you meet a Swiss businessman or woman and what not to do.’ I asked him what he would do if drove for 60 minutes and found himself in one of the surrounding countries, in Austria, Italy, or France? People working in cross-cultural environments do not need step-wise ‘Intercultural for Dummies’ training sessions, they need intercultural awareness. This will enable them to work and navigate easily with colleagues wherever they happen to be based. There are situations where they do not see their colleagues physically and there are situations where colleagues may not communicate in their language; working methods may be different in different cultures.

It is a legitimate right of an investor or a company establishing a subsidiary to homogenise the processes of their companies. This need not be done with the rigor of an army commander. No one accepts intimidation, whether intentional or incidental. One sentence I have often heard from many managers when they fail to create a good understanding with their counterparts in other countries is, ‘We need to go to another country, it is very difficult to work with them.’ As if to say, ‘we will change our behaviour in a new country.’ These are the people who need coaching, but it should begin at the top.

Most of the advertisements looking for managers for China between 1990 and 2002, which I noticed in the international newspapers and magazines, asked for one predominant qualification from applicants: fluency in the Chinese language. If fluency in Chinese made good managers then there were 1.35 billion Chinese speakers out of which at least 47 % could be candidates, because they were adults of working age and spoke the language fluently.

When I started coaching my clients would automatically ask me if I could conduct intercultural coaching. As soon as my clients heard that I had lived and worked in many countries, they also assumed that I would know or be competent in intercultural coaching. That is also a fallacy. Many people think experience is a prerequisite for intercultural training. In my experience, most expats living in foreign countries live either in gated communities or in the circle of other expats, especially with their compatriots. Even in intercultural studies, it is proposed that people look for compatriots to mitigate cultural shock. During my studies in English Literature in the University of Delhi, India, I learnt from the works of Francis Bacon (1561–1626) that in a foreign country one should avoid compatriots if one wants to experience the richness of the culture of the host country. In his essay 'On Travel' (1625, p. 64), he advised the traveller, 'Let him sequester himself, from the company of his countrymen, and diet in such places, where there is good company of the nation where he travelleth.' I followed Bacon's principle in all the countries I lived and worked in. I can confirm it gave me a better insight into how people live and interact in different countries.

However, this method is not sufficient to be an intercultural coach. Experience may sometimes be an idiosyncratic survival strategy, nothing more. To enhance my intercultural experience, in 2015, I enrolled in the course, 'Culture Communication Skills', in Munich. The course was developed by Professor Dr. Juliana Roth, Head of the Institut fuer Interkulturelle Kommunikation (Institute for Cultural Communication) at the Ludwig Maximilian University of Munich (LMU).[4]

During the first 2 days, at the beginning of the course, the instructor, Ms. Gesine Mahnke, asked us to participate in a simulation of interculturalism, which I describe below. It is a good example of how cultural misunderstandings arise and also how insights have a powerful impact, both of which are fundamental to coaching.

6.5 An Intercultural Simulation

The Set Up

A male participant, Michael, volunteered to play the part of a male protagonist and Gesine played the part of the female protagonist. The setting was the fictive island of Albatross. Michael sat on a chair and his posture was very peculiar. He had the tip of his feet on the ground but his heels were raised. His arms rested on the armrests of the chair and he had his head raised and tilted back slightly. All the other participants, I think 11 of us, sat in a circle around them to watch them and also to participate as foreign tourists in a new culture. We had to take off our shoes. Men sat on chairs copying Michael; women sat on the floor.

[4]The course was delivered by the Bayerische Volkshochschulenverband in Munich, in English Bavarian Federation of Folks' High Schools. Information on the course can be found at http://www.xpert-ccs.de/info/Default.aspx.

The Simulation
Gesine arrived in the room with a serving tray in her hand and her head covered with a cloth, as women wear head coverings in many Asian countries. On the serving tray she had a plate with a couple of biscuits on it and a cup filled with something to drink. As soon as she was close to Michael, she knelt down on the floor to the right of him. She offered the biscuits to him. He barely nipped at it and then he nodded. Gesine gave him the cup. He took a sip and then he nodded. During this enactment, Michael did not look down. Next, Gesine ate the biscuits and drank from the cup. Soon after Michael kept his right hand on her head and she bowed down to the earth touching her forehead to the ground.

The simulation goes on further, but the part I have narrated here is sufficient to demonstrate the intercultural aspects.

6.5.1 Simulation Questions

At the end of the simulation Gesine asked every participant individually what they thought of it:

- 'What had happened?'
- 'What did we think about how the society was organised on the fictive island called Albatross?'

6.5.2 Simulation Responses

- 'The woman is inferior to the man.'
- 'She is suppressed.'
- 'She needs to feed the man before she can consume anything.'
- 'She is not at the same level as the man.'

Gesine interrogated the responses. She asked, 'what do you mean, not the same level?' The response was that the women had less value than the men in the society of Albatross Island.

- 'The man is arrogant and does not look down while the woman has to sit on the floor.'
- 'The man has to be served by the woman, as in many countries.'

The list was long, but one thing common to all statements was, '**A woman had lesser value**.' Feedback from the participants reflected our experience of our society and the normal behaviour or interpretation of other cultures: '**Women are inferior elsewhere and it is a male-dominated world**.' This is what we learn from TV news, magazines; it is enculturation, our habituation. In short, we know it!

When my children were still very small, I think they were seven and six, respectively, we would go for long walks from the top of a hillock where our home was down to Lake Garda, in Italy. We would discuss whatever came to mind and very often during my explanation one of them would say vehemently, 'I know that'. I recall telling them that once you claim 'you know' you close your mind to new learning. In coaching, I call it terminating an intellectual cognitive process for future explorative learning.

When it was my turn to give my interpretation of the simulation on the fictive island of Albatross, I said that I would like to speculate, even at the risk of being wrong, that the man is inferior and serves a purpose that endorses woman's higher status. Notice I said 'speculate' not that I knew it. I said, I think that he has to taste all the food and drink and confirm by nodding that it is appropriate for the woman to consume it. Gesine wanted to know why I had thought this. She wanted to know the precise reasons. She said that no one up till that moment in all her training experience had ever come to that conclusion. I explained that in one of the Hindu Epics called the *Holy Ramayana* there is a character called 'Shabari' who is a semi-civilised person. She was an ardent devotee of the God Rama and had prayed for a long time wishing that he would someday visit her. While in exile in a forest with his wife Sita and younger brother Laxman, he does visit her. She, in her limitless joy, offers him the choicest fruit of the forest: berries. Before giving the berries to God Rama, she bites each one of them individually to examine whether they are sweet enough and appropriate for God Rama.

6.5.3 Simulation Result

After listening to my explanation, Gesine exposed the truth of the simulation. The fictive island of Albatross is a matriarchal society: the man is subordinate and needs to wait till the woman has eaten. He tested each piece of food and drink to verify whether it was appropriate for the woman to consume it. On Albatross, a man is not permitted full contact with the earth. He is not permitted to sit on the ground and that is why he sits on a chair. He may not touch the earth with his feet, only the tips of his feet to support his posture, that is why his heels are raised. He may not see the earth directly and has lifted his head to avoid direct contact. Only a woman is permitted to be in contact with mother earth. Both the woman and the earth give new life and food to sustain life for humanity. A man draws his energy from the earth by means of touching the head of the woman when she bows down with her forehead touching the earth directly. Only she draws the life-giving energy directly from the mother earth.

Imagine what happened to the participants. They experienced something that is very important in coaching when it comes to measuring efficacy: perspective shift. Nobody told them they were wrong in their responses; nobody shamed them on their misinterpretations. They were left to reflect on the facts alone. Everybody reported that they had gained an insight into the new culture of Albatross, and about their own limitations in interpreting the culture based on what they thought was normal. They all concluded that what they saw or thought as normal was not necessarily normal everywhere. This was the beginning of questioning their paradigms and the beginning of explorative flexibility. This is what effective coaching also achieves with the clients.

After a silent pause the realisation triggered a lively and critical discussion on culture and intercultural issues within the class. The result was an agreement that people focus on their own culture and make it a reference point for everything; it is a benchmark for everything else, everywhere they travel.

Ethnocentricity opened its doors wide for all of us for the first time. The main impediment in an intercultural communication is not how different a foreign culture may be. It lies in our ability to see it as strange when we compare it to our own experiences.

In coaching, as soon as my client has come to such a realisation, a very pensive and productive cognitive process begins in her and the process is very subjective for her. What it will change, I do not know as a coach; only the client will decide what she wants to accept or reject.

A very important lesson for a coach is he does not know what is best for his client. A coach should not begin to make interpretations based on what he knows. This is the reason why I think diagnosis is counterproductive and damaging in coaching. Diagnosis is based on what I know: a set of rules, a list of indications, symptoms, not what a client wants. Every client in a coaching environment is a new island of Albatross.

The lessons from Henri Tajfel, Francis Bacon, and the fictive island of Albatross should make every manager rethink the importance of intercultural awareness to avoid an unnecessary waste of resources and also avoid humiliating people who come to work with them. I think intercultural management is one of the biggest challenges facing many companies and very few companies address this issue appropriately. In the near future, companies will lose ground to their foreign competitors because of poor management in their handling of intercultural issues, unless they begin to accept one fact: normal is not what we think is normal in our home country. It is that which is perceived by people from other cultures included in our own culture. If individuals can move to different countries and accept new cultures and still respect their own to create a third culture what should stop companies from doing it? Only our own insistence on what is normal. If the CEOs and other decision makers see that accepting these differences will improve their global performance, that would be a beginning to create a new normal where a global company has only in-group.

References

Bacon, F. (1868). *The essays or counsels civil and moral*. London: Bell & Daldy.

Bennet, J. M. (2014). Cultural marginality: Identity issues in global leadership training. In J. S. Osland, M. Li, & Y. Wang (Eds.), *Advances in global leadership* (Vol. 8, pp. 269–292). Bingley: Emerald Group Publishing.

Colvile, R. (2016). *The great acceleration: How the world is getting faster, faster*. New York: Bloomsbury.

Koeck, C., & Roth, J. (2009). *Culture communication skills* (P. Andersen, Trans.). Ilmenau: Educational Consulting GmbH.

Koptelzewa, G., Roth, J., Sterzenbach, G., & Tuschinsky, C. (2011). *Interkulturelle Kompetenz-Handbuch fuer die Erwachsenenbildung*. Ilmenau: Educational Consulting GmbH. English Edition.

Pennebaker, J. W. (1997). *Opening up: The healing power of expressing emotions*. New York: Guilford Press.

Tajfel, H. (1969). Cognitive aspects of prejudice. *Journal of Social Issues, 25*(4), 79–97.

Online Sources

Boyatzis, R. *Inspiring leadership through emotional leadership*. Online course materials. www.coursera.org. Accessed 25 June 2013.

Boyatzis, R. *Inspiring leadership through emotional leadership*. Lecture 5: Stress and renewal. Online course materials. www.coursera.org. Accessed 25 June 2013.

Building Rapport, Empathy, and Mindfulness in Coaching

7

During a coaching session conversational techniques such as active listening can be applied for some time, but these conversations must be handled carefully. It can be disturbing and counterproductive for a client if it is implemented mechanically. Professionals providing disaster relief or support to traumatised people are trained in a version of this method adapted to trauma counselling. In May 2015, I attended 'Psychological First Aid: Johns Hopkins RAPID PFA', an online course conducted by Professor George S. Everly, Jr., with the Johns Hopkins Bloomberg School of Public Health. Professor Everly demonstrated how the RAPID conversational method works in trauma situations to reassure people and to give them a sense of security. The acronym 'RAPID' in the course title is an abbreviation of five different expressions:

RAPID

1. Rapport and reflective listening
2. Assessment
3. Prioritisation
4. Intervention
5. Disposition and follow-up.

In my coaching practice, I adapted Everly's 'R' by inverting the order to, 'Reflective listening and Rapport building'. In my experience, reflective listening is very important. I also find this method is more effective than active listening, which I learnt in the original coaching course with CourseU (See Sect. 2.2). What is different about reflective listening? The coach is not just listening to the client and acknowledging mechanically as a way of demonstrating that he understands her. The coach is reflecting on what the client is saying and beginning to interpret the feelings behind her words. Why is the client using certain words? He notices her gesticulations and facial expressions. What do the words and other signs of the speaker mean to her? Is it sorrow, shame, joy, hope? Is there more than one? While interpreting all these accompanying signs during a conversation, the coach must not

A. Kohli, *Effective Coaching, and the Fallacy of Sustainable Change*, Management for Professionals, DOI 10.1007/978-3-319-39735-1_7

speculate on how a client is feeling as such a speculation would be counterproductive. The coach interprets and then goes on to seek confirmation from the client whether she intends to say something more by expressing her state in certain chosen words, such as, whether she is also experiencing a particular feeling because of the events.

Let me give you an example: on the 'RAPID' course, Prof. Everly simulated reflective listening using the fictive example of a person who had survived a disaster. The survivor says, 'I have lost everything'. She makes a sad face while saying the words aloud.

In active listening, a coach may have asked, 'You mean you have nothing left?' I think that would not demonstrate appropriate concern for her feelings. If a coach asked a client, 'are you feeling very sad about your loss?', and the client was feeling sad, she would confirm that she is sad and remove the element of speculation from the coach. Or she will expose to the coach what she is really feeling. If a coach is able to show concern for her feelings, she will react with more confidence.

The moment a person thinks that they are being understood the process of building a stable rapport begins. Their feelings of sadness or any other disturbing feeling also begins to diminish. When a client is able to vent her feelings and is understood, the feelings begin to change in intensity. Rapport building has to be carried out carefully and it needs to begin within the first few minutes of the meeting. Reflective listening is listening mindfully.

Ever since Dr. Jon Kabat-Zinn, a medical expert, scientist, and founder of mindfulness-based stress reduction, provided empirical evidence that mindfulness meditation in a clinical environment is effective in relieving pain and reducing stress, it has become another buzzword, like sustainable, which many readily attach to everything. Mindfulness is also found in ancient Buddhist meditation.[1] The method of reflective listening in a coaching situation leads a coach to listen to his client with adequate mindfulness. This method of listening may have to be practised for a while because it does not come very easily to everyone, but once mastered the rapport with the client is built on very stable terms.

If a coach is implementing the reflective listening method, he will get a deeper understanding of the client's issues. The phrase 'active listening' brings to my mind an image of activity, which could be limited to physical gestures, such as nodding consistently, or making other movements. These may disturb the client. Reflective listening, on the other hand, is slow thinking that retards or delays reactions on both sides, which contributes to creating an environment of genuine concern. We know from many scientific studies[2] that slow thinking allows better reflection. There is another very positive effect that this method brings with it as a side effect. The

[1]For those who are interested in more information on Mindfulness and how it is practised in Buddhism I recommend books from Thich Nhat Hanh or by Bhante Henepola Gunaratana.

[2]See, for example, Daniel Kahneman (2013). *Thinking Fast and Slow*. New York: Farrar, Straus and Giroux.

coach, without any conscious effort, begins to display genuine empathy for the client's cause due to a deeper understanding. How does that happen?

If you ask practising coaches or clients who have been coached what empathy is and how the coach creates a feeling in the client that the coach is genuinely empathic, they will not be able to name a method. In contrast to diagnosis or analysis, it is subtle. In Professor Everly's course, I discovered that this method is good for creating genuine empathy. I have not adapted other parts of RAPID to coaching but there are similar steps that exist in different intensity. Once the client can recognise that she is being listened to and also being understood with sincerity, she is able to lower her self-created inhibitions and interact with the coach in an atmosphere of confidence. There are no more compunctions about the choice of words. There is also no effort to project one's person in a better light by deliberately avoiding giving answers that may not be right, but which are socially desirable or correct. This makes coaching very effective in a shorter span of time because little time is needed to get down to the real issues that a person wants to discuss. Reflective listening creates a secure space for a client and she begins to explore her own questions. That is exactly one of the aims of coaching.

7.1 Self-Reflection in Coaching

By implementing the 'rapport building method' discussed above, a coach not only begins to facilitate the process of exploration he begins to strengthen a good rapport with the client. A good rapport is the basis of effective coaching. When would you notice that you have established a good rapport? I rely on spontaneous and unsolicited feedback. For example, when a client tells me: 'We have just seen each other for two meetings but I have a feeling that I have known you for ages.' Or if a client reports to me, 'I have told you so much that I do not think I have any friend who knows so much about me.' Or a client says, 'It is a good feeling to feel safe talking to you.' Or one statement that I often hear, 'It seems like I have known you for ages, even though you have not told me anything about you.'

Another factor that helps in building good rapport is when a coach does not give answers to everything a client says. What is the reason that a coach should refrain from giving too many answers or advice if the client trusts him? As soon as a coach begins to give answers, he interrupts the cognitive process that the coaching method triggers in the client and cuts short the exploration. Let the client indulge in her thoughts. That is my *Leitfaden* for this stage of coaching. People in their normal routines tend to get in to automatism and have little or no time to indulge in assisted explorations. If people repeat the same tasks every day or have been struggling with the same issues for a while, by default, they are inclined to think that they are right in their assumptions. In writing about 'learning with response', George Kelly states in his book *A Theory of Personality* (1963, pp. 8–9):

> Man looks at his world through transparent patterns or templates which he creates and then attempts to fit over the realities of which the world is composed. The fit is not always good. Yet without such patterns the world appears to be such an undifferentiated homogeneity that man is unable to make any sense out of it. Even a poor fit is more helpful to him than nothing at all.

If we know that we may not be right in our thinking, we seek advice or an opinion. However, our efforts are focused on verifying what we already think. We do not approach the matter in the manner of a scientist, to falsify them. How often do friends share their experiences of daily events or conflicts just to end the sentences with the question 'don't you think I was right?': 'Even a poor fit is more helpful than nothing at all.' From an evolutionary point of view, this comes from our basic instincts. We need to be right to go through our life without having to ask another's opinion about everything. For example, if we did not think we were right we may just end up asking people about very banal needs, for example, what is the right time to drink water or should I eat if and when I feel hungry? While feeling right about things is helpful to sustain ourselves, it has a downside to it too. If I think that I am always right, I may not need a coach but a psychiatrist to treat my narcissism. If I think I am always wrong, I may again land up with a psychiatrist treating me for depression. This is what I discussed in the 'Mid Zone' (Fig. 5.1: See Sect. 5.1).

Normal, non-pathological people interact within the fictive −15 to 15 and the people in two conditions mentioned above tend to go far beyond that zone. Whatever the non-pathological people think, whether they think they are right or they think they are wrong, whatever they do, they also nurture a healthy degree of doubt. Where would such people go if they wanted to clarify their doubts? Whom, then, do we have to turn to? Our friends and our family. What if I am a single person or someone shouldering very large responsibilities and I have to exercise self-restraint to talk only to a selected few and only on selected issues? With whom do I discuss my feelings, thoughts, and doubts?

It is a fact that executives at many levels have a very limited circle with whom they may discuss their true professional concerns freely. If there was a question about what a coach does, I think this answer should clear all doubts now. A coach contributes to increasing the number of options a client can generate to reflect about their issues, doubts, problems or whatever they need to discuss confidentially. An external view and a certain discernment on the part of the coach facilitates exploration. A coach can bring a client out of automatism and stimulate self-reflection. If a coach shows understanding and compassion, the client feels supported and protected to indulge in self-reflection. Self-reflection can be carried out alone in the quiet of an office or home. The big difference is that a coach enables the client to stay within their own values and capabilities, which differentiates self-reflection from daydreaming. The process of self-reflection can be long and mostly pleasurable for a client because it opens up new perspectives. I receive unsolicited self-reports from my clients who in their subsequent meetings say that the one thing that changed for them was they are now reflecting over the issue in a way they never did before. How long can this process last? Depending on the issue the client wants to discuss, I have seen evidence of this kind of self-reflection going on for 6 to

8 weeks. Very often, this is what leads people to self-realisation. Some of them discover that they have been asking too much of themselves. Others may discover they were underestimating themselves in some areas. They may come to an understanding about themselves and this understanding leads to change that is neither motivational nor goal achieving. They begin to accept themselves as they are in many areas where they had not done before or for some time. This method instils a newfound confidence in one's own abilities and that confidence is not shaken very easily.

7.2 What Leads to Insight in Coaching?

Let me take you on a journey to elaborate the last part of the definition of coaching I have created, especially what is meant by the word 'insight' and what it means to 'enable' a client. Let us not indulge in fatalism and lead you to think nothing can be done if people think only from their point of view. Human beings are adaptive and are able to learn new associations. Now I am addressing human beings in the context of coaching and referring only to adults. The problem is that no one learns anything if told straight or with an additive 'I told you so' or 'I knew it all the time and you never listen.' They are willing to accept the new perspective on things if they realise it themselves or it makes sense to them without duress: through insight. This may not be valid for the complete domain of learning in psychology but this is definitely the case in the context of coaching. The intensity may vary from person to person depending on the interest of the individual but an insight will be gained if a client can slow down their thinking.

Insights are the Backbone of Coaching Insight is an effective method of coaching. It is a method of shutting off cognitive deceptions to create a moment of personal subjective truth for the client. With insight, clients perform self-realisation and self-reflection on their behaviour relative to their environment. No amount of goal setting or assessment tests can improve the condition of a client in the way that insight through methodical coaching can achieve for her. If a client gains an insight to events relevant to her and also on her way of thinking on her own terms and she decides how best to proceed, then coaching has been effective in her case.

Another concept Gesine and subsequently two masterful instructors, Dr. Roth and Dr. Sterzenbach, imparted to us on the 'Culture Communication Skills®' course (See Sect. 6.4) was the concept of a 'Backpack'. Gesine explained that the more reference points a person brings with himself to an interaction, the larger the number of options he has at his disposal with which to interpret and subsequently react to a situation. The concept frees a client from whatever is holding back their development. Coaching through insights can take a client to a spot where they change their thinking or behaviour, if they choose to, based on how they interpret their environment. Once someone has gained an insight it is extremely difficult to imagine that the person would regress to her previous ideas. Insight can trigger personal change.

In the context of the 'Backpack', the other participants who took part in the simulation on the fictive island of Albatross (See Sect. 6.5) had one reference point: their own cultural background. I had what everybody else had, but also teachings from the *Holy Ramayana*. The likelihood of navigating with more flexibility in a new situation increases with the number of options of interpretation. In other words, each one of us is carrying a 'backpack' full of our experiences: from our culture, or cultures we have lived in; our life and work experience; our social interactions; our education, and our very personal interpretation of our world view. Our reaction to a new situation is based on many such factors: they all play a part in formulating our convictions. Up to the moment we gain a new insight we insist that we know how things are. The more substance that we have in our 'backpack' the more likely we will be free and at ease when we encounter new situations. If your experience and knowledge has widened your horizon, then you may be able to cope with more situations more easily.

Let us now translate this idea to coaching. The more methods that a coach has in his backpack, the more exposure he has to different methods, the more effective he may be. This is the first place where I would give experience some credibility in the context of coaching. If the experience and the knowledge of your coach has enhanced his horizon, and contributed to filling up his backpack, you stand to gain more benefit from him. There is a general tendency among coaches to call assessment tests, goal setting templates, and various kinds of popular games as coaching 'tools'. I have not found an explanation of what these tools can do for a client. Every new idea is sold as a coaching tool. I find the word 'method' more appropriate because a method has to be learnt and implemented methodically, i.e. scientifically, whereas a tool sounds mechanical if not manipulative to me, such as a tool that anyone can buy without a guarantee that he can also use it properly (let us not discuss whether a tool can deliver the desired results).

Gesine did not use words such as benchmark or culture or our past experience but we all realised it ourselves and that is the insight we gained from the simulation. Just as Gesine silently delivered the message that our own culture is not the benchmark for everyone in the world, the key word in coaching should be competency combined with method: **'Methodical Competency'.** The advantage of a method is that it is also open to intersubjective criticism. In my opinion, coaching would benefit from such intersubjective criticism instead of relying on whimsical tools and assessments. Personally, I would like to see coaching rid of tools and assessments and be rich in methods.

Coaching Encourages Flexible Thinking Many people offer coaching under the motto: 'I help people to find their best'; there are others, when you ask them how they coach, who say, 'I support my coachee to unleash his potential', or 'attain his best in self-development'. In the early years of my coaching practice, I would put such superlative and ambiguous statements on my brochures and website, such as, 'Unleash your potential'. However, I could not discover any clients looking for superlative changes.

So what does a coach do? In my opinion, a coach does not propose to do any of the statements above.

A coach can contribute to the self-development of his clients, trigger insight, expand their horizon, be available to talk confidentially, if possible, and to trigger a perspective shift and perhaps a paradigm shift; increase the number of options for interpreting events and thoughts.

7.3 What Makes an Effective Coach?

Simulations, such as the simulation on the fictive island of Albatross (See Sect. 6.5), are difficult to implement in an individual coaching setting. They are more beneficial to group work. There are other methods that work well in person to person coaching. The most important aspect of coaching, which should be kept in the forefront of any discussion of coaching, is that it is a conversational explorative method. Is it enough to qualify someone as a coach if he can converse methodically? My answer to this is not only a clear yes, but this is what goes in to making a masterful coach. If a coach is able to impart insight to the client, thus enabling the client to make her own decisions, then the coach has been successful. If you set goals, they work in a linear fashion, whereas insights work on many dimensions. A person who gains an insight is able to make changes in many areas simultaneously. Her understanding of her own misconceptions can trigger a change in more than one aspect, and in her entire approach as a person.

Depending on the flow of a coaching conversation, a masterful coach has a number of methods at his disposal. Besides the different methods explained above, I will add other methods to the list. For example, Critical Incident Technique (CIT), and the Vignette Method.[3] I have adapted three methods from the 'Culture Communication Skills' course (See Sect. 6.4), for example, the Analytical Method, Creative Method, and the Open Case Method. Out of all these methods there is not one which could be called the best method for effective coaching. The needs of different clients are the best guide to which method may be most appropriate; therefore, knowledge of a wide range of methodical techniques is of great advantage to a coach.

Below I list a few methods, but without going into the details of each one, because this is not a Do-It-Yourself coaching book or a book on coaching methods. The list is also not a final list. As with most new concepts, once a process begins to take hold, it is open to scrutiny and validation, some may reject parts or all of the methods, while others will add new methods. The list is open to such amendments if it serves the purpose of supporting effective coaching in its methodical development.

[3]Originally known as 'The Vignette Technique in Survey Research': See Rossi and Berk (1985).

- Explorative conversational method
- Insights Method
- Self-Realisation Method
- Vignette Method
- Critical Incident Technique also called CIT Method[4]
- Observational Method
- Analytical Method
- Creative Method
- Open Case Method
- Narrative Method
- Parables Method

With a range of proven methods in their 'backpack', a coach is equipped to conduct a person-centred, non-diagnostic, explorative conversational method with the sole purpose of facilitating client self-reflection that leads to insight of his behaviour relative to his environment. Irrespective of the methodology, the focus remains on enabling the client to gain insight so that she can make her decisions based on her value system and capabilities.

As my client, Mark, asked after his coaching: 'does it go any higher?' (See Sect. 3.2.3) it depends on you. Similarly, if you are satisfied with the level of coaching training you have achieved it is your prerogative to stop there and relish your successes as a coach. However, if you want to 'go higher' then you will have to look at the existing available knowledge. Is there anything else in other disciplines, such as philosophy, psychology, leadership etc., that can contribute to making coaching a more predictable and reliable method at a higher level? Is there anything coaching could learn and adapt from other social disciplines to broaden its scope of implementation?

Psychology, with its more than 140 years of experimentation and detailed studies, offers great opportunities in a coaching perspective. I personally use some parts of psychology research methods, methods of measurements, how to build good questionnaires along with mathematical models in coaching. If applied prudently, psychological methods could give a boost to coaching and relieve it from the 3-day coaching myths. The discipline of psychology offers a treasure chest filled with theories and studies on personality, developmental psychology, behaviour and many other phenomena. The question, would that not make it too similar to psychology, is an appropriate one to address. The depth and the intensity with which a psychology student studies the subjects named above are not needed in coaching. She is studying to become a social scientist, a psychologist. Some basic knowledge of a few subjects would avoid the common pitfalls that trip up contemporary coaches. Which tool to use, which test to use, should tests be used at all? With additional knowledge from the discipline of psychology coaching could achieve new heights and the kind of efficacy that is needed by many businesses,

[4]Colonel John C. Flanagan of the US Army Air Force is attributed to have created this method.

especially the larger corporations. Once again, a coach need not know how to conduct a factor analysis, or, for example, significance tests, or be familiar with testing hypothesis, but it would be helpful if he had a methodical system with which he could recognise irrelevant questions from relevant ones in a questionnaire. If he could use mathematical regression models aimed for personal development, for example. Formal knowledge of the discipline of psychology could serve the coach and client if a coach had it in his metaphorical 'backpack'. I use these subjects in my coaching, if needed, and they give very effective results—saving time and resources for my clients.

References

Kahneman, D. (2013). *Thinking fast and slow*. New York: Farrar, Straus and Giroux.
Kelly, G. (1963). *A theory of personality*. New York: Norton.
Rossi, P. H., & Berk, R. A. (1985). Varieties of normative consensus. *American Sociological Review, 50*, 333–347.

8 The Basis of Coaching

We have looked at coaching, how it works, who needs it, and what impedes an effective coaching service. Let us take a look now at how coaching evolved. To understand any concept unambiguously it is useful to examine the aspects that went in to determining its basis. To understand the basis of coaching, however, we also need to indulge in a philosophical exploration of the basic assumptions of human nature that went into formulating that basis. In my opinion, coaching has been led into a terrain of uncertainty and as a result, most people do not know what to expect from it. Ideally, a service that has been created for the benefit of the general public should involve very little effort for its consumer to understand what it promises to deliver. If you look at coaching presently this is exactly what is blurred and as a consequence giving everyone the feeling that anyone can define their own concoction of it as a new magic potion. To clarify this confusion, therefore, understanding the basic assumptions of human nature that formed the basis of coaching is an important starting point. Once the basic assumptions of human nature that formed the basis of coaching are identified, coaching practitioners are automatically obliged to validate them. Such validation will come from observing the manifest behaviour of clients who utilise the service. After these two steps are complete, the logical outcome will be to create comprehensible guiding principles that can serve as a beacon for a practising coach to propagate his service, and also to reassure clients that there are certain norms to which all coaches adhere.

Why is all this necessary? It is necessary in order to prevent the continual renaming of the old professions as coaching, or peddling them as new services under the name of coaching. Some services seem so absurd and unique in their own way that no one understands what they will do for us. This method of proceeding will also go a long way to ensure a certain quality in the delivery of the service.

Finally, the guiding principles will create invisible fault lines for the practising coach. Irrespective of what his clients want or expect from him, a coach will inherently lead them to his side of the fault line, thus creating clarity for both the coach and his clients. In simple words, if you go to a Voodoo doctor in, say, Senegal, West Africa, he is likely to perform rituals to demonstrate to you that he

A. Kohli, *Effective Coaching, and the Fallacy of Sustainable Change*, Management for Professionals, DOI 10.1007/978-3-319-39735-1_8

will pacify the spirits for whatever issue you might want to be resolved. If you had some management related improvements in mind, the Voodoo practitioner is not going to talk about Peter F. Drucker[1] or the principles of management with you. Notice, the mention of Voodoo may sound foreign to many but use of the word is in no way judgemental or evaluating. The stark contrast will help to convey to my readers that all service providers follow certain methods to deliver their services, irrespective how exotic they may sound or how little you know about them. The aspects that go in to making a Voodoo ceremony may not be overtly visible to the consumer but he is more than likely to be aware of what to expect from the Voodoo doctor. If you now ask yourself, what would you expect from a Voodoo ceremony, even if you do not know the details you have an approximate idea of what it is going to be.

Every time I tell someone I am a coach by profession, they ask 'what do you coach?' This is one of the many reasons I am compelled to create a clear picture that a coach does not coach some*thing* but some*one*. Whoever it may be, coaching is always the same: person-centred.

8.1 The Guiding Principles of Coaching

During my first coaching course, I learnt the CoachU nine 'Guiding Principles', which are laid out in *The Coach U Personal and Corporate Coach Training Handbook* (2005, pp. 47–48). These formed the basis of the tuition I initially received.

The Nine CoachU 'Guiding Principles'

1. People have something in common
2. People are inquisitive
3. People contribute
4. People grow from connections
5. People seek value
6. People act in their own interest
7. People live from their perception
8. People have a choice
9. People define their own integrity.

The CoachU 'Guiding Principles' were further elaborated on a personal and corporate level in the original text; however, for the purposes of my book I will stay with the personal aspect of them. The reason is simple: individuals are major determinants for the outcome of corporate results. The results are not restricted to

[1] An Austrian born (1909–2005), American author, professor and management consultant. A self-styled 'social ecologist'. According to *Business Week* he was 'the man who invented management'.

financial interests, but also relate to governance, the treatment of people working in a corporate environment, its benefits to society and the world in general.

If the CoachU 'Guiding Principles' were relevant, I reasoned that I should be able to validate them in practical coaching with my clients; they would be visible with at least more than 50 % of my clients. I would not discount principles and basic assumptions below 50 % as irrelevant, but I drew a distinction of what would guide a coach without confusing her. This line is also necessary in order to avoid manifestations of rare behaviour or traits that are outliers. I concluded that a coach should be able to focus on aspects that appear most frequently in interactions and the aspects that people are likely to bring to a coaching meeting. Although the CoachU 'Guiding Principles' seemed to make sense when I first encountered them, I was unable to validate all of them in my coaching practice, while others were visible without any effort. Let me tell you how I validated those that had any scope of validation.

People are Inquisitive ('Principle 2') People are inquisitive only about what they do not know and particularly when it fascinates them. I could not validate this in my coaching practice. I could not see any indication that people come to coaching because they are inquisitive. I have mentioned it for a particular reason which you will encounter later.

People Contribute ('Principle 3') I did not encounter this principle during coaching. Despite that, I think it needs to be mentioned because I have noticed others talking on the same lines. Dr. Michael Loebbert,[2] in his SWR2 radio broadcast[3] titled, 'Real help or Humbug. The sense and senselessness of Coaching', was also of the opinion that people want to do something for society and the world in general. During my coaching sessions, no one asked or expressed their feelings about doing something to contribute to society and the world in general. While this may be true, we cannot reject the notion that people wish to contribute. At the same time, we need to be cautious and avoid implying that humans are only selfish: that is not the case. If we look at it in the context of the nine 'Guiding Principles' of coaching advocated by the CoachU schools, then it is not appropriate to use this principle because a coach would have a difficult time identifying when a person wishes to contribute.

People Act in Their Own Interest ('Principle 6') I was able to validate this in every meeting with every client. From an evolutionary point of view, it seems legitimate for our survival and the propagation of our species. People come to coaching because they are acting in their own interest. The inquisitiveness and curiosity that I could not validate as a standalone principle became interesting as

[2]Dr. Michael Loebbert, a coach, supervisor, an organisation consultant, and a programme manager and lecturer for coaching at the high school for social work in North West Switzerland (FHNC).

[3]A radio station based in the south west of Germany.

soon as the discussion turned to the client and his interests. If a person's own interest is needed in order to instigate inquisitiveness, it should not be an independent factor, but a dependent one. If it is dependent, it cannot be a guiding principle, but a consequence of another principle.

People Live from Their Perception ('Principle 7') This statement may not be new to many but it demarcates the line between psychoanalysis, behaviourism, and coaching. As a matter of fact, it also separates it from all advisory and management consultation services. In psychoanalysis or behaviourism there is no discussion of the person's perception. Both know some behaviour exists because of the fact laid down in each school of thought. Management consultants normally contradict the perceptions of a manager by providing him with what they think is a correct solution. They are experts dedicated to their particular business. In coaching it is all about what a person perceives himself to be or how he perceives his environment.

People Define Their Own Integrity ('Principle 9') This principle is omnipresent in coaching. People will decide what is right and permissible based on their own values. A coach will encounter this very often. That is another reason why coaching cannot promise to deliver a sustainable change when it is the client who defines her own values and what is right for her.

8.2 Basic Assumptions of Human Nature in a Coaching Context

The basic assumptions of human nature that I have observed so far and which I have also been able to validate through coaching are listed below. Each validation is demonstrated with at least one real case drawn from my coaching practice.

The Basic Assumptions of Human Nature
1. People act in their own interest
2. People define their own integrity
3. People live from their own perception
4. People nurture their own assumptions
5. People predict outcomes
6. People seek to understand
7. People trust their own decisions
8. People have answers.

8.3 Case Studies

The following case studies demonstrate the basic assumptions of human nature in observable manifest behaviour in a coaching context.

1. People Act in Their Own Interest

The main reason for someone to seek coaching is the first simple validation of the fact that people act in their own interest. Only if people think they stand to gain something personally from coaching do they meet with a coach. Why would someone visit a coach if she was not acting in her own interest? I have not encountered anyone who came seeking coaching in the interest of others. Since this is too simplistic let me share with you what validates this assumption. Before beginning a coaching relationship all my clients fill out a pre-coaching questionnaire wherein they specify why they want to be coached and what they want to discuss. The most frequent questions that the clients want to discuss are:

- How can I discover my own limitations, overcome my weaknesses?
- How can I improve myself in my private and professional areas?
- How can I understand and improve the effect I leave on others?
- How do I know how people perceive me?
- How can I reduce stress in my life?
- How can I motivate my team?
- How can I stop falling in to the same trap over and over again?

And many more such concerns with one common denominator: personal interest.

There are many other aspects of their life they wish to discuss too. The ones I have listed above are concerns of the majority of my clients, irrespective of whether they are from Germany, India, the UK, China, or elsewhere.

What about the managers who are recommended by their bosses to seek coaching? The mandate I receive from any large corporation is clearly defined. Coaching is offered by them to their employees for their personal development. The expectation behind such a mandate is that the employee will improve his own behaviour and affect the overall interaction within the company, resulting in better performance. I receive feedback after the coaching both from the CEO and the person who was coached. They confirm what improvements were visible and what made an impact subsequent to coaching. In most cases the feedback from the CEO is, 'it is much easier to work with him; he is able to cooperate with others without the unnecessary frictions that existed prior to coaching'.

In all fairness, I must mention one case which violates this rule. I have experienced one case in Germany where the CEO of a company asked me to coach a senior manager, even though he was going to retire after 18 months. His intentions were purely altruistic. He wanted his manager to experience coaching because he was of the opinion that coaching does not impact just the working area but primarily the person himself. This manager was facing a very difficult situation at home and his boss wanted to help ease some of his difficulties. Aside from this one case I have not come across any altruistic motives for someone seeking coaching on behalf of another person. This is manifest before coaching begins and throughout the coaching process. I could cite numerous cases here to give evidence of the first assumption, I will refrain to do so for one reason: all the cases cited below are also appropriate to validate this assumption that people act in their own interest.

2. People Define Their Own Integrity

Philosophers could spend a lifetime discussing the meaning of 'integrity' and still leave the unambiguous meaning to be discovered by successive generations. For the purposes of coaching, it suffices to say that everyone has a self-image and everyone is convinced they are acting in the correct way, perhaps not all the time, but in areas that are important to them. If it were not so, every person would struggle with very small things in their everyday lives. For those who are interested in a deeper discourse on integrity, I recommend Timothy D. Wilson's book, *Strangers to Ourselves: Discovering the Adaptive Unconscious* (2002). Wilson explains why, from an evolutionary point of view, it is necessary that we recognise what is known in business jargon as 'constructive deception'. Every person has created a threshold of honesty and other moral values for herself, which she will not cross. It is this threshold that judges her in her own eyes whether she is honest, whether her uprightness is still intact or not. This generates self-confidence that drives a person to face her daily challenges on her own terms. In his online Coursera course, *A Beginner's Guide to Irrational Behaviour* (2014), Dan Ariely, a professor at Duke University, USA, calls it the 'Fudge Factor' (Week 3, 'Lecture on Dishonesty'). Ariely takes the example of a person with no inhibitions picking up a pencil that costs 10 cents from his office and taking it home. However, if you ask the same person to open the cash box in the office and take away 10 cents, he will call it stealing. There are a few thresholds that every person builds up and creates as his own markers. If they are violated, the person questions his integrity. It has also been examined by social scientists that people will conveniently move the threshold to another level as long as they do not feel threatened by their own standards. While this may help us to lead our lives according to our own perception, there is a serious downside to it. People can sometimes behave in a manner that is harmful to others and still legitimise their own version of things and live undeterred with misconduct and abuse; still seeming to be honest to themselves in their own eyes.

8.3.1 Case Study: 'Tariq'

My client, whose fictive name was 'Tariq', had lived in southern France. His parents came from Tunisia, though Tariq was born in France. I met him in 2011 when he moved to Hong Kong for a period of 1 year for an assignment with a French company. He came to me for executive coaching and after about 4 months into the coaching relationship, he asked if he could talk about an issue that still bothered him even after 9 years. Even though the relationship with the coach is confidential, he requested that his life experience be kept to me. For the purpose of this book, he gave me his permission in 2015, under the condition that all the names as well as his real name be kept anonymous. Tariq had been the CEO of a perfume company. He met Sabine when she was 32-years-old. She was a designer at a fashion company in Hamburg. In her work, she coordinated product development in the south of France. After a few months of their romantic relationship, they married. Subsequently, when Sabine was expecting their first child, they made the decision that she should abandon her job and focus on bringing up children and looking after the well-being of their young family. A few years after Sabine had moved to France, her father died. Tariq, to show compassion to Sabine and her family, asked her to invite her mother Maria to France, so that she was not left alone in her grief. Sabine welcomed the idea and invited her mother to stay for 2 weeks at their home.

Sabine's mother was delighted. She promptly arrived and enjoyed her 2 weeks in southern France. When she was leaving to return to Germany, she agreed with Sabine that she would visit them more often than previously, as she loved the relaxed atmosphere of their French home.

Tariq knew nothing of these future plans. Soon he discovered that his mother-in-law was present every 4 to 5 weeks as a regular guest, spending 3 sometimes 4 weeks with them. This did not bother him at first. However, due to a restructuring measure, the complete production of Tariq's company had to be relocated to China, and he received an offer to move with his family to China. Since they now had two small children, they decided against the move. Tariq decided to look for a new job instead.

For over 2 years, he was unable to find an appropriate job. To cover all their living costs, he began to sell off his life insurance policies and other assets. Maria seemed unperturbed by these disruptive changes in the life of the young family. She did not show much concern about his financial situation and continued to be a regular guest at their home. To share her delight of visiting sunny southern France, she also began to bring her other daughter and her grandchildren with her on holiday. These visits caused additional financial burdens on Tariq's finances. He discussed the situation with Sabine and Maria and tried to convince them that, in order to contain costs, holidays had to be reduced. He asked Maria to reduce the number of her visits from nine times a year to twice a year. Instead of understanding his situation, Maria made Tariq a counter-proposal: she told him he should apply for child benefit in Germany. Under European laws and according to the prevailing law in Germany and in France, the state paid a certain amount of money to support children up to a certain age. She said, although Sabine and the children were not living in Germany, Sabine could claim the state benefit if she registered herself at Maria's German home to show her residency in Germany. Tariq rejected the idea as not the correct thing to do.

Convinced that such a step would alleviate the stress on Tariq's finances, Sabine registered herself and the children at Maria's home in Germany, although she continued to live in France. After 3 years of unemployment, when Tariq was still unable to find a job to match his qualifications, he started looking closer at his resources. He recalled that he had not seen the child benefit, which his wife told him she had applied for the previous year. He asked Sabine if she knew what had happened to it. She said she had not heard from the authorities. He then asked Maria whether she had received any notification from the authorities about the child benefit allowance his wife had applied for. She said she had no idea.

One morning, when Maria and Sabine were out sightseeing, Tariq came across bank statements in the guest room, with an entry, 'children's benefits allowance'. They were bank statements from the bank account Sabine maintained in Germany. He noticed that child benefit had been credited to the account for two children for the whole of the previous year and the amount had also been withdrawn in cash every month.

Tariq placed these figures before his wife for an explanation, but got none. Only after Tariq threatened her with separation, did Sabine admit that, with her consent, her mother had used the child allowance for her personal use over the last 12 months. Maria's explanation was simple: 'I had no money for living'.

Although all of them knew that this behaviour was illegal and cheating the state, as well as depriving the children of their benefit, Maria was convinced that she was right to take the money. In a country like Germany, the social network takes care of everyone, at least to the minimum sustenance level; her statement was therefore incredulous.

Tariq asked me whether he should have separated from his wife then. Within the process of coaching, a coach should not be party to any side. A coach should not give his opinion of what he thinks is right because he does not know how a client weighs the problem based on his integrity. I asked him how he had decided about the separation. Tariq told me that he had not wanted his children to grow up with a single parent. Another disclosure he made was his apprehension that if the children grew up with a single mother the influence of their grandmother may be very damaging.

I asked him if he was aware that this was a criminal offence. He said yes, and added that he had returned the money to the state of Germany. He had added up the whole amount taken by Maria and sent an anonymous donation dropped off by his friend in April 2006 to the finance department in Hamburg without mention of name or cause. I asked him if he knew if the amount ever reached the authorities. He said, he did not know that but he did not want to have anything to do with the act and wanted to clear his own conscious. 'So why are you talking about it now, after 9 years,' I wanted to know. 'I think a lot about it and would like to resolve it together with my wife,' he said. I asked him what he had on his mind. He said, 'I thought you could coach my wife on this matter too.' You may recall I had mentioned earlier if a coach discovers that the client needs help in an area, which may be beyond the scope of coaching, he should refer his client to the appropriate professional (See, for example, Chap. 5). I asked him if he had considered talking to a psychologist or a marriage counsellor. He asked me if they could help. I told him that it was definitely worth meeting them as they are best trained to respond to such situations. After a few months, when he returned to his home, he sent me a message that he was seeing a psychologist along with his wife.

Tariq made his decision based on his integrity. I can imagine there are people who would react with extreme measures and take punitive actions to satisfy their anger. The main purpose of this case is to demonstrate that a coach can never know how his client will decide, because everyone defines the limits of his own integrity.

For those curious about the outcome: My last information about Tariq was that they are still happily married and their children are growing up in a healthy family atmosphere. Sabine regretted and to this date she says she regrets her wrongdoing. Maria did not think she had done anything wrong and continued to visit them for holidays; until one day, Tariq, with the consent of Sabine, asked Maria not to come back to their home. Tariq's wisdom that Maria's dishonesty was not the reason to reprimand Sabine was the saviour of their marriage.

As a side issue that also demonstrates the basic assumption that 'people define their own integrity' (See Sect. 8.2), even now, when we meet, he talks about his coaching and the events with a sense of lessons learnt. He claims that he learnt from the events that neither age nor relationship, not even the financial security provided by a national social system, stops people from creating their own interpretation of what is honest: people define their own integrity; if convenient, they will move the threshold to the level where they can legitimise their actions.

This example should not leave behind the impression that in a coaching context a coach would only encounter clients with such extreme dilemmas. It should not surprise a coach if a client comes up with such an experience. The basic assumptions of integrity help to identify what moves, what motivates the client, and makes the coach think that no solution provided by him may be the right one: the client defines his own integrity. As a further issue, if we wanted to validate the very first assumption, this case could also validate the assumption that 'people act in their own interest'. Tariq made his decision because he wanted to provide his children with a family environment comprising both parents.

3. People Live from Their Own Perception

This basic assumption manifests itself in clients' behaviour, although it is not as visible as the previous mentioned principles. I have a battery of real-life cases to cite under this principle. For the sake of parsimony, I have limited the narration to the case of Mark (See Sect. 3.2.3).

4. People Nurture Their Own Assumptions

First of all, we need to distinguish 'a person's own assumptions' from the 'basic assumptions of human nature'. While making assumptions about human nature we are assuming certain aspects of human nature confined to the context of coaching and those we should encounter with the majority of clients. 'Own assumptions', I may also call them 'personal assumptions' or 'individual assumptions', may arise out of personal experience, fears, hopes, pessimism, and optimism and there is a whole battery of other attributes that can influence a person's individual assumptions. A coach may encounter identical personal assumptions in two different clients; even then they would have different causes and each client would have their own different perceptions of their specific issues. For example, a client shows exasperation with his employer. One person may be disgruntled because of his assumption that he is very competent but not respected for it. Another person may say she is discriminated because of gender issues. Before I validate this assumption with a new case, let me take you back to Mark (See Sect. 3.2.3). Based on the abusive behaviour of his boss, Mark perceived that he was not wanted and was worthless to the company from his individual assumption; however, there was no proof: no one had ever said or done anything to give him a reason to assume that he was not wanted. That is the reason that a coach must look for this word 'own'. These assumptions are private and normally not accessible to others and that is why in a privileged area not even his wife knew about his concerns.

8.3.2 Case Study: 'Moritz'

Moritz was a 57-year-old finance manager. In his pre-coaching questionnaire, Moritz said he wanted to know how to motivate his team and instil his initiatives into them. These two areas are often clubbed together or confused by many in business as being one issue. Motivating others would mean that you do something externally that moves people to do something you have on your mind. A person's own initiative is intrinsic, otherwise it is not personal: you most probably cannot expect someone to generate their own initiative simply because you think that it is the solution. Many managers believe that both are interlinked. One attribute may lead to the other, but to reach that point, motivating people may be the wrong place to start.

Moritz told me that he had a team of 17 people and did not know what to do about his present situation. He had been working up to 7:00 p.m. every day for as long as he could recall and he did not want to do so anymore, but did not know how to change his working hours. In the office, he could not get a handle on how some people behaved and he was most dissatisfied with a few colleagues. His bosses sent him new assignments and they were always extremely urgent. How to master all of this?

According to Moritz, he really did not need to work anymore. He said, even if he retired the next day, there was no financial threat to him, as he owned a few houses and received a handsome earning from them. Although his concerns were all related to his work and his colleagues, in the very first meeting, he said that he would also be seeking a divorce from his wife. During the first two sessions, I found out that his wife had suffered from a serious medical condition some years before. He complained that when he left his home in the morning, she would promise to do some chores in the household, but when he got back, he found out that she had done nothing. He asked her why she had not done the chores they had agreed. She responded mostly that she either had fallen asleep or just did not want to work or that she forgot. He said there was a whole mountain of his clothes that needed to be ironed and he had been ironing and washing his stuff in the morning for the last few years. According to Moritz, it was making him mad.

Without going in to the details of every coaching session with Moritz, let me take you fast forward to the end of the coaching relationship. During the last session, Moritz told me that he and his four children were taking his wife on a holiday. When I asked where they were headed, he said the spots his wife loved the most before her medical conditions had worsened. I asked him why he was doing so. He said that he had realised during coaching that it was not she who was not willing to do the household chores. I found his words very moving. He said, 'The poor woman has been unfortunate to be in such a situation, it is not her fault. I have to live with it and I will see to it that she receives good care, I have the means to provide for her.'

This was also the first contradiction that had struck me in the very first few minutes of our meeting. He had the resources but was waiting for his wife to do the household chores. On the professional front, he asked me what I had done to him. I was curious and wanted to know what he meant. He said he left at 5:00 p.m. on the day when the financial reports had to be completed. He had never left on such a day before 10:00 p.m. and he had always been all by himself to complete the submission in time. This time his colleagues prepared a report and presented it to him a day before he presented it to his bosses. He asked me how is it possible that his bosses came down to see him every day before the reporting deadline to ask him if he needed any help? They were the same people he had known for years, but they had never asked him earlier if he had needed help. I asked him, 'What about your clothes?' He said he had found three external services and there was not a single piece of apparel left to be ironed or washed. He had found household help to relieve his wife of that burden. He said to me, 'It is a very tall order if you leave home in anger and stress every morning and think of motivating people in the office, it just does not work.'

His assumptions had been that his staff needed motivation and he did not know how to do that. His focus was on what he did not know, not on whether his assumptions were wrong. Further, he had assumed that his wife was not doing what she promised to do because she had turned lazy. All this while he had been confusing the source of his frustration.

After the coaching sessions were over I received feedback from Moritz's boss who reported to me that Moritz had asked him a question he could not answer. He had asked, 'Why did I not meet Mr. Kohli 29 years back, my life would have been half as difficult.' If this was the feedback from my client, I had reason to believe that working on his assumptions he was able to resolve his most pressing issues. This is evidence that people nurture their own assumption.

Moritz's case provides further evidence that there prevails a fallacy in coaching that the client will tell the coach his issues and the coach will discuss with him how to resolve them. One very important factor I have noticed in all the 5 years of coaching: in the pre-coaching questionnaire, most clients reported the consequences and not the source of their irritations. Lee D. Ross, a social psychologist at Stanford University, in an article titled, 'The Intuitive Psychologist and his Shortcomings: Distortions in the attribution process', in *Advances in Experimental Social Psychology* (1977, p. 183) has conceptualised and assimilated evidence about what he refers to as 'the fundamental attribution error', which he defines as 'the tendency for attributors to underestimate the impact of situational factors and to overestimate the role of dispositional factors in controlling behavior'. As Ross notes, Heider (1958) originally discussed this tendency as a cognitive error or bias. Importantly, however, he did not call it a fundamental error. Rather, Heider (1958, p. 96) qualified his position by suggesting that 'under certain conditions, there is a tendency to attribute the outcome of an action to the person, even though its source may reside in the environment'. Moritz was demonstrating exactly this attribution error: relating the cause of his irritations to the disposition of his wife and ignoring her medical situation. With due respect to all my clients this is not a criticism on them but a lesson for a coach. It is the capability of a coach to nudge the client to think about other attributes and possibilities, enhance his coping strategies and let him discover the solutions himself, but contribute to his discovery in a constructive manner. Only when that process has borne fruit has coaching been successful.

I would like to spend a few words on motivation because I have seen a very big misconception that prevails in the professional environment. People like Moritz believe that you can motivate people to work as you think they should. Humans have an ability to adapt to most situations. After living in any particular environment, it becomes the norm for a person to adapt to their new surroundings. Unless he can see some compression to trigger an urgent need for change, he can stay in that situation for years. People living in dire poverty adapt to it and consider it as the norm. I am in no way propagating that it is right for us to let people live in poverty. I am also not insinuating that nothing should henceforth be done against poverty. My focus is on our mental ability to accept our environment or the state of affairs and consider them as normal.

To me, motivation creates a spike similar to that which a person experiences when they are happy. Recall the words of Viktor Frankl from his book *Man's Search for Meaning* (2004, p. xx): 'For success, like happiness, cannot be pursued; it must ensue and it only does so as the intended side-effect of one's dedication to a cause greater than oneself.' If you spend your day in the normal range, which is defined by your experience, a spike could occupy a couple of minutes to a couple of hours. In some cases, certain events or thoughts can cause euphoria for a few days. The spike represents the point of motivation (Fig. 8.1).

Let us speculate how this state is achieved. Perhaps someone surprises you with a gift or says something good about you that you were not expecting: you feel happy. There is a spike in your emotions. This spike is manifest in a simple measurement: you feel more elated than you would for a part or the whole day, this makes you more willing to do more for others. Elation is a great feeling, no doubt; it can change your attitude toward the person who presented you with a gift or paid you a compliment. This internal, personal emotion was stimulated in you by an external factor. How long can that feeling be sustained by a normal person? Let us not include the special cases of those under the influence of psychotropic drugs. Let us for a moment imagine that the elated feeling could last for say 1 month. How would the person function in that state? We know it without relying on studies in social sciences: when you feel happy or elated you are likely to be more generous

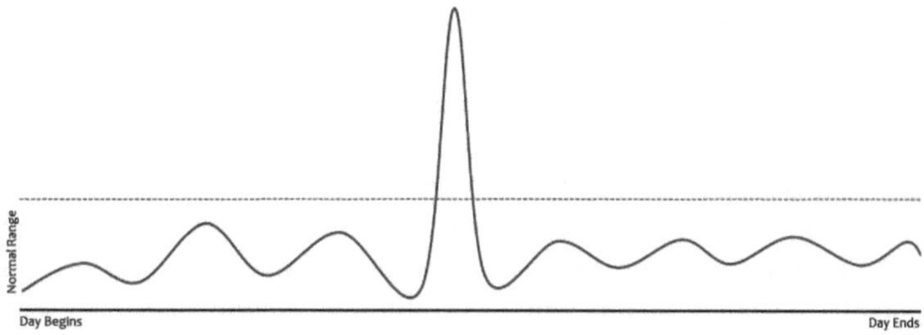

Fig. 8.1 Spike

than when you are not. If that was the case, you would not take care of your own interest at all and as a consequence of your exaggerated generosity, you may find that you have created a situation you cannot cope up with. Can such an emotion last for a long time? Can it be so prolonged that it can change you in a dramatic fashion so that your behaviour changes toward everyone, forever? I will leave you with your answer.

There is another problem with these kind of spikes. After you received a gift, a raise, a bonus, or any such appreciation, you are not only feeling acknowledged you also have reason to develop an expectation for the future. I cannot count how often I have heard that a bonus given to sales managers became a benchmark for the next year. If the bonus was lowered in the future, there was a bigger disappointment than the joy of receiving something additional and unexpected. This is one reason I am not a great follower of finding happiness or motivating people in a mechanical or synthetic sense: of providing short bursts of spikes. It is my observation that a spike is a temporary surge; it can be an emotion or a thought, a dramatic rise in attention, which is not likely to sustain itself so as to make a lasting difference in the behaviour of a person.

I believe in long-term motivation that is intrinsic; it has a lower probability of disappointment and is predictable for all concerned. In 1908 two psychologists, Robert M. Yerkes and John Dillingham Dodson, demonstrated the empirical relationship between arousal and performance. The Yerkes-Dodson Law demonstrates that performance improves to a peak from mental stimulation but only to a certain point; it then begins to regress. People quickly adapt to a new state. Anyone who has worked long enough in the corporate world must have faced a similar situation at some stage where someone says that to retain good people we need to pay them whatever they ask for: higher salaries or bonuses. If anyone has done that, then he must have also faced the situation that after some amount of increments no amount of money worked to improve the performance or loyalty to the company.

Is it then hopeless to consider motivation in the working environment? No, but there is a better and a sustainable method, which you have read in the case study of my colleagues in Hong Kong earlier (See Sect. 4.1). If we are only looking for higher performance, we need to consider that a certain amount of stress and nervousness contributes to heightened awareness and performance too.[4] If we look at studies on stress, a certain amount is necessary for us to perform at our best. Excess of both is damaging. Ideally, a person moves in a certain area, which she has discovered herself and calls it her own comfort zone (Fig. 5.1, the 'Mid Zone').

As a comparison, if I were to receive a great surprise, I may move beyond 15 and if I were humiliated, I may descend beyond −15. In normal circumstances my behaviour should be more like a pendulum between the fictive −15 and 15, depending on many factors, such as traffic jams, arguments with the kids or spouse; some people are weather sensitive and their moods fluctuate accordingly. What is it that one can possibly do to maintain employees beyond their own 15 for a stretch of time? I do not think it is possible in simplistic terms. It is possible that, if they are inspired and see a higher sense in something or understand why something should be done, they are more dedicated to their work while remaining in their −15 to 15 areas. That is, if they do not feel they are being treated badly. If the bosses are extravagant and talk about people being the most valuable assets, people do not believe them. If the bosses demonstrate through their actions that they care about the company and the people working there, it is contagious. That is when people will be motivated to work on their own initiative.

Imagine you were able to bring someone to the peak of the spike (Fig. 8.1) and also sustain him there. This is purely hypothetical; practically you would have to administer psychotropic drugs to sustain someone there for long periods. After a while, the person will see that state as normal and will have to look for new methods for a higher high to create a new spike from a previous spike. This is how adaptive drugs work on the human brain. A person consumes drugs to get a high; let us take consistent alcohol consumption as an example. The brain adapts to the quantity of alcohol consumed the last time. The amount that gave you a high in the beginning stops giving you a kick. You need more to get the same high.

My purpose as a coach, my concern, is at the micro level: most people living in their normal conditions become oblivious of the fact that there could be another way that would satisfy their own values system. That is where the coach comes in and no other profession comes to my mind that has helped people in large numbers. I also do not know of any people who are in good health and pursuing their profession who would get up and say, let me meet a psychologist, or any other professional for help.

5. People Predict Outcomes

If we accept that people nurture their own assumptions and that people live from their own perceptions, the logical consequence of this is that people predict outcomes based on their assumptions and perceptions. Predictions should not automatically be related to an astrologer or the horoscope you may read in your

[4]As suggested by the leading neuroscientist and researcher at Stanford University, Dr. Robert Sapolsky: see also, Professor Richard E. Boyatzis of Case Western Reserve University, USA, online course *Inspirational Leadership Through Emotional Intelligence*.

favourite magazine. If we have a meeting with someone, we begin to plan how to reach the venue. If the meeting is at a spot we are familiar with, we will predict how long it will take to get there. Based on our previous experience we have made an assumption that it will, for example, take 25 minutes. We know how the traffic at the hour of our departure is normally and we know the road conditions and the speed limits and so we make a prediction of how long it will take us to get there. If in our family, we are expecting a child to be born in the next 7 months, in anticipation we start making predictions of how it is going to be for us when the child is born. If we are building a home, we are willing to sign a hypothecation contract, predicting our financial status for the next 15, 20, or even 30 years. These examples demonstrate how we are predicting the outcome in different time frames, but we are making decisions of many kinds based on our expectations of the future. For the sake of simplicity, I would say predictions are assumptions that are based on expected future outcomes. As long as people are predicting probable outcomes, they are also manifesting hope. Some radical sceptics might call it speculation but I prefer predictions. The difference between speculation and prediction is that speculations are based on wishful thinking and not probable outcome whereas the latter has an element of hope. It is also the basic difference between gambling and investment. In gambling, you are wishing to get rich very fast. In investments, you are relying on various factors and expecting a probable outcome. Predictions also have another function: if they are manifesting hope, they have a motivational function and that will keep us moving toward our desired outcome. The motivation I am talking about here is not the spike I mentioned earlier in daily behaviour, as in the case of my client, Moritz (See Sect. 8.3.2).

It becomes problematic when people stop making probable predictions and begin making definite predictions.

I think we could see similar symptoms when we talk about disillusionment: when you have been disappointed continuously for a while, either in consequence of a person or as the results of some activity, you no longer entertain any illusions about the person or activity and no longer nurture expectations of predictable enjoyment from that person or activity. Similarly, in a coaching sense, it is my experience that people who have faced rejection in a sequence of events tend to stop predicting probable outcomes and begin to predict definite outcomes. It is very often evidence of frustration; they display a certain pointlessness in undertaking steps that they know they should actually be taking to change their situation: they get stuck with their situation. They also tend to lose sight of the source of their problems and attribute it, very often, to external factors. People who think they cannot control issues normally display a helplessness accompanied by phrases like 'I know it' and 'I can do nothing about it anymore.' This begins a process of retardation of all constructive activity. When that happens it is like a tsunami: it affects many areas. Strangely, when things are moving as they wish them to, they are convinced that they are in control of everything and things are going as they should because of their capabilities. In such situations, when they make a prediction of a probable outcome and it does not work out as they expected it to, they may be disappointed but not dejected. Some people can come out of this dejected state quickly and carry on as normal. I think that this could be one crucial factor that distinguishes the resilient person from others, although these claims are based on my own observations and I am convinced about them due to the evidence I have seen in my coaching practice and in the business world. In *A Theory of Personality: The Psychology of Personal Constructs* (1963, p. 12), George Kelly writes that man is like a naive scientist who creates his own constructs, 'through which he views the world of events. As a scientist, man seeks to predict, and thus control, the course of events'.

In the case below of Susanne, here is an example of a person denying herself better prospects in life because of linear thinking and who needed a nudge to get back on track by ending her practice of definite to probable predictions.

8.3.3 Case Study: 'Susanne'

Susanne was 40-years-old; an elegant young woman, who cared about what she wore and how she behaved in public. Although a self-confident person, she was unable to find an appropriate job. She had worked for years in the management of different world famous luxury brands. To explore some new opportunities, she had left her job in Germany and moved abroad for a while. When she returned to Germany she found it very difficult to get back into her previous profession and she began to lose a grip on her finances. When she contacted me for coaching, she was doing four small jobs to sustain herself and her children: cleaning staircases, gardening, distributing pamphlets at night, and working as a part-time help in a fashion boutique. I must say, she was a very determined person, because she did not have any money to pay a coach but came with a determined promise to repay.

During her coaching sessions, everything she told me sounded very logical to me. One thing I was unable to understand was what was holding her back from doing everything she claimed she knew and had experienced. After a couple of meetings, she brought an advertisement that offered an opportunity of employment, which she thought would be appropriate for her profile. However, she refused to apply for that position. I asked her what was holding her back. She said she knew that she would get a rejection letter. How did she know that? Why was she making predictions about definite outcomes of her actions? I was curious to know how she could predict what would happen if she applied for the position. 'Oh, I know it from experience; it always happens like that,' she said. Here was an element of experience of disappointments in the past. She continued: 'I will call the company and they will not want to meet me or give me an appointment that is 3 months away. If they meet me, they will offer me a salary that is far below my expectation.' The list of reasons, or better still, definite outcomes, and her conviction was very elaborate. For some time, she refused to undertake anything.

A coach who believes in goal setting as a tool for coaching would have failed miserably with Susanne. How do I know it? I discovered that methodical coaching is much more effective than goal setting. Besides, if I am setting a goal I am practically prepared to accept the problem of my client as she reports it to be. What if the source of the problem identified or believed by the client was completely wrong?

Susanne did not want to agree to dates by which she would have completed any task. It was not possible to challenge her to complete her tasks. She left the coaching meeting with a promise that she would, despite all her pessimism, apply for the job. In the subsequent meeting, she said that she could not write too well. Slowly, in the true sense of coaching, I was able to nudge her to start the process and get her to apply for the job. To her surprise, bewilderment would be more appropriate, she received a call from the potential employer to see her within the next 2 days. She watched her distorted assumptions and predictions of definite outcomes falling apart and I could see a person beginning to rejoice in the small successes. Before her meeting she had another elaborate list of issues that she predicted would all go wrong: she was predicting the outcome once again.

After another meeting with me, she went to meet her potential employer and received an offer that was very close to her expectations. She signed a contract to begin her work. She was back in her world of luxury brands again.

Six months later she came back to me with a problem that most people looking for a job would love to have. She had received an offer from a headhunter who said that she would be an ideal candidate for Christian Dior. I asked why she needed to spend money to see a coach if things were going the way she had always wanted. She said through coaching she was able to regain her self-confidence. She said, through coaching she received reassurances without which she would struggle with her own doubts all alone: she needed someone to talk to. 'Why don't you talk to your friends?' I asked. 'I do', she said, 'if I keep getting the answer, you will make it, do not worry you are smart. I begin to get new doubts, perhaps it is bothering them to spend most of their time on my problems.' She added, 'despite all the talk I still do not get any further with my doubts.' She said she had struggled with these issues so long on her own, she was happy to see me to talk about her doubts and go away from the coaching meeting free of doubts. As a coach it was a very happy moment for me because it had hardly been a few months since she had first come to talk to me and was already there where she always had wished to be. After a couple of days, she called me and said she had realised that she was denying herself exactly what she wanted to achieve. She was immersed in a new habit of predicting outcomes without any concrete basis for them. After another session, she was back where she had wanted to be; working with a world class fashion luxury brand. I have reduced the narrative to her job in this case. Due to her financial situation she had also neglected other areas in her life. She had tolerated a relationship which, according to her, was not what she had wanted. Subsequent to coaching, she told me that she had also been able to improve the state of her romatic relationship. As I said earlier, changes take place in many dimension due to effective coaching.

More than a year after the coaching sessions, she came with a wonderful gift for me and I took the opportunity to ask her if she knew why she had started to predict negative outcomes for herself. I wanted to know whether she was a pessimistic person or whether it was a temporary phase which I had the privilege to experience.

Her explanation showed me that when people continue to get negative responses for particular events in their life they begin to predict definite outcomes. It is not about whether their predictions are right or wrong; it is about disenchantment: loss of hope and belief in life-sustaining necessity. This is a very stark difference between a resilient person and one who is not. A resilient person will continue to predict probable outcomes and will sustain hope for improvement. This is what will impact the significant change in her life. In the context of coaching, if a coach is able to observe and identify that a client is predicting definite outcomes and the person is not old, still in her active working age, then the person may need to be nudged back to making probable outcomes that will get her back to looking at her life and the events therein as worthwhile pursuing. Though this case may give an impression that it is effective only in cases of unemployed people, that is not true. I have seen similar behaviour with people who were unfortunate in their relationships or with financial issues or even in their work.

At the same time, it is necessary for the coach to distinguish whether a client is suffering from depression. In such a case, it is imperative to guide the person to a medical expert and abort coaching, regardless of any financial losses, in the interest of the well-being of the client. That is why this basic assumption of human nature is extremely important within the context of coaching. Some readers might argue that people with an adamant mindset or propositional knowledge also tend to predict definite outcomes. That may be so, but I would like to remind my readers that this is a discussion limited to the scope of coaching and not one to validate any psychological subject in detail.

After discussing the basic assumption above it is time to enhance the definition of success in the context of coaching:

If a coach is able move the client from predicting definite outcomes to probable ones, then both the client and the coach have succeeded in coaching.

6. People Seek to Understand

As a 16-year-old, Christian started working in a coalmine, but he wanted to do more than sheer manual labour. After work, he attended an evening school; subsequently, his career took a new turn. According to Christian, his diligent efforts took him to great heights and made him the person he was when he met me: a benevolent and a generous human being; a high performing manager and a much respected expert in his business. The following case study is a good example that shows how people seek to understand.

8.3.4 Case Study: 'Christian'

You have met Christian before in the case of Mark (See Sect. 3.2.3). As a matter of fact, after being coached by me a couple of years earlier, it was Christian who had asked Mark to seek coaching. Besides being the co-CEO of the same company, Christian carried a much larger responsibility of being the CEO of a multinational company. He was one of the first ones to say how he was happy to see that as a coach I did not come with a stencil 'F' for him to pass through as a measure of being a successful manager.

It is in the nature of hard-working people that they are singularly focused, extremely dedicated, and disciplined. While these are all inspiring attributes, they can sometimes have a serious downside to them. They often lead the owners of these habits into a downward spiral. The person starts by working hard and wanting to achieve the next higher level in their profession: studies, game, or the chosen pursuit. If this focused practice continues over an extended period of time, let us take a hypothetical time frame of 3 years and more, slowly they are likely to disconnect from other social activities, one after the other. This steady disconnect continues to move them down the spiral until they are standing alone. Standing alone can also be part of the experience of being at the top. It is not a new idea that top executives can feel isolated and exposed to excessive stress. Over the years I have observed many colleagues and business friends who have suffered from excessive stress. Imagine the peculiarity of the bottom of the spiral. The person does not even question or wonder what happened. The worst part comes when a person begins to consider the state of affairs at the bottom of the spiral as a normal way of life. Here, they probably do not even ask how to come out of it.

You may recall that I referred to the adaptive ability of human beings in the case of Moritz (See Sect. 8.3.2). Going back to Christian, he met with me because one of his women colleagues noticed that he had been increasingly isolating himself over a number of years and, in her opinion, he was spending too much time in the office. I am once again going to disappoint the followers of the sect called 'Work-Life-Balance Coaching'. To balance something with another thing it is necessary that they have to be two different entities. I do not accept the idea that work is outside of my life. Work is not an outside threat or an event outside of my life. I will address this topic in detail later in the book, in relation to 'Work-Life Balance Coaching' (See Sect. 9.6) but for now let us focus on Christian.

When I first met Christian, he narrated his very inspiring rise from a simple manual labourer to an international manager. He said he wished to get married and have children and create a family. I asked him what was stopping him from doing what he wanted. He had all the resources and the financial stability to sustain and nurture a family. In my opinion, he was good looking: an eligible bachelor. He disclosed he had a friend of the same age who was living 550 km away. During the conversation, he admitted that the probability of having a child with a 42-year-old woman, living so far away, was very low. I asked whether he was with his friend for a utilitarian reason: to have a child. Apologetically, he explained that it was not so and went on to explain that he had not been paying any attention to what he was doing in the social areas of his life, except to play regular sports. He found it absurd to have a distant relationship where he met his friend once every 3 weeks. He thought it was wrong because it was also not fair on his friend.

Being a very conscientious person, Christian started discussing ways of not hurting his friend and ending their relationship. I wanted to know why he had decided to end the relationship. He said he was not being fair to her. He felt she could perhaps get to know someone in her own town and lead a normal life, instead of meeting a romantic partner every 21 days. He showed a lot of care and sensitivity toward her feelings and told me that he was going to be honest with her. He was not going to wait and get to know some else and then end the relationship. He was going to do this because he felt it was wrong on his part and it was not coherent with his values.

As soon as people understand that what they are doing is not in line with their personal values, one of two reactions may emerge: conscientious people will make amends and ensure that others are not harmed because of their actions; others, like Maria, as cited earlier (See Sect. 8.3.1), will move the threshold of their integrity to legitimise their actions. They are insensitive to the feelings of others: whether they harm others or not, their own interest is served.[5]

7. People Trust Their Own Decisions

Irrespective how much advice or evidence of proven facts you provide to a person, as I have discussed in earlier cases in Hong Kong or in Italy (See Chap. 4), a client will do what she thinks is right, that is why, as explained earlier, coaching works on insights and does not rely on explanations. That is not a description of a stubborn person or a narcissistic personality. This can be observed in the behaviour of humans right from the beginning: as soon as small children can express themselves, they will express their own will. This will take the form of a decision as soon as the caregiver accepts their will as their decision.

My wife and I have raised two children and irrespective how incredulous it may appear to the readers we did not face the famous ‘adolescence blues’ with our kids. There is no denying that children get more aggressive during that phase of their life. They do not do it because they have morphed from Jekyll to Hyde. It is their biology, hormones, and their growth process. If we, as parents, are capable of facilitating our children to see that the decisions they are making in this phase are their own, or at least make sense to them, the intensity and the duration of aggressive outbursts are predictable: very short and easy to accommodate. They need help in this stage, not disciplinary measures from their parents: they need effective coaching.

Let me take you to a professional environment: have you ever considered the reason why many employees of any company feel stressed? It could be owing to the absence of their decisions or their convictions. Irrespective of how well they are trained or paid many employees complain about being stressed. Most of the time, employees are performing work duties that someone else decides that they will do. On the other hand, it is in the nature of organisational structures that someone has to decide what the employees need to do. That is the reason why we have

[5] I am aware that this explanation of the latter comes very close to the definition of a sociopath but that is an area reserved for the psychologists and not for a coach.

dedicated people responsible for certain areas and have created hierarchical structures. It would create an unmanageable chaos in a company, if not anarchy, if everyone was to decide what he or she wanted to do.

In the midst of this tension between personal decisions and acceptance of authority lies the secret of leading people: effective leadership. This needs flexibility in action, conversation, and thinking. This is where most of the concepts and services that offer fixed sets of steps and a linear approach to people, such as time management, change management, Work-Life Balance, goal setting, and other external 'heal all' methods fail to provide effective thoughts and ideas for self-development in leadership. As demonstrated through the case studies, coaching provides effective solutions to personal development.

8. People have Answers

This is a basic assumption about human nature that you can notice at every step in coaching. Irrespective of your occupation, whether a CEO or a school-going youngster, everybody has an answer to whatever is going on in their life. In the coaching world, it is extremely damaging if a coach has an answer. This is probably one of those difficult skills that a coach needs to master: a coach does not have answers.

Some clients have answers, while other clients who do not have answers can give legitimate reasons for the absence of answers. This is not being sarcastic about my valuable clients. It is a fact I see in my daily practice. The efficacy of coaching is measured in stimulating critical self-reflection. This has one crucial reason: it encourages the client to question her questions and subsequently to find her own solutions. If you go back and see all the basic assumptions about human nature, you will notice that they all converge to this point:

People act in their own interest because they have an answer to how to act in their own interest; they define their integrity because that is their answer about how they wish to shape their self and their life. They live from their own perception: that is the answer to how they interpret how things are. They nurture their assumptions because they want answers and they make their own assumptions. The prediction of outcomes is an exercise solely aimed at giving an answer—whether the outcome is definite or probable.

An answer may not always be black and white; it may sometimes be the simple understanding of facts, or better still, a closure, a way of making peace with one's situation. It all serves the purpose of being a response and an answer to enable the client to move on in life.

8.3.5 Case Study: 'Angela'

I first met Angela at hypnotherapy classes in 2012. Angela was 34-years-old and worked at the world famous Automotive Company in Munich. During the course of hypnosis, she asked me if I would coach her. She had just separated from her partner after a 12-year relationship. She said that the person had been abusive. She was now looking, very carefully, almost apprehensively, for a new romantic relationship. During the course of coaching, she got to know a young man and was thrilled at the prospect of not living a single life. After a couple of weeks, she went on a holiday to Switzerland with her new friend and returned extremely perturbed and wanted to see me immediately to talk about her experience. This is what she told me:

On the way to Switzerland he asked me if I could lend him some money to fill up with gas as he had forgotten his wallet at home. We reached the small village in the Swiss Alps that my friend had chosen and started looking for a hotel. I asked him why he had not booked it in advance: he had told me he would. When we returned to Germany he asked me to add up all the costs and offered to pay half of all the expenses. I was disappointed because it was his idea of going on a short holiday and I considered it as an invitation.

She complained: 'I seem to attract only this kind of man: grown up men who behave like students.' I asked her what she wanted. She wanted to have a romantic partner who was stable in his profession and could afford to go on holidays or undertake other activities without having to draw on her resources. She wanted to go to the Maldives; she also wanted have a family. I asked her what her plans were with her present friend. She said nothing, and indicated that she would accept things the way they were.

Angela was not predicting any probable outcomes. She went on to say that he is loving in some ways. I asked her what she meant by that. She said, 'When I go to see him at his home he is very loving with his dog.'

You will notice she has all the answers and if there is any dissonance between what she wants and what she has, there is an answer for that too: she finds legitimisation for her reasoning. I have formulated a proverb for myself that reminds me that I need to look for a better method whenever I see myself resorting to legitimisations: 'legitimisations are crutches that falsehood needs to walk'.

This is not uncommon. People sustain such relationships for years. It is not only in romantic relationships. I have encountered numerous people who will stay in a job they want to leave. It is a dichotomous situation: they say, 'I want to leave' but they hold on to it. This kind of situation gets people into very sticky situations where their answers legitimise their actions. I did not tell her what I thought of her answer or situation, but I can share it with you here. She deduced that if her friend loved his dog he was a loving man. I recall when I was a student in New Delhi, India, a friend once gave me an example of ambiguity of logic, or fallacy of equivocation, that still makes our kids laugh: 'Love is God, love is blind, therefore God is blind'. If you ignore your dog for a couple of hours or, I hope you do not do it, kick him in anger, the dog will come back wagging his tail and lick you all over the moment you call him again. A dog is a faithful animal and not resentful to his masters. A human reaction cannot be compared with that of a dog. John Gottman is an authority on relationships by virtue of his long clinical trials and research into relationships and married couples. I read his studies a few years ago in which he claims that a human does not forgive abusive or negative treatment so easily. Gottman says it takes five good deeds to balance one bad. In his book, (2011, p. 21) *The Science of Trust: Emotional Attunement for Couples*, Gottman notes, 'in our own research we found that all three styles. . .[.] were actually functional (stable and happy) if the positive to negative during conflict was greater than or equal to 5:1.' A dog is a very gracious animal when compared to humans in this sense. He forgives abusive behaviour instantly. The point I want to make is that people have answers but their answers may be addressing the wrong source of their trouble, or they may be indulging in an ambiguity of logic. The more encouraging part of the client's problem, and the one a coach should have his focus on, is the part that people have the ability to find answers and also the right solution for themselves. A coach's main focus should be to stimulate critical self-reflection in his client and not influence it with his own answer. Can this be done? Here is the evidence that is self-explanatory.

Angela separated from her friend on her own accord and lived with her apprehensions and doubts whether she would have to live alone for the rest of her life. This is the part where people begin to think in a linear fashion and interpret a long time gap in very short intervals. Angela defined a prediction for her whole life based on one event. A couple of weeks passed and soon after that she got to know another person.

Six months later she sent me an email: 'I am going to the Maldives.' Ten months later she sent me a note: 'I am pregnant.' Fifteen months later she sent me a note: 'We are getting married.' She had found all the answers.

A coach should trust the capabilities of his clients. If a coach thinks he has the answers, I have very serious doubts if his coaching is effective. I am certain that is not coaching. A coach can only facilitate introspection, critical self-reflection, and strengthen the client's efforts to find her own solution, one with which she is happy. The biggest moment for a coach should be to relish the success of a client. If a coach is basking in personal glory, he should change his profession because that is not the right attitude to coaching.

References

Gottman, J. (2011). *The science of trust: Emotional attunement for couples*. New York: W.W. Norton.

Kelly, G. A. (1963). *A theory of personality: The psychology of personal constructs*. New York: W.W. Norton.

Leonard, T. J. (2005). *The Coach U personal and corporate coach training handbook*. New Jersey: Wiley.

Ross, L. (1977). The intuitive psychologist and his shortcomings: Distortions in the attribution process. In L. Berkowitz (Ed.), *Advances in experimental social psychology* (Vol. 10, pp. 173–240). Orlando, FL: Academic.

Sapolsky, R. M. (2004). *Why zebras don't get ulcers*. New York: St. Martin's Griffin.

Wilson, T. D. (2002). *Strangers to ourselves: Discovering the adaptive unconscious*. Cambridge, MA: The Belknap Press.

Online Sources

Ariely, D. (2014). *A beginner's guide to irrational behaviour*. Week 3, Lecture on Dishonesty. Coursera. https://www.class-central.com/mooc/424/coursera-a-beginner-s-guide-to-irrational-behavior. Accessed 14 Mar 2014.

Boyatzis, R. *Inspiring leadership through emotional leadership*. Online course materials. www.coursera.org. Accessed 25 June 2013.

Byrne, J. A., & Gerdes, L. (2005). *The man who invented management*. http://www.bloomberg.com/news/articles/2005-11-27/the-man-who-invented-management. Accessed 10 Oct 2012.

Loebbert, M. http://www.fhnw.ch/personen/michael-loebbert/publikationen. Accessed 2 Nov 2015. http://www.fhnw.ch/personen/michael-loebbert/profil. Accessed 15 Mar 2016.

Loebbert, M. (2015). *Real help or humbug. The sense and senselessness of coaching*. Radio Broadcast, SWR. Broadcast at 4 Minutes 40 seconds. http://www.swr.de/swr2/programm/sendungen/wissen/hilfe-oder-humbug-sinn-und-unsinn-descoachings/-/id=660374/did=16437268/nid=660374/1h9sg7/index.html. Accessed 6 Nov 2015.

The Drucker Institute. *Peter Drucker's life and legacy*. http://www.druckerinstitute.com/peter-druckers-life-and-legacy/. Accessed 12 Oct 2012.

The Gottman Institute. https://www.gottman.com/about/john-julie-gottman/. Accessed 3 Mar 2014.

Short Survey of Coach Training and Coaching Companies

9

The following short survey examines different coaching courses and coaching that are currently marketed as coaching. The research was often conducted as a 'participant observer'.[1] I was careful with this approach, as I was aware that I could easily slip into the role of an intrusive or critical observer and become a nuisance to others on the courses, or worse, take upon myself the role of obtrusive judge, trying to find faults to prove that they were all wrong. If they were all wrong, I would prove I was right. I decided, in all fairness, that if I found something that was really disruptive and something that was worth learning for coaching, I would adapt my practice accordingly. If that was not the case, I would come away with an objective explanation of why their courses were not coaching.

The question I wanted to address was, how would you distinguish or decide which coaching course offered under the name of coaching is also really coaching. In order to research the different kinds of coaching methods available, I conducted a survey, as if I were a potential student coach. I also contacted coaches and invited them to be my coach mentor. When approaching other coaches, I declared very clearly that I was a coach. Out of the 17 coaches I approached, five refused outright. I rejected six of them on the basis of my own criteria. Two never responded despite a promise to call back after their holidays. In the end, I worked with five coach-mentors. From the long list of various coaching providers, I abbreviated it by sifting out the most frequent results a coaching student may encounter on a search.[2]

- Hypnosis Coaching
- NLP Coaching
- Systemic Coaching
- Work-Life Balance Coaching
- Energy Coaching

[1]This expression has its origins in anthropology. It was coined by Bronislaw Malinowski.

[2]The search was conducted during September 2011.

A. Kohli, *Effective Coaching, and the Fallacy of Sustainable Change*, Management for Professionals, DOI 10.1007/978-3-319-39735-1_9

I began by investigating a few courses being offered by some of the schools in Munich. To get a good understanding of various coaching courses I decided to get a full immersion as a 'participant observer': be a part of them and do as they do; by learning as they do, I learnt what they know.

9.1 Hypnosis Coaching

From the 18 different schools in Munich and the surrounding areas, I enrolled on a course at the Hypnosis Zentrum; a school with a good reputation for teaching Hypnosis Coaching. The course was split into three phases or levels and taught over 6 months: it was a serious course because many people recommended it. During the course, my contributions were thoughtful and non-intrusive. Evidence that I behaved and was treated as a genuine student is that Rainer Schnell, the school's owner, offered to forego the payment for the last phase of the course: he gifted it to me. I asked him why he had gifted me an expensive course. He said my contributions were an enrichment for his course; he had learnt something new from me and he and his wife, Daniela, decided to gift me the last level. I was able to develop a cordial relationship with both of them during the course. I took the liberty of asking Rainer Schnell what kind of coaching he provided through hypnosis. He told me very honestly that it was a fad he had followed and a co-therapist offered, but he was soon going to discontinue with it. I noticed soon after I left the school that he had removed the word 'coaching' from the list of services in which he provides training.

Hypnosis is often tagged as entertainment. As children we are awestruck by how people fall into a trance. In fact, hypnosis is a serious and a reliable therapeutic method, often used in a clinical environment. The psychiatrist named Milton Hyland Erickson developed new ways of therapeutic hypnosis. In the clinical environment it is a very effective method to help people overcome pain, fear, and many other aspects which they cannot overcome themselves. As it is with most things, the moment you learn something you are likely to hear within the circle of your family and friends that such and such person underwent hypnotherapy and stopped smoking with its help. I have a high regard for this therapy as it helps people in a very effective manner. It has nothing to do with coaching, though.

After receiving my certificate of completion in training as a 'Hypnotherapist', I wanted to distinguish hypnotherapy from coaching, but in a manner that did not undermine the former in any subjective opinions. I started my comparison between coaching and hypnotherapy by examining the basic assumptions of human nature and also the observable manifest behaviour in both disciplines to see where they have commonalities. The basic assumption of human nature, according to the hypnotherapeutic method, is that you are unable to make certain changes in your life, such as stopping smoking or overcoming fear, and hypnotherapy helps by putting you in a trance and giving you constructive suggestions, while in a trance. When you come out of the hypnotic state, you will have little difficulty in changing the desired habits. Rainer Schnell told me that his success rate was about 80 %. I will not discuss hypnotherapy in a clinical setting. The intervention of hypnotherapy is external: the method assumes that in human nature a person is unable to resolve her issues without external help. This is the first contradiction to the basic assumptions of human nature that coaching adopts. In coaching, taking the basic assumption of human nature described above, it is accepted that the client will decide the time and method of how he wants to improve, change, or mend the part of his life he considers needs to be mended. The focus in hypnotherapy is on intervention: in coaching, the focus is on leading the client to insight and self-reflection. In coaching there is complete faith in the capacity of the client to resolve her issues; in hypnotherapy, the probability of effectiveness of the induced hypnosis is the premise of the therapy.

I learnt some vital lessons through hypnotherapy training. One is that people are easily influenced by suggestions. Such a concept is of serious concern in coaching, because clients could be susceptible; the coaching session could be manipulative, if hypnotherapy was performed on clients by unethical coaches. I do not use hypnotherapy, as my main concern is with coaching. Based on these observations it would be safe to claim that hypnotherapy has nothing in common with coaching. It would also be safe to assume that if anyone is using these two expressions in conjunction then he is either unaware of the meaning of either or both of them together.

Hypnotherapy is a therapy: a treatment intended to relieve or heal a disorder. In contrast, a coaching client does not, by default, seek therapy, healing, or treatment. There are many other aspects that clearly separate the paths of hypnotherapy and coaching. It would be unproductive to go into the fine details, because the case has been made that distinguishes coaching from hypnotherapy. There is no visible overlap. There is no reason to label hypnotherapy as 'coaching'.

During the course at Hypnosis Zentrum, I took the opportunity to discuss with at least seven participants what their views of coaching were, and how they would implement hypnotherapy in coaching. Two were practising coaches; one had changed his profession from a sales manager to coaching, because he thought he could share his business experiences (he also thought the work of a coach would not be as strenuous as that of a sales manager). This person disclosed that coaching alone was not a lucrative business for him. He did not know how to recruit new customers easily and thought perhaps enhancing his service with hypnosis would expand his client base. Eleven months after this discussion I received an email from him telling me he had abandoned coaching and returned to the corporate world. I learnt later that 85 % of coaches abandon their practice within the first 10 months of starting up. One person was a spiritual consultant and had wanted to add something new to her services. The other four were not certain what they would do with it and had begun to learn hypnotherapy to start something new on their own. The other of the seven people questioned, who was also a coach, told me he was already practising another form of coaching called 'Hypnosystemic Coaching', in German it is called 'Hypnosytemische Coaching'. He had praised it a lot and told me where to buy the course, which was available on CDs. I studied this course and found it a very good course on hypnosis, therefore I did not analyse it further.

9.2 NLP Coaching

With the relief of discovering that a form of hypnosis coaching being offered had nothing to do with coaching, I moved on with a renewed confidence to explore other courses. The effect of new confidence was that I was willing to spend 6 months and more to go into deeper detail: read books and research, as I did for hypnotherapy; however, if I found the evidence I was looking for early, I aborted the course. The focus of the study was solely to compare courses offering coaching, but it had to be conducted in a way that was both cost and time effective.

NLP is an abbreviation of 'Neurolinguistic Programming'. NLP is 'a system of alternative therapy intended to educate people in self-awareness and effective communication, and to model and change their patterns of mental and emotional behaviour' (*OED*).[3] J. O'Conner & J. Seymour in their book, *Introducing NLP Psychological Skills for Understanding and Influencing People* (2002, p. 2) explain how 'Richard Bandler and John Grinder created NLP in the 1970s in the USA.' The inclusion of hypnotherapy in the methodology is reason enough for me to consider whether it is a method of coaching, but let us look for other attributes before drawing a conclusion. I recall that many people in sales and also human resources were claiming to have found the Holy Grail with NLP in the 1980s and 1990s. I was curious even then to find out more about it, but now it was relevant to my study, because it was now also called 'NLP Coaching'. From the 12 results that showed up in my search, after some discussions with other coaches, I narrowed my choice to the mindSYSTEMS: Institut für strategische Kommunikation (mindSystems: Institue for strategic communication), in Munich. I began my training with the plan to complete the full course up to the level of Master-Coach (INLPTA, DVNLP).

NLP methodology claims to help people alter their habits, overcome fear, phobias, programmes, scripts, patterns. It is claimed that an NLP Master can re-imprint impressions in the brain of the client and help them overcome traumatic or undesired experiences from their memories. All these and other techniques leave an impression with the participants that they could be in possession of certain skills that could influence the client to do what the NLP practitioner thinks is the right course of action to take. Many participants on the course were human resources managers. They were of the opinion that NLP could offer them solutions to personnel problems. Even after the course had ended, I noticed that NLP seemed to attract many people as practitioners who interacted with personnel. On the one hand, it was fascinating to watch how, through certain techniques, my actions could influence the behaviour of my counterpart without him noticing how I am influencing him. On the other hand, it gave me the impression that I was imposing my intentions on someone without him knowing that I was indulging in such an exercise. I had previously encountered many conversational techniques in

[3]Richard Brander compiled the *OED* entry defining NLP.

coaching: re-framing, paraphrasing, mirroring, and a few others. These techniques are also used in counselling conversations.

Besides these conversational techniques and hypnosis, in NLP I was taught that imitating physical movements of the client can also influence their behaviour. For example, when a person crossed his legs and I did that too, if he put a hand under his chin and I did that too. It created a kind of synchronisation effect, which NLP claims can create sympathy for practitioner and client. In my experience, over time, it was extremely arduous to try to imitate the client. It was also a mechanical method. I felt I was running a risk of irritating the client if he noticed that all I was doing was imitating him. I am a staunch believer in the autonomy of my clients. I don't believe that anyone should be put under the mercy of some mechanical techniques to influence their psychological faculties in order to do things that I may consider good for them.

NLP includes concepts they have adapted from educational psychology. According to NLP, people are divided into three different kinds of learners: kinaesthetic, visual, or auditory. I find it problematic to categorise people into learning types. I have concluded that there is one type of learner: the human type. We learn when we see meaning or necessity or when something seems to mirror our values. This is, as discussed earlier (See Sect. 8.2), important within the context of coaching. At the beginning of 2015, I heard a TEDyouth talk, titled 'Ten Myths About Psychology, Debunked', by Dr. Ben Ambridge, a psychologist and a senior lecturer in psychology at the University of Liverpool. He is also the author of a few books: *Psy-Q: A Mind-Bending Miscellany of Everyday Psychology* (2015), *Child Language Acquisition: Contrasting Theoretical Approaches* (2011) and numerous research papers he has written on language and development. Ambridge had some interesting things to say, which confirmed my ideas of learning types. In his TEDyouth talk (2015) he said:

> It means that you're a kinaesthetic learner that you learn best when you get stuck in and do things with your hands. [. . .] the whole thing is a complete myth. Learning styles are made up and are not supported by scientific evidence . . . [.]. Could you learn to drive a car, for example, just by listening to someone telling you what to do with no kinaesthetic experience? Could you solve simultaneous equations by talking them through in your head and without writing them down? Could you revise for your architecture exams using interpretive dance if you're a kinaesthetic learner? No. What you need to do is match the material to be learned to the presentation format, not you.

I was able to find out very quickly that NLP was not what I would be willing to practice as a coach.

NLP is also combined with more than coaching. In J. Sutton and W. Stewart (2009), *Learning to Counsel*, it is classified as 'counselling' and offering 'Work-Life Balance with NLP' (pp. 6–7). According to these limited findings, NLP is a set of techniques; it is Neurolinguistic Programming; it is coaching; it is counselling; it is work-life balance coaching.

During the NLP course, I took the opportunity to talk to five other students during the lunch breaks to find out what they expected from learning NLP. Three were personnel managers and their expectation was very clear: they wanted to be in a superior position to better handle the issues of their personnel. They wanted to know if they could decipher the new applicants more effectively through NLP. The other two students, a married couple, were entrepreneurs and claimed that they thought they could coach their employees better using NLP. In all my discussions with the five students I got the sense that they wanted to learn something secretive or with the power to influence others. Coaching does not nourish any such misconceptions and that alone is a very important reason to ask whether NLP is coaching. The basic assumptions about human nature in the context of coaching and NLP differ as they did with hypnosis. That is why I aborted my course on NLP after two courses.

9.3 Coaching Mentors

I mentioned in the introduction to this section that I had engaged five coaches as mentors. My agreement with them was that we would meet for two sessions within 45 days. I was not surprised to see that in coaching they all used techniques such as re-framing, paraphrasing, mirroring, and acknowledging. None of them got beyond these methods. It was unfair on my part, because I knew these techniques. With two mentor-coaches, I also took the liberty of asking if they were only repeating what I was saying. They were immediately embarrassed and apologetic. Three asked me what I wanted. After I told them I wanted to know how to set up my coaching practice in Munich, they jumped straight to goal setting with a timetable and insisted that some points had been agreed with me. That is all there was to coaching and mentoring. I think there is a very big misconception that prevails in coaching even with practising coaches. These coach-mentors did not use methods to stimulate insights. I asked myself, what if the goals I express are out of necessity to say something that sounds great because I do not want to appear to be inconsequential? What if all I said I wanted to achieve were only dreams? What if I realised that the goal I achieved was not what I really wanted but only what I interpreted as my goal? All in all, I was not very impressed at the coaching I received because it was too shallow. Most of the coach-mentors used straightforward sentences and quotes from Steve Jobs and other famous people that made very little sense to someone trying to establish a coaching practice. I did not know how to use them in my life. There was one coach who had a few sentences straight from Tony Robbins too. I asked this coach, 'Ok I will take 100 % responsibility for what is happening to me, where do I go from here?' He had no answer. Next, he said wanted me to find the purpose of my life. I said, I do not need to find it; I want to give my coaching practice a meaning: that is the purpose of my efforts and research into coaching. Coaching cannot be full of clichés, quotations, and sentences from other people. Its primary aim should be to stimulate self-reflection and then insight so that the client feels that he has gained something of value from the process.

9.4 Systemic Coaching

Systemic Coaching and the service offered under the banner of coaching was introduced to me by a trainer in Wolfsburg, the home of Volkswagen. Systemic Coaching is known as a family therapy, based on the methods of Virginia Satir. Her method was successful in the resolution of family issues, and she became a role model for many for years. The coaching offered as Systemic Coaching was from the family setting, but converted to a business environment. As far as I know, that was not the original idea that Virginia Satir had in her mind. I will not name the school I visited because my comments may discredit them and that is not my intention. On 'The Virginia Satir Global Network' I could not find any coaching courses. Even though I searched for the word coaching, I found that the purpose of her work is clearly described in their statement:

> Purpose: to provide a broad educational context including classes, workshops and seminars in which persons may experience and learn in depth the Virginia Satir systemic growth model in order to understand, develop and use the Satir Model in their personal and professional lives. [...] The Satir Transformational Systemic Therapy (STST) training programs (Levels I, II and III) are for practicing counsellors, therapists, psychologists, psychiatrists, family physicians, nurses, clergy, instructors of family studies and family therapy, child care workers and graduate students in the above fields who are presently working with clients. The focus of the programs is on facilitating transformational change through Virginia Satir's Growth Model. The approach is applicable to working with individuals, couples and families.

This is how Virginia Satir was known and still admired for her pioneering work for families and children. I wonder if the introduction of family resolution therapy to the business world as coaching is particular to Germany? As if there was no difference between therapy and coaching or between emotion-laden family issues, where sometimes people received very effective therapy in cases of child abuse or other traumatic experiences, and repackage it as coaching in a business environment. I aborted this venture as irrelevant after the first day of school.

Going back to my method of comparing the basic assumptions of human behaviour, this method assumes the need for diagnosis and therapy (See Sect. 8.2). A person is unable to get over his traumatic experiences and conflicts through his own efforts. The person with whom I may have conflicts is made present in representation so that I can tell that person what I experienced and how I felt.

You may have by now noticed that many methods that call themselves coaching tend to gravitate either to hypnosis according to the Ericksonian thesis, or family therapy, according to the methods of Virginia Satir.

A woman friend's father died and while she was grieving, she encountered aggressive discussions with her mother. She wanted to know why her mother couldn't leave her in peace at such a difficult period of sorrow. Another of her friends is a Systemic Coach (also 'Familien Aufstelleung' or 'Family Constellation'). In this method, you imagine that the person from whom you are estranged is present, in front of you, represented by a chair or some other object, and you talk to her. According to Virginia Satir's family therapy methods, venting your thoughts may diminish the grievances and provide a relief. In the Systemic Coaching sessions that my grieving friend attended, the coach gave her a diagnosis. She said, 'Your mother does not want you. She does not like you and that is why you are having these issues.'

I do not stop to wonder where they learn such insensitivity. I think anyone could have told our friend that her mother is probably having more difficulty losing her husband after 57 years of marriage than probably she herself was facing. As if such fast-food kind of diagnosis was not sufficient, all this was undertaken over the telephone. Such practices damage the reputation of coaching. They can only be stopped by propagating methodical coaching.

The website for SystemicCoaching.com offers 'Systemic Coaching, Relationship Counselling, & Therapy'. They claim, 'Our work is client-centered, solution-focused and success oriented. Like consulting, systemic coaching is outcome oriented—we examine your visions, action plans … [.] How does systemic coaching work? Our systemic coaching begins with diagnosis …'

The definition of effective coaching that I have formulated does not diagnose people. What is the problem with diagnosis? As discussed earlier it is a highly specialised field reserved for medical and clinical psychological experts when it comes to the well-being of people, at least, as far as I am concerned in the context of mental health, preventive measures, and coaching (See Sect. 5.1). The purpose of diagnosis is to find out whether there is a mental or biological disorder that may be limiting a person's normal function. The diagnosis has a clear purpose: it should lead to an intervention. The purpose of the intervention is to mitigate the suffering and if possible cure the person of the illness. What if a diagnosis is being conducted in the coaching or business environment and the person conducting it does not possess adequate competency to diagnose illnesses?

There is one form of Systemic Coaching that deserves to be mentioned here also. Even though it is called Systemic Coaching it does not lean on family resolution as mentioned in reference to Virginia Satir. I wonder why they carry similar names if they have different purposes? Konstantin Korotov et al., authors of *Tricky Coaching* (2012, p. 53) find that Systemic Coaching is

> Although critically important in coaching, a systemic approach can be described quite succinctly: Know the client, and know the client's business. Surprisingly, we find that many coaches focus too much on one or the other, cutting themselves off from important background information and avenues for exploration.

My contention after all the research is that effective coaching is not as complex as it is made out to be through its new names. The confusion is evident even in such a small area as Systemic Coaching. Sometimes the concept of Virginia Satir is sold as Systemic Coaching and other times there seems to be another Systemic Coaching.

9.5 Case Study: 'Matt'

Matt was an accomplished 47-year-old CTO in a well-known company in the north of Germany. The company's annual turnover was double digit billion euros. The story begins before he came to me for coaching. He had approached the human resources department (HR) in his company looking for help as he was not very happy with the way things were going for him in his department. Matt asked the HR manager to allow him to select his own coach as he knew one in whom he confided. His request was turned down and he was told they cannot evaluate new coaches every now and then. The HR manager allocated a coach to him from the 'pool of coaches'. The coach selected from the 'pool' was 72-years-old. This man was a retired HR manager, with a lifetime's experience and reputation in well-known companies. It is necessary to note his age and his profession because both aspects contribute to another prevailing fallacy in coaching: if the coach is old, he is experienced and the prevailing presumption goes that he is automatically good. Secondly, if he is from HR then he is also automatically considered a coach because he has experience of dealing with personnel and their problems. There is nothing that could be further from the truth than these assumptions about what kind of person and qualities are needed to coach effectively. What is not unimaginable is that an HR manager could become a coach. I have not, in my 35 years of corporate world experience (up to 2010), employed or seen a single HR manager who was also a coach by virtue of his profession as an HR manager. They have their dedicated area of expertise: coaching, by default, is not included in it. If there is anyone who claims that she or he is an HR manager and does a great job in coaching their personnel, then it may be an exception.

First, let me tell you how I know all these details. After completing the coaching that was paid by his company, Matt came to me privately for coaching, as according to him, he had 'a gut feeling' that his coaching had not been good. Within the first meeting with me, after his confidence level was high enough, he wanted to show me what had happened in the last coaching and wanted to know if he had been right in feeling lousy about his previous experience. I did not comment on the nature of his previous coaching or his previous coach. He was a mature person and has a company with a whole army of experts to support such a decision for him; they should know what they are doing or getting into. A couple of weeks later he voluntarily sent me all the correspondence he had exchanged with his previous coach by email, together with a request to look at them. For a while I left it lying in my archives as I was not interested in their correspondence. My focus was on building my own practice and not looking critically at how other coaches were conducting their sessions. Much later, when I was looking for evidence for a few facts for this book, I wanted to explore how people were coaching. I thought it would be a good opportunity to see the decision-making processes of a large corporation in their selection or recommendation of coaches, such as, the criteria they applied to select the person most suited to coaching their most valuable assets. These are world famous companies; they must have some best practices to learn from to inform their selection methods.

I was amazed at what I read in the email exchanges. In my opinion, the unprofessional coaching service handed out to Matt was extremely shoddy. Within the first two meetings Matt had to undergo a questionnaire. From this, he received an assessment and a diagnosis. Summarised, it said: 'Since you are second-born in your family you have a tendency to hold yourself back. You should fight back and learn to push your way more aggressively.' Pseudo psychoanalysis that suggests that a person is disadvantaged in life because of his place within the family grouping is not coaching. It is well-established that not even our own memory is reliable when recalling events from our past. How can a person claim to give such a precise diagnosis to a mature client based on a three-page questionnaire? This is the stuff pseudo coaches are made of: they are damaging people. Generally speaking, assessments are part of HR. It seems normal that a person who has spent all his life as a corporate HR will use assessments. There was no mention of any intellectual property or its origins on Matt's questionnaire, which I examined to determine what the coach could have had in his mind while using this type of questionnaire, and what it was that he had wanted to possibly achieve.

Each question had three choices. If you checked the first one you were awarded with three points, two points for the next, and one point for the last. According to 'Test Construction', a subject that forms part of psychology studies, under such conditions, the person taking the test can easily manipulate the outcome. Matt knew that three was higher than one: he would most likely answer in such a way that he would be awarded three points for every question. I investigated whether the points given were sometimes inverted: three for a bad/wrong answer; one for a good answer. The questionnaire did not have any such mechanism built in to it. It was all very simple and straightforward, almost naive.

I looked for the source and owner of this questionnaire for some months, but did not find anything relevant. After about 6 months passed, I was looking at some books on stress management and accidentally stumbled across an identical test. The book was written by a well-known professor in Germany. How does stress management assessment relate to coaching assessment? In the area of stress management, it may be appropriate to assess whether or not a person is exposed to excessive stress. Stress can lead to pathological outcomes and may need medical intervention. Is there a need for such an assessment in coaching? I do not think so.

Assessments are a sham in coaching. At best, they demonstrate that a coach does not know what to do with a client. Such a coach conducts dubious typological or ideological tests, which are absolutely irrelevant within a coaching setting. The most unfortunate part of all this is that you would expect that world class companies would have people who are capable of making good decisions on the coaching service providers they employ, and the assessments they carry out. Is that not what HR managers do all the time? But relying on such assumptions seems to be wrong when it comes to coaching. A large number of people, whether HR or not, still do not know what coaching is, or who is capable of coaching. As a result, company personnel are left to the mercy of fallacies such as 'an HR manager must be a good coach'.

During the interviews I conducted, one of the questions I posed was whether people really wanted to be assessed during coaching. I found that they are averse to it. They are willing to undertake a test if it brings out some comparative study to demonstrate whether they are good leaders, whether they are right in their perceptions of various things in the company or not, but they do not want to be assessed for the sake of being assessed. They accept feedback from their colleagues, customers, clients, and other important interlocutors.

The assessment that Matt underwent made him think that he needed to change his demeanour. This was the result of the assessment conducted by a coach who was still stuck with the concepts of psychologists from the 1900s. I noticed that every day, Matt had forwarded to his coach all the emails he exchanged with his boss, asking him what to do. The coach responded to Matt, telling him exactly how to respond to every situation. There was always a word of reassurance: 'You did this well and you will soon improve there.' There was no mention of how he would improve, just that it would happen. Reassurance and confidence-building measures are good but they alone do not make up for the deficiency in methodical coaching. One day, Matt narrated to his coach that his boss, a woman, had made him wait for 1 hour and 10 minutes in front of her office before receiving him, despite an agreed appointment. When he finally met with her, the first thing she did was to point out all that he had not completed as agreed previously. As a comparison, she pointed out that all that she had agreed with his colleagues was completed on time, and was done well despite time constraints. The coach responded to Matt, 'oh, she is now doing a pissing competition'. For another situation he responded that 'she is name jobbing'. When a coach becomes party to the struggle of a client, they become comrades-in-arms or co-combatants. When your coach becomes your buddy in your disputes and sympathises solely with your side of things, he has lost sight of his obligations. I thought that expressions like 'pissing competitions' belonged to adolescence; the way boys between 12 and 13 years of age talk and perhaps undertake such competitions. I wondered what image would have emerged in Matt's mind listening to his coach. How was he relating that image to his boss's behaviour? I could not find the meaning of the expression 'name jobbing'.

Language plays a very important role in coaching or for that matter in any other verbal human interaction. This is not a new concept that I am introducing but I am convinced that the language of a coach is, besides other vital methods, critical to the delivery of good quality coaching. According to the Sapir-Whorf hypothesis (Reprinted in D. G. Mandelbaum, (ed.) (1958, p. 69). *E. Sapir: Culture, Language, Personality. Selected Essays*), the structure of language determines and/or influences our thinking and our world view.

> Human beings do not live in the objective world alone, nor alone in the world of social activity as ordinarily understood, but are very much at the mercy of the particular language which has become the medium of expression for their society. It is quite an illusion to imagine that one adjusts to reality essentially without the use of language and that language is merely an incidental means of solving specific problems of communication or reflection. The fact of the matter is that the 'real world' is to a large extent unconsciously built upon the language habits of the group. [.] We see and hear and otherwise experience very largely as we do because the language habits of our community predispose certain choices of interpretation.

Earlier than Sapir, the German philosopher, thinker, and linguist, Wilhelm von Humboldt said that language is the medium that gives expression to the inner life and knowledge of its speaker. I am a strong believer of this aspect of language and its use. I studied English Literature at the University of Delhi and have learnt 12 languages, so that I have personal experience of how words can change people's perception across the world. Appropriate words change the emotions of the listener. Humboldt said that words may remain incomprehensible sounds until and unless some meaning is intended to be conveyed by the speaker. His thoughts are still valid; he is often quoted by Noam Chomsky, who is known in the US as 'the father of modern linguistics'. My main concern in this book is not of linguistics but these references have been made to prove my point that language displays the level of knowledge the speaker possesses in the area of his expertise. Now try to imagine what Matt understood from the words of his coach?

Further if you recall my experience with hypnotherapy and my comment that I learnt some important aspects related to coaching from it, one was that people are easily influenced by suggestions and the second is to do with language and words. Have you ever considered the most important instrument that hypnosis has at its disposal to put people into a hypnotic trance? Words: there are no special words used in hypnosis. Do not expect to hear words such as 'Abracadabra' or any other words from fairy tales. You will hear simple words such as 'now you are completely relaxed and feeling your body is pressing against the ground under your own weight'. And you will relax and have a feeling of sinking to the ground. These are simple selected words spoken by the hypnosis master or therapist in a soothing tone, at times accompanied by soft music. Any healthy person, or the majority of them, can be induced into a trance. Imagine simple words can make you lose control over your consciousness and put you into an induced state very close but not identical to sleep. Try one exercise yourself in your personal environment: try to talk about faeces at the dinner table and in the same breath ask the others how the food tastes. You are very likely to receive either disgusting looks in response or no answer at all, with heads shaking in disgust. You may risk being declared gross. This should validate how your choice of words and your language affects others. As a matter of fact, many of the coaches I interviewed think that building a relationship or confidence with a client in coaching is based on paying nice compliments to give them a feeling of being understood.

While reading the comparisons above of hypnotherapy, NLP, and other disciplines with coaching, if I gave the impression that I was trying to put coaching in a better light than the other disciplines, then it is time that I said it is wrong to assume that. Irrespective of what a person does, whether NLP, motivational coaching, Systemic Coaching, or hypnotherapy, it should be based on a competency that is easily comprehensible by the client. No one should get the kind of shoddy treatment that Matt experienced under the pretext of coaching or conducting sham diagnosis based on fragmented knowledge. No company should be vulnerable to it either. Presumptions about coaching are extremely damaging and expensive for all concerned. One of the ideas behind writing this book is that people should not think just because coaching is not a regulated profession that anyone should chisel one subset to fit their own abilities or rather inabilities. Distributing your personal opinions is not coaching. It is also imperative that HR departments and managers abandon the illusions of what coaching is and begin to create measurable checks of quality. They should examine their 'pool of coaches' and ensure quality of service.

9.6 Work-Life Balance Coaching

The concept of 'Work-Life Balance Coaching,' the phrase first coined in 1977, is accepted as part of normal language. In casual conversation it is not unusual for people to use the phrase. That does not mean they know what it is. It offers to optimise your life and make your working life more efficient. The expression alone is sufficient for me to decide that there is something missing here for it to be coaching. The first thing you discover when you look for explanations on it is that you can prevent 'burnout' if you do not balance your working life and your home life. The term 'burnout' suggests that these are psychiatric and psychological disorders. It is irresponsible to play around with offering to treat serious conditions through coaching.

The first thought that comes to mind is if you are balancing anything the whole has to be divided into two equals. Life on one side with an equal weight for work on the other. Some definitions I found for this form of coaching included these expressions, which are self-explanatory. Work-life balance means a balance between the health, psyche, body, social aspects, family, and work. Five aspects of your life to balance two parts: Work-Life? I am not convinced that you need to balance your working life with your personal life. If you balance one object with another then they are two independent entities, physically separate from each other. You take a balance and put one entity on one side and the other on the other side and add or reduce weight until they are balanced (Fig. 9.1).

Let us consider the round object as work and the square object rounded off at the edges as life. I am aware that there are proponents who say but this method of looking at it is a bit of black and white way of looking at it. Well it is in the nature of the definition that forces the reader to look at it as black and white. It is the inherent obligation of the author to articulate the definition in a manner so that it is

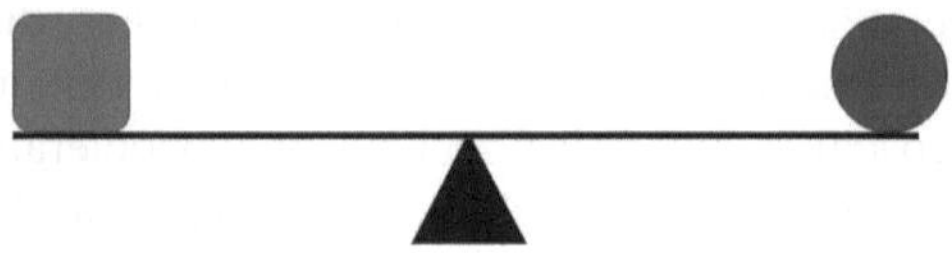

Fig. 9.1 Work-life balance

understood as it was conceived to be and be able to deliver the message unambiguously.

Let me give you some more examples of balancing. If you hear someone say I need to balance my intake of alcohol what do you understand? The speaker is not talking about any second entity, he is indulging in the ambiguity of human language, but even then a normal person would understand that the speaker means to say that he wishes to reduce the frequency or the quantity of his alcohol consumption. I do not think anyone ever plans to increase the consumption of alcohol and then goes to propagate openly that he needs to balance it. You may hear someone say, my daughter needs to balance her diet: eat more fruits and vegetables. The speaker has not talked about reducing something to increase fruits.

Work-Life Balance will automatically be understood as reducing work to have more personal time. To do this there must be some techniques and skills to learn that will reduce your stress or make your life better. That would also mean that a concept such as this would assume that human beings and their moods, behaviour, reactions, and emotions remain static. What if you plan to reduce your work and spend more personal time, but your plans are disrupted by events beyond your control: illness, natural catastrophes, accidents in the family—there is a large catalogue of events that everyone knows are not predictable. Under such circumstances you have even less personal time. Do you then give up your work? Every few years there is a new concept to teach us how to reduce stress, tweak some part of our life, optimise our lives, and improve the state of all busy people. The problem is that all these systems have one thing in common: they assume a human being can improve some units of his being—that he is static and will always live as a constant.

In the 1960s it was marijuana and free love; in the 1980s it was 'Time Management'. In the 1990s it was goal setting. It is assumed that a person—irrespective of his moods, illness, fatigue, the weather, changes in his life; birth of a child, death of a loved one, good news or bad—will continue to function, hence one template will apply to everyone.

When a solution is based on what Hjelle and Zeigler (1992, p. 28) have called 'knowablility' while disregarding the 'unknowability' of human nature then it may not work for all humans as a template. That is the case with work-life balance. Any system or service that assumes a person or his nature remains constant or is a rigid mechanism will fail to provide a satisfactory stimulant to personal development.

In the new millennium 'Work-Life Balance' comes packaged as a preventive measure for 'burnout' and as a solution to harness one's life issues. This also assumes that it would be sufficient to reduce work and heal all evils in life. There is another problem with such balancing acts: the moment we consider something outside of our life, our family, circle of our friends, school, football team or company, we consider it different. The question is this: is the work really outside of one's life. Can work sustain itself outside of life or without life? We need work to sustain our life as we always have. How could you balance it against each other? You can at best integrate work into your life. These are the reasons why such techniques and tools should stop creating confusion by calling themselves coaching and encroaching on an area which has nothing to do with it.

In Boris Groysberg and Robin Abrahams's article in *Harvard Business Review* titled, 'Manage Your Work, Manage Your Life', they discussed the results of their interviews of 4000 executives conducted over 5 years. They found that 'Work/life balance is at best an elusive ideal and at worst a complete myth, today's senior executives will tell you . . . [.] Deliberate choices don't guarantee complete control' (March 2014). I do not need to add anything to such a clear finding except that there is no scope for such 'elusive ideals' to be calling themselves coaching.

The basic assumptions about human nature are very different in coaching as compared to 'Work-Life Balance Coaching'. If coaching is to be accepted according to the basic assumptions of human nature, then this is not coaching; at best it offers a set of skills or techniques to teach you how to balance your work with your life: optimise you. As I mentioned earlier (See Sect. 2.1), any service that imparts skills, which are not person oriented, is skills centred: it is not coaching but training.

9.7 Energy Coaching

Energy coaching was, for years, propagated under the name of energy healing. Nowadays it is called 'energy coaching'. It did not take me more than a day and a few hundred euros to discover this method has nothing to do with coaching. The basic assumptions of human nature are that a person is unable to heal himself or reach his healing energy (See Sect. 8.2). A healer will heal you with an energy to which only the healer has access due to his mastery. There are rituals to be performed to access that energy. There are no such assumptions in coaching that are similar to these ideas, and it suffices to say that the basic premise of energy coaching disqualifies it from being called coaching.

By coincidence, while investigating energy coaching, I encountered one important lesson that is imparted in energy coaching, which is also within coaching. All the students are taught that 'The client is the solution holder.' This statement is identical to the lesson one learns in coaching. Energy coaching goes further. It made me wonder whether people coaching their clients also think like this. The second part of the lesson in energy coaching was, 'if a person is not being healed then it is probably not you, it is his belief that is stopping him from being healed'. Sigmund Freud was known for immunising his claims with similar explanations. This is the immunisation that I mentioned in the earlier part of the book (See Chap. 5). If a coach can claim that he is not responsible for the results, he has no stakes in the efficacy of coaching either. A coach, if he has learnt coaching methodically, should be able to predict the probable results that he will be able to achieve for his clients, if not immediately, at least within the first meeting.

9.8 Three-day Coaching Courses

Can someone learn coaching in 3 days? As mentioned earlier there is a very common complaint by many that anyone can become a coach after 3 days of coaching. While anyone can call himself a coach, becoming a coach is a different dimension altogether. It is true that when you enrol on a coaching course that lasts 3 days you will be trained in a method which may be new to you; thus, you may tend to think that you have learned all there is to know about how to coach. As a matter of fact, what you learn in 3 days is part of coaching, but it should be considered as a very small part of the coaching conversational method. However, this part on its own is not the whole training.

On the 3-day coaching course, you will learn that coaching is an eye-level interaction between a coach and the client.[4] If your education is limited to 3 days, you may never learn that there is more to coaching than eye-level interaction. In my experience, irrespective of how high and how important my client is they always tend to look up to me as the coach in expectation of receiving some wisdom about something they do not already know: some insight. It is another matter that a coach should treat his clients as such but it is never an eye-level relationship. It is important for a coach to understand because coaching brings certain ethical obligations for his behaviour. A coach should not try to teach his clients something he thinks is right for his client. In some coaching manuals, it is suggested that coaching is a partnership. I tend to disagree. A coach is a service provider who should respect his clients as such.

To learn more about coaching I enrolled on two different courses in two different institutes in Munich. I wanted to find out what one could learn about coaching in just 3 to 4 days of training. The fees were €760 in one school and the other one asked for €900.[5] In the 3 or 4 days, I was taught a few methods of listening carefully to clients. In my original coaching course that I undertook in 2010 this method was called 'active listening' and it was clear from the training what this meant. In 'active listening', when a coach listens attentively to what the client is saying, he stimulates a process that creates a confidential rapport with the client; it is part of the methodology that underpins a coaching conversation. As this method is based on the scientific study that people talk more than they listen, it can be problematic if a coach talks more than he listens.

Another method of coaching taught over a short time by one of the institutes I visited in Munich was how to question a client. Some call it digging to find more

[4] Throughout the book I use 'client' in place of the usual term 'coachee' out of personal preference.

[5] I will refrain from naming them as it may be interpreted as an effort to discredit them and that is not the purpose of this book.

details of what the client is saying or meaning to say; others call it revealing, there are many names to this method of questioning. It is a good method; it leads to confidence building and the client feels he is being heard and understood. Different coaching institutes and classes have their own names for this method, such as re-framing, mirroring, paraphrasing, repeating, and so on. Each one, doubtlessly, is a very good and effective method. Re-framing, mirroring and paraphrasing the client's statements help the client understand what he is saying. It is as if he observes his own statements and questions with a certain detachment; it helps the client to see the contradictions between his words and his beliefs.

Here is a very short example of a questioning session. A client complains that she has a feeling that she is not being treated as an equal and feels she is being discriminated by her boss.

The client says, 'I think I am being discriminated by my boss.'

The coach asks her, 'So you think you are being discriminated?'

She replies, 'yes. Every day I am told "you cannot do this job yet".'

The coach responds, 'you think your boss thinks you cannot do the job?'

Active listening and paraphrasing are effective methods to create a rapport with the client, which have been used in counselling for a long time; the conversational method is not a new concept that coaching introduced to the world. However, if a coach continues to repeat, re-frame, and paraphrase too frequently he might end up facing a very annoyed client who might ask if the coach is trying to make a fool of her by repeating what she is saying. Many coaches I interviewed thought that was all coaching involved. As I hope I have demonstrated in the book this is not all that coaching can offer; it is one part of coaching: the basic level of a coaching conversation. While it is a good instrument for dealing with a simple issue, coaching is about more than the conversational method. Beyond this level, a client would experience what makes a coach more proficient in his coaching

9.9 Conclusion

I recall an exchange with my paternal grandfather who was a very wise man. My recollection of him was of a sage. I think it was 1967, when I wanted to read his books. He told me when you are ready to read these books they will come to you and you will not have to look for them. I asked him, 'what do these books teach you?' He said, 'irrespective of what the books teach you, if you are able to talk with a child with as much respect and ease as you would a mature person then you have learnt one of the many secrets of living well.' Turning to coaching; if you can implement coaching properly it will give you access to this secret. Coaching is beneficial, not only for its clients, but also for the coach. A coach is able to talk to a brain surgeon as easily as he can talk to a lawyer or an executive. Coaching is not profession dependent, that is why, when people claim that you can implement coaching in personal relationships as much as with children and top executives, they are right.

We began our discussion on coaching and the ambiguity that prevails in Germany around it. As I have shown, there exists a popular belief that it comes from sports and discussions that it can be used as therapy or it is similar to psychoanalysis; there are also some claims that no one knows exactly what coaching is. At the end of our discussion I hope I have been able to convince you that in fact there is no ambiguity where coaching comes from or what it is. If, as discussed by Vikki Brock, Sir John Whitmore, in addition to my own conviction that even Socrates used this method more than 2400 years ago, then I have reason to believe that it can exist for as long as humanity has understood that there exists an effective method to learn and teach and where there is a behaviour that encourages people to grow and flourish—and that is coaching.

References

Groysberg, B., & Abrahams, R. (2014, March). Manage your work, manage your life. *Harvard Business Review*.

Hjelle, L. A., & Ziegler, D. (1992). *Personality theories: Basic assumptions, research, and applications*. Singapore: McGraw Hill.

Korotov, K., Florent-Treacy, E., Kets de Vries, M. F. R., & Bernhardt, A. (2012). *Tricky coaching, difficult cases in coaching*. London: Palgrave Macmillan.

O'Conner, J., & Seymour, J. (2002). *Introducing NLP psychological skills for understanding and influencing people*. San Francisco: Conari Press.

Sapir, E. (1929). The status of language as a science. (Reprinted from *Culture, language, personality: Selected essays*, by D. G. Mandelbaum, Ed., 1958, Berkeley, CA: University of California Press)

Schacter, D. L., & Dodson, C. S. (2001). Misattribution, false recognition and the sins of memory. *Philosophical Transactions: Biological sciences, 356*(1413), 1385–1393. doi:10.1098/rstb.2001.0938.

Sutton, J., & Stewart, W. (2009). *Learning to counsel*. Oxford: How To Books.

Online Sources

Ambridge, B. (2014, November). Ten myths about psychology, Debunked, TEDyouth@Manchester. https://www.ted.com/talks/ben_ambridge_10_myths_about_psychology_debunked/transcript?language=en#t-292375. Accessed 8 Feb 2015.

Satir Website. https://satirglobal.org/. Accessed 7 Mar 2016.

MIX
Papier aus verantwortungsvollen Quellen
Paper from responsible sources
FSC® C105338

If you have any concerns about our products,
you can contact us on
ProductSafety@springernature.com

In case Publisher is established outside the EU,
the EU authorized representative is:
Springer Nature Customer Service Center GmbH
Europaplatz 3, 69115 Heidelberg, Germany

Printed by Libri Plureos GmbH
in Hamburg, Germany